REGULATORS AND THE MARKET

An Assessment of the Growth of Regulation in the UK

Edited by

Cento Veljanovski

IEA

Institute of Economic Affairs

1991

First published in September 1991
by
THE INSTITUTE OF ECONOMIC AFFAIRS
2 Lord North Street, Westminster, London SW1P 3LB

IEA Readings 35

ISSN 0305-814X
ISBN 0-255 36248-X (paper)
ISBN 0-255 36249-8 (hard cover)

The Institute gratefully acknowledges financial support for its publications programme and other work from a generous benefaction by the late Alec and Beryl Warren.

Filmset by Goron Pro-Print Co. Ltd., Lancing, W. Sussex

Printed in Great Britain by Biddles Limited, Guildford

Filmset in Times Roman 11 on 12 point

CONTENTS

INTRODUCTION

PRIVATISATION HAS CREATED a patchwork of regulation for the telecommunications, airport, water and gas industries. The new economic regulation was based on the idea that price control, together with the terms of the licence awarded to the privatised firms, would be sufficient to protect consumers and encourage greater competition. This framework was expected to be neat, straightforward and simple – all the regulator had to do was to monitor compliance and at stated intervals the controls would be reviewed and re-set either by agreement or, failing that, reference to the Monopolies and Mergers Commission. That was the theory. In reality regulation of the utilities has proved more complex and contentious. The contributors brought together in this *IEA Readings* explore some of the issues surrounding the relatively new phenomenon of economic regulation 'UK-style'.

In the IEA's Hobart Paperback No. 28, *Privatisation and Competition – A Market Prospectus* (January 1989), the contributors were agreed that privatisation had failed to bring about adequate competition in the previously nationalised industries. These utilities were sent into the private sector with their monopoly intact, imposing a great burden on the regulator to act as a 'surrogate for competition'. The failure to eliminate monopoly has inevitably led to tension between industry chiefs and regulators. The elegant simplicity of regulation discussed by Littlechild in his influential report on telecommunications regulation and proffered by Government Ministers is, in the view of some, degenerating into a web of informal and amorphous rulings based on the predilections of the individual regulators.

The purpose of this volume is to assess the UK's experience with this new regulatory system. In Part 2 the regulators present their view of what they have done and the system in which they must operate. These papers were delivered at a conference organised by the IEA in May 1991. To these are added some introductory remarks by Professor Sir Alan Peacock and a summary of the main themes by the Chairman of the Conference, Professor Michael Beesley.

Parts 1 and 3 of the volume contain essays providing an assessment of regulatory developments and a discussion of alternative approaches. In Part 1 the contributors examine the record so far. As if to reflect the complexity of the subject, they offer a mixed assessment. In my essay the views of the regulated industries have been emphasised, as has the absence of clear channels of accountability, and checks and balances on the regulators. This can be contrasted with the views of the regulators who see the system as workable and relatively effective. The contribution by Professors Beesley and Littlechild (the latter now a regulator of the electricity supply industry but the essay was written before his appointment) provides a retrospective on the way price controls of the regulated industries have worked. The authors have written a subtle and thorough analysis of one of the cornerstones of economic regulation of the utilities. Part 1 concludes with Dr Irwin Stelzer's comparative analysis of regulation in the UK and the USA. Originally written for a North American audience, it provides a fresh view from one with considerable experience of how regulation works in both countries.

The essays in Part 3 have been included to stimulate those interested in regulation to think about the alternative ways of controlling industry. Professor Benson examines the efficiency of the common law. This is a body of law which has evolved through the decisions of judges in resolving disputes. A number of lawyers and economists regard the common law to be superior to regulation. Professor Benson explains why. This is followed by Dr Siebert's discussion of the way markets can implicitly control accidents, thereby providing an automatic method of regulation. Finally, Dr Dnes re-examines contractual methods of regulation which were explicitly rejected in the UK, other than for broadcasting and telecommunications industries. Competitive tendering for the franchise to operate a monopoly, argues Dr Dnes, offers the possibility of effective regulation.

The IEA is a research and educational charity and therefore does not hold a corporate view. It nonetheless commends the contributions in this *IEA Readings* as original and stimulating analyses which will enliven the debate over privatisation and regulation of key service industries in the UK economy.

August 1991   DR CENTO VELJANOVSKI
Senior Research Fellow in Law & Economics,
Institute of Economic Affairs

PART ONE

OVERVIEW
AND ASSESSMENT

THE REGULATION GAME

Cento Veljanovski

Director, Lexecon Ltd.
Senior Research Fellow in Law & Economics,
Institute of Economic Affairs

'When designing and setting up regulatory agencies, the British way has been to muddle through ...'

ROBERT BALDWIN (1985)

'The greatest danger to liberty today comes from ... the efficient expert administrators exclusively concerned with what they regard as the public good.'

F. A. HAYEK (1960)

WHATEVER THE RHETORIC accompanying Britain's privatisation programme it was always clear that for some industries the hawsers of state control would remain to prevent customers from being gouged and competition smothered. In the telecommunications, gas, electricity, airports and water industries, privatisation entailed the replacement of public ownership by regulation. It recast the state's rôle from that of a producer of goods and services to that of the regulator of the producers. Since the privatisation of British Telecom in 1984, these five key industries have been regulated by a patchwork of controls, whilst others, such as broadcasting and the financial sector, have also experienced major regulatory reforms.

This growth in regulation has always been the subject of unease and confusion. At a simplistic level it could be, and has been, asked why the state should be better at regulating these industries compared with its performance when it owned them. With over half a decade of experience, there is a growing demand for a fundamental reassessment of regulation 'UK style'. The purpose of this essay is not to bemoan the fact that privatisation was not perfect and that regulation could be better than it is. Rather it attempts to make a clear statement of the key features of the new economic regulation in the UK and to begin, in a preliminary way, the task of developing a model of regulation which fits the facts more closely.

1. Regulatory Rumblings

Regulation is the new border between the state and industry. It is also the battleground for ideas on industrial policy and how the economy should be run. No government will ignore the privatised utilities, nor will they be immune from politics or politicians. This has become apparent to industry chiefs as they grapple with regulation. The greatest threat facing their independence is not the prospect of re-nationalisation but the tightening corset of regulation. The fear of management and shareholders is that regulation could easily be the device for the re-socialisation of the utilities, and for government to achieve political and social schemes at shareholders' expense.

Two opposing views of regulation can be identified. Each is an exaggeration but nonetheless each captures the conflicting interpretations of experience to date. The first camp sees the *ad hoc* development of regulation, the high profits of the utilities, the absence of genuine competition, and the supposed deterioration of service levels as evidence of inadequate regulation. For this view the present experiment with regulation has failed, pointing to the urgent need for reforms which will both rationalise the patchwork of watchdogs and give greater powers to the regulator. This camp would ideally like the consolidation of regulation in one public utility commission, perhaps under the auspices of the Monopolies and Mergers Commission (NCC, 1989; Waterson, 1991).

The other camp feels disappointed and betrayed. The management of many utilities regard the recent actions of some regulators as a breach of the implicit 'regulatory bargain', struck between the Government and the shareholders of the privatised industries, that the rules-of-the-game would not be radically changed. The regulators, seeking greater powers, have spread their net wider and are challenging managements' right to manage. It is sometimes gravely suggested that industry and regulator are on a collision course over the question: 'Who runs the industry – management or regulator?'

These views reflect a fundamental dilemma inherent in privatisation. On the one hand, the overriding purpose of privatisation was to propel the new entities into the private sector with new and greater freedoms to pursue commercial objectives and improve efficiency. Yet, unfettered, they have every incentive to charge customers high prices, reduce the quality of services and prevent competition. Regulation is required but invites other difficulties. The bureaucratic second-guessing of managements' decisions and price-setting against shifting goal-posts and policy objectives creates regulatory uncertainty, reduces competitive pressures (by removing the profit incentive for entry) and, given the wide power of regulators, encourages the urge to increase controls. Moreover, the process of regulation raises concerns not only about the vexing relationship between the state and private property, but also about 'due process' – the accountability and constitutional legitimacy of the new regulatory watchdogs, and the absence of an open system of rule-making and decision-making (see Baldwin and McCrudden, 1987).

Clashes as Regulators Flex Their Muscles

These concerns have until recently smouldered under the surface or have been the subject of hushed comment among Government Ministers and civil servants wondering whether they got it right. Now flare-ups are occurring with some regularity. In July 1991, *The Financial Times* reported daily clashes between regulator and industry chiefs: 'Water Regulator Makes Waves . . . Row over dividend paid by privatised utilities'; 'British Gas given ultimatum on prices'; 'BT escapes MMC referral with Oftel deal';[1] National Power reported to be seeking judicial review of OFGAS's actions in forcing low-price gas to be sold to gas turbine power stations; OFFER is undertaking a study to find out whether the privatised electricity generating companies are 'abusing their huge market clout'. By the end of July 1991, Robert Evans, Chief Executive of British Gas, had clearly had enough of his 'acerbic' regulator:

> 'Few companies, I suspect, have had to take the apparently bizarre challenge which British Gas has faced over the past two years. Having built up a thriving market for gas in industry and commerce we are seeking every opportunity to give a substantial proportion of that market to competitors.'[2]

The situation has been neatly summed up by Jeremy Warner, the City Editor of *The Independent on Sunday*:

> 'Over the last couple of months regulators have been cracking down on privatised monopolies with increasing severity as if engaged in some kind of regulatory virility contest – each seems intent on outdoing the other.'[3]

---

[1] *The Financial Times*, 24 July 1991.   [2] *The Financial Times*, 30 July 1991.

[3] *The Independent on Sunday*, 4 August 1991.

The regulators have not been without their own problems. Mr John Bowman, Chief Executive of the National Rivers Authority, unexpectedly resigned. Lord Chalfont resigned as Deputy Chairman of the Independent Television Commission after a row over a conflict of interest. This was followed by pressure for him to resign as head of the Radio Authority after the revelation of another conflict of interest. Casting the net wider, there has been mounting public criticism about the competence and effectiveness of the financial regulators, not least the rôle and authority of the Bank of England in the recent BCCI fraud, and that of the Department of Trade and Industry in the Barlowe Clowes affair.

Whether all this amounts to a crisis in regulation is a moot point. But what is evident is that the experience of regulation is leading industry, politicians and informed commentators to ask a number of searching questions about regulation 'UK style'. These questions, some of which are illustrated in Box 1 below, provide the basis for the inevitable reassessment of privatisation and regulation.

2. The Development of Regulation

Regulation, even of the utility industries, is not new to the UK. What is new is the present *form* of regulation and the private sector provision of basic services. Under nationalisation these monopoly firms were controlled internally and externally by Ministers and government departments. The management of the nationalised industries and the rôle accorded to that most enigmatic of British political institutions, ministerial accountability, ensured that the political end of regulation was hidden behind the anonymity of central government departments.

As part of their monopoly, the nationalised industries had regulatory functions combining the rôles of defendant, judge, jury and prosecutor in protecting their operations, especially from competition. Industries were subject to unclear and conflicting objectives, poor systems of control, and capture by trade unions and politicians. The successive White Papers on the nationalised industries[4] sought and failed to ensure that these industries were run in a commercial way. By the end of the 1970s the politicisation of the nationalised industries was complete, and the principle that they should operate independently of the government had been replaced by one premised on comprehensive and detailed direct control of their activities by Ministers.

---

[4] White Papers: *Financial and Economic Obligations of the Nationalised Industries* (1961); *Nationalised Industries: A Review of Economic and Financial Objectives* (1967); and *The Nationalised Industries* (1978).

BOX 1

A Question of Regulation

o Is there too much or too little regulation?

o Do we have the right type of regulation – that is, is it effective in achieving the goals set for it?

o Are the goals of regulation the right ones?

o Are the procedures of regulation effective, fair and democratic?

o What criteria should be used to assess regulatory effectiveness?

o What should be the scope for the regulators to maintain social aspects of the services which are provided?

o Should the regulators be more open?

o Should there be an appeal mechanism from the decision of the regulator?

o Does the Monopolies and Mergers Commission provide an adequate forum for licence modification and price control revision?

o Are the regulators being excessively meddlesome and breaching the regulatory bargain entered into on privatisation?

o Are the shareholders of the privatised utilities being expropriated by tightening regulation?

o Who is running the utilities, the management or the regulator?

o What recourse does a utility have from arbitrary and unfair decisions by the regulator?

o Is regulation sufficiently immune from political interference?

In large measure the crisis in the nationalised industries was a failure of 'regulation'. The defects of the control system were highlighted in a damning study by the National Economic and Development Office (NEDO, 1976). The NEDO study painted a picture of ad hocery, confusion and blatant political manipulation. The regulatory framework was described as 'unsatisfactory and in need of radical change'. Among the deficiencies were lack of trust and mutual understanding between government and management, confusion about rôles, and the absence of an effective system for measuring performance and managerial competence. To remedy the unsatisfactory relationship between the management of the nationalised industries and the government, the NEDO report recommended that a Policy Council be established for

7

each industry. This and the other recommendations of NEDO were never implemented.

Privatisation the Radical Solution

Privatisation was seen as a radical solution to the crisis in the nationalised sector. The profit motive constrained by regulation, capital market controls and increased competition would make these industries more efficient and more responsive to consumers. The political practicalities of large-scale privatisation meant that competition could not be maximised. The political trade-off was rapid privatisation and less competition for more regulation (Veljanovski, 1988 and 1989). This, as we shall see, has bequeathed to the regulators the difficult task of acting as a 'surrogate for competition'. The Directors General of the newly formed regulatory 'watchdogs' have a duty to promote effective competition, ensure a 'level playing field', and protect customers, at the same time as ensuring that the social aspects of the utilities' operations, such as universal service, are maintained.

Faced with the political trade-off in favour of regulation, a new system had to be devised. This did not follow any coherent plan nor, despite claims to the contrary, did it evolve into greater coherence with each successive privatisation. This interpretation can be disputed by arguing that the significant differences in regulation among the five industries can be seen as customised or purpose-built regulation fitted to and based on the experience and learning by government from past privatisations. There is undoubtedly some truth in this. Nevertheless, each Minister responsible for privatisation had considerable independence to determine the privatisation plan for the industry against a political imperative to do it rapidly. For the most part any studied approach to regulation was rapidly overtaken by the political necessity for a 'quick fix', the necessity to bargain with the nationalised industries over industry structure and regulation, and the limitations of departmental skills in dealing with complex industries like electricity generation and transmission.

The record speaks for itself. British Telecom may have been a test bed for ideas about regulation, but it is generally accepted that the privatisation of British Gas, which followed, was a retrograde step in terms of promoting competition and effective regulation. British Gas was privatised as a vertically integrated monopoly from well-head to gas tip with a significant proportion of its market unregulated. Paradoxically but predictably, most of the Director General of Gas Supply's efforts have been directed at the 'unregulated' industrial market for gas because the conditions for effective competition are not present.

Even if there were truth in the claim that regulation has been finely tuned in the UK, the outside observer would be none the wiser. One of the less appealing features of UK regulation, and indeed British government in general, is its secretiveness. In some cases the new regulatory framework was ushered in by reports by independent experts and White Papers. Yet in others there was no such independent view and no serious attempt to foster informed public debate. Again, the privatisation of British Gas stands out for its lack of openness. It was preceded by neither a discussion document on economic regulation nor a White Paper. The telecom privatisation White Paper (1982) – two pages reproducing a DTI press release – was embarrassingly short on details. Similarly, electricity privatisation was notable for the absence of any serious attempt to air the issues. The much-vaunted electricity White Paper (1988) consisted of no more than chapter headings. The consultants' report on economic regulation of airports was buried (DTp, 1986). The concerned citizen would have done better to have bought the *Financial Times* than to rely on government to provide even basic information on what form of regulation was to be employed.

3. Regulation 'UK Style'

Until recently the word 'regulation' was not part of the common vernacular. It is not a separate category of law; it is difficult to define; and it is often difficult to find. Much of the law is informal, consisting of guidance notes, codes, determinations, and negotiated modifications to the utilities' licence and the price cap. This amorphous approach makes regulation an elastic and ill-defined term; and this before the lawyers have been asked for an opinion.

Regulation UK style is, in practice, a complex affair. The discussion in this section develops several related themes:

o Regulation is evolving into an informal system of rule-making which operates through negotiation and bargaining in the shadow of the law.

o This development has an economic explanation. Regulatory strategies are the predictable outcome of maximising behaviour by the parties involved subject to resource and institutional constraints.

o And that economic regulation UK style is evolving into a system of controls which are at odds with the original intention of privatisation; namely:

(a) that the 'regulatory bargain' struck between government and

9

shareholders at the time of privatisation would remain the basis for the future commercial operation of the privatised utilities; and

(b) that for the most part the regulatory system would be a rules-based one with intervention along agreed lines.

Structure of UK Regulation

The new economic regulation ushered in by privatisation is designed to protect consumers and promote competition (Veljanovski, 1990). Initially these aims were seen as requiring little more than the expansion of the rôle and functions of the Office of Fair Trading (OFT), which is responsible for monitoring competition in the UK. This the OFT declined, setting in motion the growth of separate regulatory agencies charged with administering what was conceived as a rules-based, non-discretionary approach to regulation (see Table 1).

British Telecom, as the first of the privatised utilities, was regulated by the Telecommunications Act 1984, a licence and a new regulatory agency, the Office of Telecommunications (OFTEL), headed by Professor Sir Bryan Carsberg. He was the first of the new breed of regulators. Excluding the new regulatory system governing financial services, a further three new watchdogs have been created: the Office of Gas Supply (OFGAS), the Office of Water Services (OFWAT), and the Office of Electricity Regulation (OFFER) (see Table 2). The Civil Aviation Authority (CAA) has had its rôle expanded to administer the regulation of the privatised BAA plc operations of Heathrow, Gatwick and Stansted airports, and Manchester Airport plc owned by the City of Manchester and other local authorities. Other regulatory agencies have been set up whose concern is with quality regulation and the licensing of new entrants. The National Rivers Authority (NRA) and HM Inspectorate of Pollution (HMIP) have been established to enforce and develop environmental standards. In broadcasting, *two* 'quangos' have been abolished (the Independent Broadcasting Authority and the Cable Authority) and *three* new ones established under the Broadcasting Act 1990: the Independent Television Commission (ITC), the Radio Authority, and the Broadcasting Standards Council (BSC). The ITC and the Radio Authority are responsible for licensing broadcasters and cable operators under a new scheme of auctioning licences to the highest cash bidder.

General Features of Regulation

The new regulation for each industry has the following main features:

o   On privatisation each industry is regulated by a new regulatory

TABLE 1

REGULATORY WATCHDOGS, 1991

AGENCY	DATE FORMED	INDUSTRY	STATUTE
Economic Regulators			
Civil Aviation Authority	1971	Airports	Airport Act 1986
Office of Telecommunications	1984	Telecommunications	Telecommunications Act 1984
Office of Gas Supply	1986	Gas	Gas Act 1986
Office of Water Services	1989	Water	Water Act 1989
Office of Electricity Regulation	1990	Electricity	Electricity Act 1990
Quality Regulators			
National Rivers Authority	1989	Water	Water Act 1989
HM Inspectorate of Pollution	1987	All	Environmental Protection Act 1990
Independent Television Commission	1991	Terrestrial, Cable & Satellite Television	Broadcasting Act 1990
Radio Authority	1991	Radio	Broadcasting Act 1990
Broadcasting Standards Council	1990	Broadcasting	Broadcasting Act 1990
Competition Regulators			
Office of Fair Trading	1951	All	Fair Trading Act 1973
Monopolies & Mergers Commission	1948	All	Fair Trading Act 1973; Competition Act 1980

11

TABLE 2

REGULATORY AGENCIES' STAFF & BUDGET 1989-90

Regulatory Agency	Budget £m	Staff	Self-Financing
Established Agencies			
Office of Fair Trading	14.7	360	No
Monopolies & Mergers Commission	5.8	116	No
Civil Aviation Authority	442.0	7,500	Yes
New Agencies 1984 onwards			
Office of Telecommunications	6.9	134	Yes
Office of Gas Supply	1.6	28	Yes
Office of Water Services	4.3	112	Yes
Office of Electricity Regulation	12.6	220	Yes
National Rivers Authority	450.0	7,500	Yes
Independent Television Commission	19.3*	225-250	Yes
Radio Authority	2.6	27	Yes
Broadcasting Standards Council	1.3	14	No
HM Inspectorate of Pollution	-	200	No

Source: Annual Reports.   *Approximate figure.

watchdog charged with administering economic regulation and consumer protection. Formally, these watchdogs are non-ministerial government departments headed by a Director General (with the exception of the older CAA which has a Chairman and is technically a nationalised industry because it also supplies air traffic control services).

o   The legal authority to regulate the industry is contained in the 'privatisation' statute. This lists the duties of the Director General and the general regulatory framework. However, the real power to control the utilities is found in the terms of their licences.

o   The cornerstone of economic regulation is the price-cap formula, known as 'RPI minus X'. This forces the real price of services to fall by X per cent, X being a factor reflecting the government or regulator's estimate of the scope for increased efficiency of the utility. In later privatisations (e.g. gas) the formula was modified to permit direct pass-through of unavoidable costs (the Y factor) to price increases to customers, and in the case of water a K factor, to encourage new investment in the industry (see Table 4).

o Review of the licence terms and price cap is the responsibility of the Directors General and the Monopolies and Mergers Commission (MMC), as are general competition matters (see Table 3 for MMC investigations involving privatised industries). The MMC acts as an 'appeal court' for licence revision and re-setting of the price cap if the regulator fails to reach agreement with the industry.

The regulation of these industries exhibits an interesting diversity and division of responsibilities which can be only briefly illustrated here. For example, OFTEL is responsible for economic regulation and consumer protection in telecoms, whereas in the gas industry these two areas are separated, OFGAS being responsible for economic regulation and The Gas Consumers' Councils dealing with consumer complaints and service. In the water and sewerage industry there is a different division between economic regulator (OFWAT) and environmental regulation by the National Rivers Authority (NRA).

In theory, the MMC appears to be the most powerful regulator because of its power to impose modifications of licence terms and to re-set the price caps. The exception is economic regulation of airports where the MMC's rôle is limited to making recommendations to the CAA on the re-setting of the price cap; it is the CAA which takes the final decisions. In practice the MMC's rôle is limited because of the tendency of regulator and industry to negotiate and agree licence modifications and price-cap revisions. Government departments still often have significant powers especially over entry (in the case of telecommunications) and production (nuclear power, which has remained in the state sector).

Regulation by Bargaining

As indicated above, it is a mistake to regard the formal legal framework as regulation. The legal framework provides only the scaffolding of regulation in practice. No legal system, apart from the most totalitarian, operates a penal strategy with automatic recourse to the formal law. Rather the law operates as the sanction of last resort against which compliance is sought through negotiation, bargaining and threats. *Regulation in practice is better understood as operating in the shadow of the law*; as a complex interaction between politicians, civil servants, industry, consumers, interest groups and regulatory bodies.

This model of regulation is particularly appropriate to the UK. It is

Table 3

REGULATED INDUSTRY REFERENCES TO THE MMC, 1983-91

Date	Reference	Company/Report	Recommendation
July 91	Airports	BAA PLC: A report on the economic regulation of the South-East airport companies (Heathrow Airport Ltd, Gatwick Airport Ltd and Stansted Airport Ltd)	*RPI-4* price control formula on average revenue per passenger. Permitted pass-through of 85% of cost of additional Government security proposals. Price formula to be changed to *RPI+1* for Heathrow and *RPI-1* for the group in 95/96 and 96/97 on condition that 5th terminal at Heathrow is started. CAA imposes higher cap of *RPI-6*.
July 90	Merger	British Airways PLC and Sabena SA	Approved. EC investigation running in parallel.
July 90	Nationalised Industry	Civil Aviation Authority: a report of an inquiry into the supply of navigation and air traffic control services to civil aircraft	Efficiency Audit
July 90	Merger	General Utilities PLC and The Mid Kent Water Company	Blocked
July 90	Merger	Southern Water PLC and Mid Sussex Water Company	Approved
Apr 90	Merger	General Utilities PLC, The Colne Valley Water Company and Rickmansworth Water Company	Blocked
Feb 89	Telecoms	Chatline and Message Services: a report on the provision of Chatline and Message Services by means of the British Telecommunications public switched telephone network	Provision of reference services against public interest as customer has inadequate control. BT to provide, when feasible and economical, itemised billing; notice of bill exceeding a given ceiling; call barring of premium rate services. BT also to develop facilities for Calling Line Identification throughout the network and to make chatline service providers act according to a code of practice.
Oct 88	Gas	Gas: a report on the matter of the existence or possible existence of a monopoly situation in relation to the supply in Great Britain of gas throughout pipes to other than tariff customers	BG to publish schedule of tariffs; not to refuse a request to supply; supply gas for combined heat and power schemes on same basis as other users; to offer a single contract for users with multiple premises; publish calculations underlying common carriage terms; maintain confidentiality of potential third party users; not to contract for more than 90% of deliveries from new UK fields.
Dec 87	Airports	Manchester Airport PLC: a report on the economic regulation of the airport	*RPI-1* price control formula on average revenue per passenger. Permitted pass-through of 75% of cost of additional Government security proposals.
Jan 86	Merger	British Telecommunications PLC and Mitel Corporation: a report on the proposed merger	Merger approved, subject to BT undertaking not to acquire Mitel products for UK use: not to cross-subsidise; to renegotiate certain exclusivity terms in contracts; not to joint market or sell and to keep staff structures entirely separate; not to force distribution by other manufacturers through Mitel.
Oct 83	Nationalised Industry	Civil Aviation Authority: a report on the supplying by the Authority of navigation and air traffic control services to civil aircraft	Efficiency Audit

Source: MMC and CAA.

14

also well documented.[5] Vogel (1986), for example, offers the following comparison between the USA and the UK. US regulation is relatively rigid, rule-bound, adversarial and open, with opportunities for third parties to participate. In comparison, UK-style regulation is informal, discretionary, co-operative and closed. The UK system tends to be quick, cheap and flexible.

The preceding contrast is deliberately stark. To claim that bargaining and negotiation are not major features of the US legal system is to turn a blind eye to reality. The prevalence of out-of-court settlements and plea bargaining in criminal cases indicates not only that it is endemic but that it is a central feature of Anglo-American law (Posner, 1986). Indeed, some have suggested that bargaining rather than 'command and control' is an even better description of the procedure of Public Utility Commissions in the USA (Spulber, 1989).

Nonetheless, the extent of bargaining and informality is more striking in the administration of the new economic regulation in the UK. Graham and Prosser (1991, p. 230) state:

> 'It is not too extreme to say that negotiation and bargaining are institutionalised in the regulation of privatised enterprises in Britain.'

Licence modifications and the re-setting of the price controls (i.e. the RPI minus X cap) using the formal procedure of reference to the MMC is clumsy, time-consuming and unpredictable. The different Directors General thus have considerable leeway to negotiate a 'deal' with industry chiefs on terms and in a manner which is determined by the regulator.

Regulatory Strategy is Predictable

The emergence of different regulatory styles and strategies between legal systems and between different industries is not a haphazard occurrence. It is the predictable consequence of the political process, and the economic and institutional constraints facing the parties.

Economics can be (and has been) applied to examine the factors which influence regulatory behaviour and strategies.[6] Most of these models assume that the regulator and other participants in regulation act rationally in the sense that they maximise their own self-interest subject to resource and institutional constraints. Regulators are assumed to define objectives which they pursue in the most cost-effective way by selecting from the legal and extra-legal devices available to them. It

---

[5] Hawkins (1985), Fenn and Veljanovski (1988), Veljanovski (1983a and 1983b), Peacock (1984). *Cf.* Owen and Braeutigam (1974).

[6] Ehrlich and Posner (1974), and the empirical work drawing on McFadden's framework: McFadden (1975 and 1976), Magat (1986), and Fenn and Veljanovski (1988).

would be quite reasonable to assume that the present group of regulators has, as a major priority, consumer protection and competition. The way the regulators implement these objectives is influenced by the law and by the particular industry's structure but not pre-ordained by them.

For some industries the legal system may be sufficiently in tune with policy objectives and the formal law cheap to apply. In this setting one would see a more legalistic enforcement strategy employed by the regulator[7] (as with police and magistrates enforcing the system for punishing traffic offences). In the more general case, however, there will be a mismatch between the law and the most effective method of regulation. In such cases there is a clear economic reason why negotiation and informal methods are preferred – they are cheaper, and result in joint gains to regulator and industry.

Why is UK Regulation so Discretionary?

It directly follows that since negotiation and co-operation are generally cheaper, the inclination of a regulator will be to adopt this strategy first. This will be the case particularly where formal procedures are expensive and cumbersome and/or where the costs of informality are significantly lower because the regulator is subject to weak checks and balances. Where accountability is weak and adjudication, enforcement and detection are contained in the same agency, one would expect that the use of non-legal techniques will be more widespread and that there will be a tendency for more intense regulation.

This is the case in the UK. The new watchdogs are constitutional anomalies which do not fit well into the framework of controls, checks and balances. The regulator therefore has the latitude to use informal negotiated strategies and incurs very low costs in so doing. This is because of three critical features of the legal, or lack of legal, constraints on the regulator – weak accountability, weak judicial review, and the absence of procedural safeguards.

1. *Weak Accountability*

Regulators in the UK have weak channels of accountability. While they are technically accountable to Parliament there is very little structured supervision. The Select Committee system offers one channel but in general the regulators have a free hand to put their own interpretation and stamp their own mark on the regulation of the industry.

---

[7] For a model of mixed regulatory strategies and the determinants of when an agency employs a penal or compliance enforcement strategy, see Fenn and Veljanovski (1988).

2. *Weak Judicial Review*

The prospect of judicial review by the courts generally prevents the agency from acting *ultra vires* (beyond the scope of its legal powers) or in breach of natural justice. Although the scope of judicial review has increased in recent years, its impact on the quality of decision-making by regulatory agencies is weak and offers no real protection. First, English courts are not prepared to evaluate the merits of the case or the quality of the regulator's decisions. Secondly, the remedies available under English administrative law are entirely discretionary and most often do not afford the applicant adequate safeguards. In rather crude terms, they amount to no more than procedural protection that the regulatory agency complies with its own rules or procedures. But if an agency is given discretion, the English courts will generally not interfere on the merits of the decision. In practice, English administrative law acts as a positive inducement for regulatory agencies *not* to state clear criteria nor to give reasons for their decisions, thus preventing the courts from reviewing their actions.

3. *Absence of Procedural Safeguards*

The third factor which enables the system to operate in such a discretionary way is the absence of procedural safeguards. Much lip-service is paid to the idea of transparency in the discussion of regulation. I take 'transparency' to mean sufficient information for the regulator and the public to decide whether prices reflect costs and whether the commercial strategy of the privatised utility is an abuse of its monopoly position. Yet the regulators have shown that they are prepared to keep crucial facts away from the public gaze on grounds of 'commercial sensitivity', particularly on key matters such as whether the prices charged bear a reasonable relationship to the costs.

This is endemic in all UK regulatory proceedings with the notable exceptions of the CAA's route licensing which is trial-like and based on detailed criteria, and the reporting procedures of the MMC. The newer regulatory agencies have been particularly bad at providing a clear framework for their decision-making. This is especially the case in the licensing of television and telecommunications operators. The procedures for the award of cable franchises by the now defunct Cable Authority stood out for their cavalier disregard of the need to explain decisions, as did those of the also defunct Independent Broadcasting Authority (IBA). Indeed, regulatory reform of broad-casting regulation led to the frank admission by the IBA that it had been less than open in the procedures it had followed and had deliberately failed to give reasons for its decisions to avoid litigation and judicial

TABLE 4

PRICE CONTROL REGULATION, AUGUST 1991

Industry	Telecommunications	Gas
Affected Companies	**British Telecom**	**British Gas**
Regulated	Switched inland calls, line rentals, international calls.	Gas supplied to domestic users (those using no more than 25K therms per annum).
Unregulated	Payphone calls, customer premises equipment, telex, mobile radio, VANS, leased lines, etc.	Price of gas supplied to industrial and commercial users, connection charges, appliance sales, etc.
Price Index/Average	The weights in the price index for year *t* are proportional to contributions to turnover in the previous year.	Average price per therm.
Re-Balancing	BT has undertaken that *RPI+2* will apply to domestic rental charges and to reduce international calls by 10%. Oftel has investigated rebalancing between local and trunk call charges, and has investigated some other individual prices.	The standing charge (ie the fixed element of the charge to the user) cannot increase by more than *RPI* in any year.
Efficiency Factor ('X' Factor)	6.25%	2%
Cost Pass-Throughs ('Y' Factor)	None	Changes in the cost of gas supplies to British Gas.
'K' Factor	None	None
Regulatory Review	After five years, licence modification either agreed with BT, or imposed on BT after an MMC investigation on public interest grounds.	Price control reviewed after five years following MMC investigation. 1991 review led to significant proposed changes, e.g. *RPI-5*.

Source: Lexecon Ltd, London.

review.[8] The new procedures for the award of franchises to the applicant offering the highest cash bid were in many ways a direct response to the failings of franchising in the past. Yet old sins die hard. The ITC (1991) statement of the criteria and procedures to be complied with begins:

---

[8] The IBA (1988, p. 9) conceded that in awarding licences it 'made a public announcement about the basis for its selections, but did not give detailed reasons. This avoided the possibility of legal challenge . . .'.

TABLE 4 (Continued)

Airports	Water	Electricity (England & Wales)
BAA, Manchester Airport (MA)	34 Water & Sewerage Companies	12 Regional Electricity Companies (RECs) & National Grid Co (NGC)
Airport charges (for departing passengers, aircraft landings, etc.) at Heathrow, Gatwick, Stansted & Manchester Airports.	Standard domestic and non-domestic supply.	Prices for transmission, distribution and supply. Overall price to customers <1 MW.
Airport charges at other airports. Commercial activities (e.g. retail).	Bulk supplies to other undertakers, Water Infrastructure charge.	Generation business, overall prices to customers >1 MW, electrical contracting appliances, etc.
Average revenue per passenger.	Average charge per chargeable supply for unmeasured water; increase in charge for measured water.	Average charge per KWh supplied or distributed or transmitted.
BAA: Heathrow limited to *RPI+1* and group to *RPI-1* in 1995/96 & 1996/97 on condition that 5th terminal at Heathrow is started.	None	Price control applies to 0-0.1 MW customers as well as 0-1 MW customers.
MA 1%, BAA 4%	None	One for distribution (0% to 2.5%) and one for supply (all 0%) applied to each REC; NGC for transmission 0%.
75% (MA) and 85% (BAA) of additional costs arising from Government airport security requirements.	Very wide range of expenditure, e.g. metering charges, rates and land disposals.	Cost of purchasing generation from the pool.
None	K factor per company: 1991/92 factors range from 3% to 22.5%.	None
Price control reviewed after five years (in 1992 for MA, 1996/97 for BAA) by the Civil Aviation Authority following MMC investigation.	At least every 10 years, every 5 at request of company or Director General.	NGC charges for transmission under review. Price control to be reviewed after 3 years in 1992. RECs monopoly reduced from 1MW to 0.1MW in 1994.

'The ITC disclaims all responsibility for the accuracy or otherwise of the information contained in this document.'

The Subversion of Simplicity

The consequence of this setting is clearly seen in the operation of price control regulation. The criteria and philosophy underlying good regulation was spelt out by the Littlechild Report (1983) on the

19

regulation of BT's profitability (also see Littlechild, 1986 and 1988). This report led to the adoption of the cornerstone of economic regulation, the RPI minus X formula. As already explained, RPI minus X is a price cap which only permits a defined basket of services to rise by the retail price index minus X per cent. The X factor is designed to put pressure on the utility to cut costs and improve productivity. RPI minus X focuses attention on what consumers ultimately care about – the price they have to pay – and makes that price fall in real terms. With a known price cap fixed for five years, the company can get on with reducing real prices to captive customers while at the same time retaining the fruits of its efficiency gains. And it also has the freedom to rebalance the prices of individual services within the average price cap (see Table 4).

Price-cap regulation was intended as a 'temporary regulation' – a stop-gap until fully fledged competition emerged. As Professor Littlechild (1983, para. 4.11), the originator of this form of regulation, stated:

'Competition is indisputably the most effective means ... of protecting consumers against monopoly power. Regulation is essentially a means of preventing the worst excesses of monopoly; it is not a substitute for competition. It is a means of "holding the fort" until competition arrives.'

The great attraction of this approach was its non-discretionary nature which minimised the burden of regulation and the likelihood of agency capture: 'Once X has been chosen,' states Littlechild (1988, p. 56),

'the regulatory authority does not need to approve price changes nor vet the company's investment programme. There is less intervention in the company's business. Fewer regulatory staff are required. Regulation is cheaper. Decision-making is not held up or distorted by bureaucratic inertia or political pressure.'

Clearly the formula must be reviewed and reset to ensure that prices bear a close relationship to costs and the potential for further efficiency gains. In Littlechild's judgement a review every five years met these requirements whilst at the same time preserving the utility's incentives to make the gains. More frequent reviews would simply tax the gains away and make the utility indifferent to improving efficiency.

The Evolving Role of RPI Minus X

We are now in a position to review whether, within the evolving style of UK economic regulation, RPI minus X operates in such a simplistic way.

First, it has been turned into a permanent feature of the regulatory landscape. In large part this arose because in BT's case the Government failed to introduce the maximum feasible amount of competition. As Littlechild (1988, p. 60) later conceded: 'permanent regulation is more complex than temporary regulation'. The formula has been applied to all five privatised industries and has increased in complexity (see Table 4). There are now Y factors, K factors, limits on rebalancing, voluntary price caps inside and outside the 'basket', and so on.

Secondly, the price cap is being undermined by the regulators. The major attraction of the formula is that it would be set and not revised during its initial five years and that the company's rate of return would not be taken into explicit account in determining the price formula. However, during the first five years of BT's privatisation the Director General of OFTEL has threatened to revise the formula at least three times in the light of BT's 'high' profitability. The degree of scrutiny of BT's tariff structure and profits has been much more intense than originally envisaged. OFTEL conducted detailed inquiries into the rebalancing of BT's tariffs in 1985 and 1986. It has reviewed individual price increases within the controls (rental charges, differentials relating to time of day and discounts for long-distance routes), and some unregulated prices (access lines, private leased lines, payphone rentals and telex services), and has reviewed the general level of BT's prices. Indeed, Professor Carsberg has stated that price caps are a species of rate-of-return regulation, and therefore require BT's rate of return to be taken into consideration in its revision (OFTEL, 1988). James McKinnon, the Director General of OFGAS (and another professional accountant), shares this view.

There are three dangers with this emerging belief: it is totally opposed to the original intention of the approach, raises the spectre of cost-plus pricing which would have detrimental effects on customers, and by threatening to take away the utility's profits every time they increase undermines both the company's incentive to cut costs and improve productivity *and* at the same time reduces the possibility of introducing more competition by removing the profits which would act as an inducement for other firms to enter as competitors. Thus we have the perverse result that a regulatory approach which in the short run benefits customers, in the long run becomes its own justification.

4. The 'Regulatory Bargain'

The tensions at the heart of UK regulation are more deep-seated than the prospect of over-zealous regulators. The political imperative to get the nationalised industries into the private sector as fast as possible resulted in a significant trade-off in favour of monopoly and regulation, and away from competition. This required the regulator to act as a 'surrogate for competition'. Thus most regulators confront a situation where the structure of the industry is fundamentally at odds with the goal of competition. The present regulators have clearly not been 'captured' by their industries but they do operate within a regulatory system which was the outcome of an earlier capture. This happened in the very formulation of the agencies and the structure of the industry itself. This is seen by the failure to restructure all but the electricity industry and by the setting of prices for the operation of the price cap at their initial nationalised levels.

As a result many of the regulators have found themselves railing against the implicit understanding – the 'regulatory bargain' – struck between the utilities (read shareholders) and the Government at the time of flotation. The regulators appear to have come to the conclusion: if the structure of the industry and much of the regulation work against competition, then the 'regulatory bargain' must be broken by edging the controls against the utilities. The regulators are encroaching on more areas – prices, quality of service, access, rate of return – and scrutinising and probing more of each utility's activities. In short, they are threatening fundamentally to change the way regulation actually works.

From what has been said so far it can be seen that regulation UK style has the following features:

o   An initial 'regulatory bargain' slanted in favour of the regulated utilities,

o   Coupled with a regulatory system which was intended to be rules based, simple and transparent but which gives regulators considerable discretion and imposes few constraints,

o   Has resulted in two trends:
   (a) a regulatory system which at heart relies on negotiation and informal rule-making; and
   (b) regulators who are railing against the original regulatory bargain by progressively edging the rules against the utilities.

Costs and Benefits of Regulatory Bargaining

How is this development to be assessed? The delegation of discretion to regulators has obvious costs and benefits. It delegates to expert bodies control of complex issues which are not within the competence of Ministers or Parliament to decide. It permits flexibility, adaptation and evolution and speeds decision-making. It can under the right circumstances lead to the fine-tuning of rules to policy objectives and the incorporation of new information into the design of the regulatory system.

Balancing these are some major disadvantages. The first are constitutional ones. There is the possibility that regulation in the UK could well evolve into the rule of men (the regulators) rather than the rule of law. The regulators have been given considerable discretion immune from systematic checks and balances other than through direct Ministerial control. This is not a problem when the 'right people' are in charge, but can lead to major shifts in regulatory policies should a regulator be appointed with a different view of the world.

Secondly, UK regulators are increasingly trading certainty for flexibility, and in the process risking 'stop-go' regulation. The current high profits of the privatised monopoly industries (especially BT and BG) can quite easily create an environment for more stringent price control even though those profits have been generated within pre-set limits of declining real prices for basic services set by the regulators. The naïvety that regulation could be set on automatic pilot once every five years has been matched by the growing pressures on the regulators to intervene, investigate and report on profits, quality of service, prices and whatever else causes consumers, competitors or politicians to complain.

The discussion above and the greater commitment to consumer interests shown by the regulators (including the Citizens' Charter) could be seen as moving in the direction of more efficient regulation despite the drawbacks. The validity of this claim depends crucially on identifying the forces within the regulatory system, apart from the good intentions of regulators and politicians, which would point to the evolution of efficient regulation over time. Some see this as inextricably linked to the amount of information available to the regulator. It is argued that sound regulation is based on good information, and that the present system does not generate sufficient information, as indicated by the difficulties the Director General of OFGAS has had in extracting financial information from British Gas.

Others see the problem as more than merely access to financial information (Kirzner, 1985). Hayek (1947) in particular has expressed extreme scepticism of the ability of institutions that are the product of human design rather than evolution to utilise available knowledge. As a result, regulation is artificial and based on a 'fatal conceit' that one individual can use information in a meaningful way. Yet the above discussion has been at pains to point out the way regulation has evolved in a manner which was not foreseeable and that discretion has been used to fine-tune the law in the light of new facts. Hence the formal regulatory system can be viewed as setting general standards of conduct rather than a rigid command-and-control system. As Littlechild (1988, pp. 88-89) points out, a regulatory agency is engaged in its own discovery

23

process and adjusts to changing events and information. This, as has been shown above, leads to significant modification of regulation in practice.

Regulation and the Common Law

This adaptation does not always progress towards greater efficiency. The essay by Benson in this volume (also see Posner, 1986; Hirshliefer, 1987) argues that the common law has an in-built tendency towards efficient law because it is evolutionary, based on general standards applied on a case-by-case basis by judges who are required to listen to the merits of each party's case presented in an adversarial setting, who are bound by precedent and whose decisions are subject to review by appellate courts. The scope for judges to engage in radical changes in the law or to use it other than to adjudicate a dispute on the basis of the merits of the litigants' cases is therefore severely limited by the checks and balances of the common law system. Regulation, while it shares some of the features of the common law, departs radically in many respects, for the regulator acts as plaintiff (as an agent of consumers and competitors), judge, jury and appeal court subject to the parties' right to disagree and to seek review by the MMC.

There is reason to believe that the private gains and losses to regulator and industry do not mirror the full economic gains and losses so that the regulatory system will not evolve automatically into efficient law. There are several reasons for this conjecture.

First, as we have seen there is a tendency towards more complex regulation. This is inherent in the UK system because the monopoly problem has not been attacked at source. The regulatory historian, Thomas K. McCraw (1984, p. 272), succinctly identifies this tendency in his description of US airline regulation:

> 'Control price, and the result will be artificial stimulus to entry. Control entry as well, and the result will be an artificial stimulus to compete by offering larger commissions to travel agents, advertising, scheduling, free meals, and bigger seats. The response of the complete regulator, then, is to limit advertising, control scheduling and the travel agents' commissions, specify the size of the sandwiches and the seats and the charge for inflight movies. Each time the dyke *[sic]* springs a leak, plug it with one of your fingers, just as a dynamic industry will perpetually find ways of opening new holes in the dyke, so an ingenious regulator will never run out of regulatory fingers.'

Secondly, discretionary case-by-case regulation creates opportunities for the parties to 'game-the-system'. That is, because regulation is operated in a discretionary way, each party has an incentive to operate strategically to obtain an advantage or avoid losses. This in turn consumes resources both directly and indirectly as the industry and other interest groups seek to persuade, threaten, influence and take advantage of the regulatory system. The process by which information is generated in the regulatory system is unlike the common law under which each party in open court provides information to the court, or even like the inquisitorial system of Continental courts or the MMC. The information is not tested in public or subject to routine challenge by the parties. Industry chiefs will know that their actual decisions – to pay high dividends, give themselves salary increases, raise prices – will lead to a reaction from the regulator and a tendency to 'tax' away some of the industry's profits. The industry will react by anticipating the regulator's response, and the scene is set for a system fraught with strategic negotiations and inefficiency brought about by industry chiefs trying to outwit the regulator.

Thirdly, the combination of gaming the system by industry and the urge for the regulator to investigate more widely and deeply, will eventually lead to a merging of regulator and industry interests. Perhaps not this but the next generation of regulators may find their capture more than an accusation of academic economists. It is often observed that many agencies go through a predictable life-cycle. They begin as aggressive regulators of the industry but over time become captured by those regulated as they begin to share their views and interests. In the UK there may come an eventual tip-over point where the regulators unintentionally become the victims of their own zeal by failing to maintain an arm's length relationship with the industry. Professor Littlechild (1988, p. 55) identifies this problem:

> 'The more the regulatory authority is involved in "second-guessing" the company's plans, the more it becomes committed to defending the company when the approved plan is implemented. There is heightened danger of "regulatory capture".'

Admittedly, the list of detrimental effects is at this stage merely conjecture awaiting empirical verification.

5. Conclusion

This essay has deliberately focussed on some of the undesirable effects of UK regulation. It should not be read as an attack on regulation or the progress which has been made to date, nor as a counsel of perfection. Regulation in practice today is far superior and more open than was control of the nationalised industries. Nevertheless, there is little room for complacency. A number of trends and dangers of the new system of regulating the utilities have been identified. Moreover, it is clear that the practice of regulation departs radically from the original philosophy.

Regulation UK style is evolving into a discretionary system where negotiations and personality are becoming its most important features. It is turning into a 'game' between industry chiefs and regulators because regulation does *not* provide a clear and certain set of rules within which the industry can take economic decisions. Rather, investing in influencing regulators and changing the rules of the game are becoming an industry in themselves, consuming resources and increasing the burden of regulation. While it is premature to make any firm pronouncements and/or recommendations there is a case for a fundamental re-assessment, a stock-taking to analyse the diversity of approaches and the impact of UK-style regulation. This could begin by comparing regulation as practised against the original criteria used by Professor Littlechild (1983, pp. 10-11) to frame a sound regulatory system: protection against monopoly abuse, encouragement of efficiency and innovation, low burden of regulation in terms of information costs, degree of discretion and implementation; promotion of competition; and regulatory simplicity and predictability. A review body akin to the Law Commission or the National Audit Office should set about this task by commissioning independent research and undertaking a thorough audit of progress to date.

REFERENCES

Baldwin, R. (1985): *Regulating the Airlines: Administrative Justice and Agencies' Discretion*, Oxford: Oxford University Press.

Baldwin, R., and C. McCrudden (1987): *Regulation and Public Law*, London: Weidenfeld & Nicolson.

DTp (1986): *Economic Regulation of the British Airports Authority plc*, London: HMSO.

Erlich, I., and R. A. Posner (1974): 'An Economic Analysis of Legal Rulemaking', *Journal of Legal Studies*, Vol. 3, pp. 257-86.

Fenn, P., and C. G. Veljanovski (1988): 'A Positive Theory of Regulatory Enforcement', *Economic Journal*, Vol. 98, pp. 1,055-1,070.

Graham, C., and T. Prosser (1991): *Privatizing Public Enterprises*, Oxford: Clarendon Press.

Hawkins, K. (1985): *Environment and Enforcement*, Oxford: Oxford University Press.

Hayek, F. A. (1947): *Individualism and Economic Order*, London: Routledge & Kegan Paul.

Hayek, F. A. (1960): *The Constitution of Liberty*, London: Routledge & Kegan Paul.

Hirshliefer, J. (1987): *Economic Behaviour in Diversity*, Brighton: Harvester Books.

IBA (1988): *Independent Television in the 1990s*, London: Independent Broadcasting Authority.

ITC (1991): *Invitation to Apply for Regional Channel 3 Licences*, London: Independent Television Commission.

Kirzner, I. M. (1985): *Discovery and the Capitalist Process*, Chicago: University of Chicago Press.

Littlechild, S. C. (1983): *Regulation of British Telecommunications' Profitability*, London: HMSO.

Littlechild, S. C. (1986a): *Economic Regulation of Privatised Water Authorities*, London: HMSO.

Littlechild, S. C. (1986b): *The Fallacy of the Mixed Economy*, Hobart Paper No. 80, 2nd edition, London: Institute of Economic Affairs.

Littlechild, S. C. (1988): 'Economic Regulation of the Privatised Water Authorities and Some Further Reflections', *Oxford Review of Economic Policy*, Vol. 4, pp. 40-68.

Magat, W. A., *et al.* (1986): *Rules in the Making – A Statistical Analysis of Regulatory Agency Behaviour*, Washington DC: Resources for the Future.

McGraw, K. (1984): *Prophets of Regulation*, Cambridge, Mass.: Belknap Press.

McFadden, D. (1976): 'The Revealed Preferences of Government Bureaucracy: Empirical Evidence', *Bell Journal of Economics*, Vol. 7, pp. 55-72.

McFadden, D. (1975): 'The Revealed Preferences of a Government Bureaucracy: Theory', *Bell Journal of Economics & Management Science*, Vol. 6, pp. 404-16.

NCC (1989): *In the Absence of Competition – A Consumer View of Public Utilities Regulation*, London: HMSO.

NEDO (1976): *A Study of UK Nationalised Industries*, London: National Economic Development Office.

OFTEL (1988): *The Regulation of British Telecom's Prices – A Consultation Document*, London: Office of Telecommunications.

Owen, B. R., and R. Braeutigam (1974): *Strategic Uses of the Regulatory Process*, Cambridge, Mass.: Ballinger Publishers.

Peacock, A. T. (ed.) (1984): *The Regulation Game – How British and West German Companies Bargain with Government*, Oxford: Basil Blackwell.

Posner, R. A. (1986): *Economic Analysis of Law*, Boston: Little Brown, 3rd. edn.

Spulber, D. F. (1989): *Regulation and Markets*, Cambridge, Mass., and London: M.I.T. Press.

Veljanovski, C. G. (1983a): 'The Market for Regulatory Enforcement', *Economic Journal*, Vol. 93, pp. 122-28.

Veljanovski, C. G. (1983b): 'Regulatory Enforcement: A Case Study of the British Factory Inspectorate', *Law & Policy Quarterly*, Vol. 5, pp. 75-96.

Veljanovski, C. G. (1987): *Selling the State – Privatisation in Britain*, London: Weidenfeld & Nicolson.

Veljanovski, C. G. (ed.) (1989): *Privatisation and Competition: A Market Prospectus*, Hobart Paperback No. 28, London: Institute of Economic Affairs.

Veljanovski, C. G. (1990): 'The Political Economy of Regulation', in P. Dunleavy *et al.* (eds.), *Developments in British Politics 3*, London: Macmillan.

Vogel, D. (1986): *National Styles of Regulation*, Ithaca, New York: Cornell University Press.

Waterson, M. (1991): *Regulation and Ownership of the Major Utilities*, Discussion Paper No. 5, London: Fabian Society.

White Paper (1961): *Financial and Economic Obligations of the Nationalised Industries*, Cmnd. 1337, London: HMSO.

White Paper (1967): *Nationalised Industries: A Review of Economic and Financial Objectives*, Cmnd. 3437, London: HMSO.

White Paper (1978): *The Nationalised Industries*, Cmnd. 7131, London: HMSO.

White Paper (1982): *The Future of Telecommunications in the UK*, Cmnd. 8610, London: HMSO.

White Paper (1988): *Privatising Electricity – The Government's Proposals for the Privatisaion of the Electricity Supply Industry in England and Wales*, Cm. 322, London: HMSO.

2

THE REGULATION OF PRIVATISED MONOPOLIES IN THE UNITED KINGDOM*

M. E. Beesley
London Business School

and

S. C. Littlechild
University of Birmingham

1. Summary and Introduction

THIS PAPER examines the experience in the United Kingdom with the regulation of privatised monopolies. Its conclusions are:

o   that there are significant differences between RPI minus X (or price-cap) and US rate-of-return regulation, which provides greater scope for bargaining in the former system;

o   that UK regulators have taken seriously their duty to promote competition, but that the existing economic literature is of limited help in this task;

o   that price regulation is likely to be more effective where technology is changing slowly and/or where there are many firms in an industry, whereas the promotion of competition is indicated where technology is changing rapidly; and

o   that the case for RPI-X price-cap, rather than rate-of-return regulation, is strongest in telecommunications, gas supply, and electricity supply, and least strong in gas and electricity transmission grids.

*© 1989. Reprinted by kind permission of RAND from *The RAND Journal of Economics*, Vol. 20, Autumn 1989, pp. 454-72.

Since 1979, the Conservative Government has transferred over two dozen public enterprises into private ownership. Most of them previously operated in more or less competitive industries, but three of the largest – namely, British Telecom (BT), British Airports Authority (BAA), and British Gas (BG) – had market shares approaching 100 per cent for their core activities. These three companies now operate under licences containing many obligations and constraints. Independent regulatory authorities, each headed by a Director General, monitor and enforce compliance with licence conditions. The privatisation of the water and electricity industries has followed a similar pattern, although in these two industries there are a number of successor companies rather than a single major one. Thus, in the UK there is now a set of five major privatised industries which (in the US context) would normally be thought of as regulated utilities.

The statutory duties of the regulators include protecting the interests of producers (licensees), of consumers of various kinds, and of employees and third parties (e.g., environmental concerns). The wording varies but, for present purposes, three main objectives may be identified in the respective privatisation Acts:

(1) to ensure that all reasonable demands are met, and that licensees are able to finance the provision of these services;

(2) to protect the interests of consumers with respect to prices and quality of service; and

(3) to enable or to promote competition in the industry.

Strictly speaking, the duties of the regulator are not a direct obligation to achieve the stated objectives, but rather require the regulator to carry out his statutory functions in the manner which he believes is best calculated to achieve these objectives.

Economics of Privatisation

Economists may find it helpful to analyse privatisation as the instrument of change in a cost-benefit appraisal. The privatisation Acts, and in particular the duties of the regulators, may be interpreted as consistent with a formal aim of maximising the present value of expected net benefits to consumers plus producers, subject to a minimum profit condition and to various constraints on the distribution of benefits to ensure Pareto efficiency (i.e., no major interest group is to be made worse off). The problem then faced by each regulator is to interpret this general criterion and make it operational. In particular, the regulator has to balance the interests of present and future consumers, both against each other and against the interests of present and future producers.

This article examines the experience of the United Kingdom with regulation of privatised monopolies. In particular, we consider:

o   whether the form of price control adopted is significantly different from US rate-of-return regulation and how far this constitutes an advantage;

o   how regulators have tackled their duty to promote competition and what mode of economic analysis is more appropriate for this; and

o   under what circumstances each of the two main regulatory duties is likely to be performed most effectively and what this implies for government policy.

2. Price Control

Rate-of-return regulation is well established in the USA. There have been numerous variants across jurisdictions, across industries, and over time, but for present purposes the key features of 'traditional' rate-of-return regulation may be characterised as follows (see Phillips, 1969).

The regulated company files a tariff when it wishes to revise its prices. For an agreed test period ('frequently the latest 12-month period for which complete data are available': Phillips, 1969), the company calculates operating costs, capital employed, and cost of capital. The regulator audits these calculations and determines a fair rate of return on capital employed. These data plus assumptions about demand are used to calculate the total revenue requirement. This determines the level of the tariff. The structure of the tariff has to avoid unfairness and unjust or unreasonable discrimination. The tariff therefore has to be approved on a line-by-line or service-by-service basis, which typically requires the allocation of common costs on the basis of, for example, output, direct costs, revenues, and so on. An approved tariff generally stands until the company files to change it, usually on the ground that the achieved rate of return has become inadequate.

When making its plans for privatising British Telecom (BT), the Department of Industry's original intention was to adopt a modified rate-of-return regulation. After further discussion and investigation, however (Littlechild, 1983), a control on prices, or price-cap, was finally adopted and variants of it have been used for the other privatised utilities.

The key features of this price control are that, for a pre-specified period of four to five years, the company can make any changes it wishes to prices, provided that the average price of a specified basket of its goods and services does not increase faster than RPI-X, where RPI is the

Retail Price Index (i.e., the rate of inflation) and X is a number specified by the government. At the end of the specified period, the level of X is reset by the regulator, and the process is repeated.

Rate of Return versus RPI-X

The pros and cons of rate-of-return regulation versus RPI-X and other schemes have been frequently discussed (e.g., Littlechild (1983), Vickers and Yarrow (1988), Johnson (1989)). Briefly, the main arguments for RPI-X, as originally spelled out in the context of privatising BT and subsequently repeated in other cases, are threefold.

First, RPI-X is less vulnerable to 'cost-plus' inefficiency and over-capitalisation (the 'Averch-Johnson effect'). Because the company has the right to keep whatever profits it can earn during the specified period (and must also absorb any losses), this preserves the incentive to productive efficiency associated with unconstrained profit maximisation. Part of this expected increase in efficiency can be passed on to customers, via the level of X. Prices are therefore lower than they would be under rate-of-return control, without producers being worse off.

Second, RPI-X allows the company greater flexibility to adjust the structure of prices within the basket, and in principle there is no constraint on prices outside the basket. This is of particular importance where, as with British Telecom, initial prices were thought to be considerably out of line with relative costs, yet 'optimal' prices could not be immediately determined and achieved because of inadequate knowledge of costs and demands, as well as political constraints on speed of adjustment.

Third, RPI-X is simpler to operate by the regulator and the company. It is more transparent and better focussed on the parameter(s) of greatest concern to customers, hence providing them with greater reassurance.

The main counter-argument against the incentive and efficiency claim may be summarised as follows. The level of X must in practice be set and repeatedly adjusted to secure a reasonable rate of return. If not, allocative inefficiencies will arise (from prices being out of line with costs), and there will be political pressures from company or consumers. If the criteria for revising X are left unclear, this will increase the cost of capital and/or discourage investment. Clear guidelines must therefore be laid down, or must emerge from precedent, for resetting X. These guidelines will have to embody an explicit feedback from cost reduction to (eventual) price reduction. This will negate the superior incentive effects claimed for RPI-X. Specifically, companies may believe that the short-term advantages of increased efficiency and lower costs will be more than offset by a tougher X and therefore lower prices in the next period, and may even induce an adverse change of X within the current period. In this view, RPI-X is merely a special form of rate-of-return control, embodying no significant net advantage over the US approach on grounds of economic efficiency.

It is also questioned whether RPI-X involves as much price flexibility and transparency as claimed. It is further suggested that greater price flexibility may be a disadvantage rather than an advantage, since it allows cross-subsidisation which is allocatively inefficient and may be used anti-competitively.[1]

The key questions to pose in this section are thus whether in practice RPI-X makes any difference to regulation and, if so, whether the differences are beneficial. Our aim is to assess how RPI-X has actually operated in the UK. We make no attempt to assess its potential effectiveness in or appropriateness to the USA.

(a) Setting and Resetting X

In assessing these arguments, it is necessary to understand the procedures for setting and resetting X, and to appreciate the similarities and differences between them.

The RPI-X constraint is one of many conditions in the regulated company's licence, all of which are initially set by the government. Unlike the other conditions, it has a limited duration, typically five years, and there is no formal constraint on the magnitude of X in any subsequent period. The regulator may modify any licence condition at any time by agreement with the licensee. If the licensee does not agree, the regulator may refer the matter to the Monopolies and Mergers Commission (MMC) and has the authority to modify the licence if and only if the MMC finds the licensee to be acting against the public interest. (With certain exceptions, the licensee has no power to refer possible licence modifications to the MMC.) Renewal of the RPI-X constraint, whatever the level of X, is equivalent to a licence modification.

The initial level of X is set by the government at the time of privatisation, as part of the privatisation process, whereas X is reset by the regulator as part of the continuing regulatory process. This has three important implications.

First, the initial level of X is set as part of a whole package of

---

[1] Other issues lie beyond the scope of this paper. For example, it has been suggested that RPI-X may offer less incentive to maintain service quality (Vickers and Yarrow, 1988; Besen, 1989). The framework of regulation needs to be designed accordingly, and the Acts and licences do in fact reflect this consideration.

measures, whose parameters affect the costs, revenues, and risks of the regulated company. Some of these parameters pertain to the design of the price control itself, including the duration of the price constraint, its scope in terms of goods and services included, what costs (if any) are allowed to be 'passed through' into prices, and whether the constraint is calculated on the basis of historical or expected performance. All these parameters are embodied in licence conditions. Other parameters pertain to the wider regulatory framework, including what other non-commercial obligations or constraints are put on the company, what steps are taken to encourage or restrict competition, what policies are adopted towards suppliers, and so on. Both sets of parameters are fixed by the government more or less simultaneously in full acknowledge-ment of the interactions and trade-offs between them. They are gradually firmed up and made more precise in the run-up to privatisation, culminating in the determination of certain key parameters, including X, prior to publication of the prospectus, a few weeks before flotation. (The striking price of the shares is determined later in this last period and will be heavily influenced by the anticipated changes in the stock market level up to the flotation date.)

In contrast, the resetting of X takes place in a context where these parameters have already been determined. Admittedly they could be changed, and in practice some have been, but to make substantial and unexpected changes would have potentially adverse effects on the company's cost of capital and hence on prices to customers. Moreover, insofar as any proposed changes pertain to the company's licence, if the company does not agree to the changes, the regulator may not wish to run the risk of an unsuccessful appeal to the MMC. There are thus fewer degrees of freedom in resetting X.

Second, the initial level of X is set by the government as owner of the company, whereas X is reset by a regulator who does not own the shares. The government as owner can choose, if it wishes, to take lower proceeds in return for, say, lower prices to customers. The regulator does not have that extra degree of freedom: any shift in favour of one interest group (such as customers) will be at the expense of another group (such as shareholders). The regulator is constrained by the expectations of shareholders and customers, which were established at privatisation, and his discretion is limited to whatever range is deemed acceptable (or can be so presented).

The *third* difference between setting and resetting X, which re-inforces the previous two, relates to the effect on the company's share price. In both cases the level of X will influence the share price via its effects on expected net revenue streams, so in practice the stock market decides the yield to shareholders. At the time that X is initially set, however, this effect has to be conjectured. It is not known with any certainty how potential investors will evaluate the company put before them. Nor is there any market valuation of the previous or alternative arrangements with which to compare it. After privatisation, however, the views of investors are clearly reflected in the company's traded share price, with its accompanying dividend yield, price/earnings ratio, relative risk factor ß, etc. A change in the stock market's evaluation of the company, following any action by the regulator, in particular his revision of X, can be immediately observed in the change in share price. If the market regards the regulator's decision as favourable to the company (i.e., more favourable than expected), its share price is marked up and its cost of capital falls; the opposite happens if the decision is regarded unfavourably. The regulator cannot ignore this consideration in his decisions, and it re-inforces the greater constraints on resetting X than on setting it initially.

To summarise, when setting X initially there are many degrees of freedom. X is just one of numerous parameters chosen simultaneously in the light of the political and economic trade-offs involved. There is nothing unique, optimal, or mechanical about the initial choice of X. When X is reset, there are significantly fewer degrees of freedom. Nevertheless, there invariably are degrees of freedom open to the regulator.

(b) Two Examples

The following two examples will illustrate the above procedures and provide further insights into the characteristics of the RPI-X approach.

(i) Setting X for Manchester Airport

The Airports Act of 1986 provides for economic regulation of 'designated' airports. At privatisation, the Secretary of State designated BAA's three London airports and specified RPI-X regulation with $X = 1$ per cent. He also designated Manchester Airport, but delegated to the Civil Aviation Authority (CAA), as regulator, the task of designing Manchester's regulatory constraint. The Airports Act required the CAA, in turn, to seek the advice of the MMC.

Since Manchester Airport was not to be privatised, but was to remain in the ownership of Manchester City Council, in important respects the considerations involved were different from those where X is set or reset for a privatised company. Nonetheless, there are useful insights to be obtained from the MMC report because it sets out in some detail its reasoning on RPI-X. (It should be noted that the MMC in this context is an 'advisor' to the regulator, not the regulator itself, and by convention the MMC's report is its only means of conveying that advice.)

The MMC recommended that RPI-X be adopted rather than rate-of-return control, for the kinds of reasons given earlier. The Airports Act set the review period at five years, and the MMC was advised that the scope of price control had to comprise landing, parking, and passenger charges, but not baggage handling charges. The MMC exercised judgement on four main parameters apart from the level of X. It recommended:

(i)   that there be a single basket for all three charges rather than (say) three separate baskets or additional sub-constraints on prices;

(ii) that the formula be based on a 'tariff basket' (as used for British Telecom), with weights reflecting revenues in the previous year rather than on a 'revenue yield' basis (as used for BAA) involving predicted revenue per unit and a subsequent correction factor;

(iii) that no special allowance be made for passing-through costs associated with changes in (non-economic) government regulation, except for three-quarters of any additional airport security costs; and

(iv) that the present levels of airport charges (which some users claimed were too high) were the appropriate starting point for the formula.

In proposing a level for X, the MMC's procedure was, first, to examine four important issues: future traffic growth, the timing and financing of capital expenditure (particularly the construction of a second terminal), the development of (unregulated) commercial income, and the scope for cost reduction and productivity increases. After exploring a range of alternative assumptions, it adopted those used by the company itself (except on 100 per cent self-financing policy), albeit commenting that some of these assumptions were rather cautious. On the basis of the adopted assumptions, it used the company's financial model to make predictions, for each year over a five-year horizon, of four financial magnitudes (operating profit before and after interest and tax, net current assets, and shareholders' funds) and five financial ratios (gearing or debt-equity ratio, self-financing ratio, interest cover, dividend cover, and return on capital employed). The MMC then

'looked for a value of X which would give the necessary degree of protection to users of the airport while leaving the company in a financially sound position and able to carry through its capital expenditure plans' (see MMC, 1987).

It recommended that X = 1 per cent.

It should be noted that the MMC approach was explicitly based on future predictions, and a central problem for the MMC was to decide what those predictions should be. It felt that Manchester's assumptions were often cautious, but had no firm basis for making alternative assumptions. (Over time, a regulator would aim to secure an independent source of information on these matters, and the CAA has begun to do so, as have the other regulators in their own areas. We discuss this point further, below, pp. 52-55.)

This forward-looking approach also applied to the financial calculations. The rate of return on (historic) book capital was only one of nine financial projections and ratios that the MMC studied. It was projected to decline steadily from the present 18·8 per cent to 9·0 per cent at the end of five years. The MMC merely commented that these rates of return were considered 'consistent with our assessment of the company's financial soundness, which is also reflected in the other projections' (see MMC, 1987). Thus, in order to assess the future yield to shareholders, the MMC found it necessary to go beyond a single historic cost ratio.

The CAA proposed to accept the MMC's recommendations. Manchester Airport then appealed to the CAA, arguing for X = 2 per cent (i.e., RPI-2) and a revenue yield approach. Other interested parties also made representations. The CAA upheld X = 1 per cent, but granted Manchester Airport's request for revenue yield. The CAA report hints at the bargaining situation in which it found itself but, in giving its verdict, does not quantify (for example) the differential effect on future cash flows of revenue yield versus a tariff basket approach (see Civil Aviation Authority, 1988).

(ii) Setting and Resetting X for British Telecom

At a late stage in the privatisation of British Telecom in 1984, three parameters remained to be determined: the contents of the 'basket' (i.e., the coverage of the price cap), whether to allow unrestricted resale of BT's leased lines, and the level of X. The third parameter had clear implications for prices and proceeds, but so did the other two. Unrestricted resale would allow competitors to use low-priced BT circuits to undercut high-priced BT phone calls; this would mean lower prices, revenues, and proceeds. Restricting the basket to local calls and connection charges, for which the monopoly was thought to be strongest, would leave little scope for price reductions. Indeed, British

37

Telecom argued that local calls and connections were already underpriced. On the other hand, incorporating inland trunk calls – where competition was pending, prices were already considerably in excess of costs, and technological prospects were for yet lower costs – would give scope for greater average price reductions across the basket as a whole. (International calls, though known to be highly profitable, were not a serious candidate for inclusion at that time, perhaps reflecting the government's unwillingness to provoke issues of international liberalisation at a time when only the USA was clearly pursuing similar policies.)

There was considerable negotiation, involving a wide range of Xs. (This has been repeated in subsequent privatisations.) The eventual outcome was a package comprising no resale, inland trunk calls in the basket, and X = 3 per cent. The detailed calculations on which this figure was based have not been published. (Nor, for that matter, have any of the calculations of other Xs by government departments.) The offer price for BT's shares was set to ensure that there would be demand from a large number of small shareholders and employees. After flotation, the share price was duly bid up by institutional shareholders, who had excess demand at the offer price.

As BT's profits increased, the question was raised whether they were excessive, even though its prices were within the RPI-X constraint. The regulator published an assessment of the appropriate rate of return for BT to earn, concluding that the then-observed level of 18 per cent on book value was about right. (Director General of Telecommunications, 1986; for a debate on the adequacy of this assessment, see Beesley *et al.*, 1987, and Carsberg, 1987.) BT, in fact, held its prices below the permitted maximum for two years. The regulator also commented on BT's changing price structure, suggesting that rebalancing between inland trunk and local call prices had gone far enough. His staff published an analysis of price structure based on Ramsey pricing (Culham, 1987), although this was viewed with caution by the regulator himself.

The resetting of X in 1989 was preceded by a consultative document (Director General of Telecommunications, 1988a) in which the regulator invited comments and suggestions for modification to the whole framework of BT's price control, such as substituting rate of return for RPI-X, using revenue yield instead of tariff basket, changing the coverage and duration of RPI-X, and so on. Each of these would have required a change in the licence, and therefore allowed the possibility of a challenge by BT and reference to the MMC. An agreement was reached. The regulator reduced the duration of the subsequent review period from five to four years (to reflect the uncertainties involved and BT's own investment planning horizon), slightly extended the coverage of the price cap (to include directory services), and increased X from 3 per cent to 4·5 per cent. He rejected the option of including international calls in the basket, but indicated that he would keep this area under review. He gave no detailed explanation for his choice of X, beyond indicating that rate of return was the most important criterion, but not the only one. The other factor mentioned was the financing of investment. He stated that in determining X, he had considered the effect on growth in earnings and borrowing, as well as on rate of return (Director General of Telecommunications, 1988b).

The regulator noted that he had taken some account of current cost accounting results. Perhaps a decision based entirely on such a valuation would have indicated higher prices and therefore a lower X, which would have been favourable to BT. In explaining his position, however, the regulator stated that current cost accounting should not be used as the sole basis of regulation unless it was also used as the main basis of reporting to shareholders. BT was evidently unwilling to do this. Nor did BT think it advantageous to challenge the decision on X, which would have meant submitting to an MMC investigation. As it happens, BT's share price did not move significantly after the announcement, suggesting that changing X to 4·5 per cent did not alter the stock market's expectations of BT's future profit stream.

One may surmise that the regulator focussed the issue of the future level of X on BT's prospective or possible gains in productivity. By making effective use of the degrees of freedom open to him in redefining the formula and of BT's unwillingness to challenge his decision, the regulator was able to get agreement to a higher X than would otherwise have been possible. He thus set a target for efficiency, which BT was constrained to follow; he did not base his judgement primarily on evidence of what had previously happened in the industry.

Incentives and Efficiency
In the light of these two examples, but also taking into account the experiences of the other industries, we may now address the argument on incentives and efficiency.

RPI-X and rate-of-return regulation have certain common features. Both accept the need to secure an adequate return for the company's shareholders in order to induce them to continue to finance the business, without conceding unnecessarily high prices at the expense of customers. Nevertheless, there are significant differences between the two systems, which give RPI-X a potential advantage with respect to incentives and efficiency.

First, RPI-X embodies an exogenously determined risk period between appraisals of prices, whereas rate-of-return regulation makes the duration of this period endogenous. Admittedly, US regulatory commissions have tended not to intervene when profits are increasing, provided that prices are not increased (Joskow, 1974), but the company can file for a new tariff whenever its performance diminishes, which may be quite frequently. This last is not possible in the UK. The regulator can propose a modification of X within the risk period. BT's regulator considered doing this, but he decided not to. Apart from the disincentive effects, there would have been a risk of not getting MMC support for a contested licence modification. BT's regulator also re-inforced the concept of an exogenous risk period by reducing its duration from five to four years to limit the extent of uncertainty during the period, and emphasised that any mid-term review should be limited to major unexpected events outside the company's control (Director General of Telecommunications, 1988b).

Second, RPI-X is more forward-looking than rate-of-return regulation. The latter tends to be based on historic costs and demands, with adjustments for the future limited (at most) to an adjustment for inflation or the extrapolation of historic trends.[2] In contrast, RPI-X embodies forecasts of what productivity improvements can be achieved and what future demands will be, and is set on the basis of predicted future cash flows.

Third, there are more degrees of freedom in setting X than are involved in rate-of-return regulation. The latter system does allow flexibility (e.g., on the basis of asset valuation, the definition of the rate base, treatment of work in progress, etc.), but it would seem difficult to change these decisions repeatedly. X is initially set in the context of negotiations about the whole regulatory framework, including the coverage, duration, and form of the price constraints, the extent of non-commercial obligations, the restrictions on competition, and the

---

[2] 'Commissions base costs upon a test year due to the need for certainty – the need to avoid unresolvable factual disputes that threaten lengthy proceedings, arbitrary decisions, and court reversals. Although last year's prices will differ from likely future prices, at least they are known. One thereby avoids what would be an endless and unresolvable argument about what future costs will probably be' (Breyer, 1982, p. 50).

'The Commissions have been hesitant to make future forecasts of consumer demand, often preferring instead to assume that the test-period demand conditions will hold in the immediate future' (Phillips, 1969, p. 136).

Joskow (1974) noted that 'a few Commissions have begun to cautiously use "projected" test year results, allowing companies to predict cost and demand conditions one or two years ahead', but this does not appear to have become standard practice. Automatic adjustment mechanisms are, however, widely used (Joskow, 1974; Spulber, 1989).

permissible rate of adjustment from inherited pricing policies. In resetting X, the regulator has fewer degrees of freedom, but nonetheless can modify (at least at the margins) any aspect of this framework and in practice has done so.

Fourth, in setting X the UK regulator has more discretion and less need to reveal the basis of his decisions than does his US counterpart. The US tradition is to place all evidence and reasoning in the public record. In the UK, there is less pressure for due process. The UK regulator is deemed to be a person to whom public policy may be safely delegated, subject only to judicial review on the question of whether his actions are legitimate in terms of the Act. In the UK, neither governments nor regulators have given detailed reasons for their decisions on X. This reduces the basis for challenge (by company, competitors, or customers).

The consequence of these four differences – exogenous risk period, forward-looking approach, degrees of freedom, and less requirement to explain – is that there is greater scope for bargaining in RPI-X than in rate-of-return regulation. The level of X can reflect negotiations with the company, not only about the scope for future productivity agreements, but also about other matters affecting the company's future, including the details of the price constraint formula, the rate at which competition is allowed to develop, the provision of information, and so on. In short, X may be thought of as one of several variables in a political and commercial bargaining process.

It is not suggested that UK regulation is conducted, or even perceived, primarily in terms of bargaining. Nor, on the other hand, is it claimed that there is no scope for bargaining in US rate-of-return regulation. Spulber (1989), for example, explicitly characterised US rate hearings as a bargaining process between consumers and the regulated firm. The hearings economise on the transaction costs of forming consumer coalitions and bargaining directly with the firms. The regulatory commission establishes rules for negotiation and mechanisms for the resolution of conflicts, selects the issues that are open to debate, acts as arbiter and 'may select an outcome especially if bargaining does not yield a unique solution' (p. 270). Spulber also notes that 'rates are often set indirectly through decisions on methods of estimating costs, demand, and rates of return' (p. 272). These insights are not inconsistent with our own assessment. Our claim here is simply that the UK approach offers greater and more direct scope for bargaining, with a correspondingly more active rôle for the regulator.

There is an important implication for incentives and efficiency. The exogenous risk period and the forward-looking approach mean that the company is not deterred from making efficiency improvements either by fear of confiscation within the period or by the belief that allowed future prices will simply be an extrapolation of past costs. The regulator can take an independent view of the scope for productivity improvements and can use the discretion and degrees of freedom open to him, including the absence of a requirement to justify decisions in detail, to negotiate a better deal than would otherwise be possible.

Whether the difference between RPI-X and rate-of-return regulation is significant depends on whether the regulator is able to use the additional bargaining power effectively. This depends upon the underlying scope for efficiency improvements and upon the extent and quality of the information available to him (see Vickers and Yarrow, 1988). These factors will differ from one industry to another. We take up this issue in the final section of this paper.

Price Flexibility

Traditional US rate-of-return regulation requires each price to be individually approved. Changing a price requires the filing of a new tariff. In principle, RPI-X allows any price to be changed at any time, subject only to the price cap on the average price within the basket. The coverage of the price cap is approximately 37 per cent of BAA's total revenue, 57 per cent of BT's, 63 per cent of BG's, and probably 95 per cent or more of the water and electricity companies. Again, in principle, there is no constraint on prices outside the basket.

In practice, the regulated companies are typically more constrained than this. BAA has sub-constraints on its two major airports; the public electricity suppliers will have separate constraints on their distribution and supply activities; and BT gave a written undertaking (outside the licence) to limit the rate of increase of residential line rentals to RPI+2. The regulator has since added an additional constraint for BT's private circuits and brought directory services into BT's basket; non-discrimination provisions have also been added for gas. There are also informal constraints: BT's regulator indicated that the rebalancing of trunk and local call prices had, in his view, gone far enough, with the threat of explicit control via modification of the licence. There is always an incentive for a regulator to increase control by refining and extending the basket.

On the other hand, the rebalancing problem was in part attributable to the definition of BT's basket (which included competitive as well as monopoly services) rather than to the RPI-X concept itself. As Johnson (1989) has suggested, a key task during each formal review is to redesign the basket(s) to reflect (changing) market conditions.[3] BT's regulator did not in fact press his concerns on relative prices and, in particular, did not adopt the Ramsey pricing philosophy examined by his staff. Any new contested constraint would, in any case, need MMC approval. In effect, the burden of proof is on the regulator to show cause why the rebalancing of prices should not occur. The opposite applies in US rate-of-return regulation, where the burden is on the company to justify the price changes it proposes. There seems no doubt that RPI-X allows greater pricing flexibility for the regulated company.

Whether this flexibility constitutes an advantage depends upon how much price flexibility is required (e.g., to reflect changing conditions), how much information is available to the regulator for determining prices in detail, and what other instruments are available for dealing with anti-competitive pricing (e.g., non-discrimination provisions). Again, we return to these issues in the final section of the paper.

Transparency: Cost Pass-Through and the X-Formula

As privatisation has been extended from BT to other utilities, questions have arisen as to whether the simple RPI-X constraint is appropriate for industries with different cost and demand structures. For example, should certain costs be passed through into prices, and should the price cap be based on historic or predicted parameters? Decisions on these questions have implications for profits and proceeds, consumer prices, and economic efficiency, as well as having an effect on transparency.

Cost Pass-Through

An essential feature of any price-control scheme is the provision to be made for costs which are considered outside the control of the regulated company's management. Several options are available. A simple RPI-X constraint, based on expected costs, would expose the company to higher risk, thereby increasing the cost of capital and reducing proceeds. Setting a lower (less stringent) value of X would provide a greater margin against risk, but would imply higher prices for customers. Shortening the review period would reduce risk, but would also reduce the scope and incentive for cost savings; the cost of review would also be incurred more frequently.

The fourth possibility is to allow increases in specified costs to be passed through to customers as they occur. This does not eliminate the risk, but simply transfers it from company to customer. It therefore

---

[3] The possibility of a company cross-subsidising competitive uncapped services out of monopoly capped services is frequently mentioned in the literature (e.g. Johnson (1989), Besen (1989), Spulber (1989)), but to date this has not been a major issue in UK regulatory experience.

reduces the incentive of the company to seek lower cost or less uncertain sources of supply – for example, by signing fixed-price contracts with suppliers – and increases that incentive for customers. To the extent that prices vary more directly with costs, there may be an increase in allocative efficiency at the expense of productive efficiency. There is a reduction in transparency because of the added complexity in the regulatory formula and the reduced predictability of prices.

UK practice has varied. Both BT and BAA have zero pass-through (except for three-quarters of the unforeseen additional cost of airport security). The price controls in the other three industries make significant provision for pass-through: for BG, the costs of buying gas; for the water authorities, the costs of meeting any unforeseen government commitment such as new EC directives (subject to a minimum threshold set at 10 per cent of turnover); and for public electricity suppliers, the costs of purchasing electricity from the generating companies. In the latter case, a yardstick provision (relating a proportion of pass-through to the costs of the industry as a whole) is also envisaged.

Tariff Basket versus Revenue Yield

Another feature of price control is the precise rule for determining allowed price changes. BT's rule is based on the concept of a 'tariff basket', whereby price changes must be such that the average price of the services in the basket, as weighted by observed usage in the previous year, does not increase by more than RPI-X. The water industry has a similar rule. In contrast, price regulation for BAA and BG (and prospectively for the privatised electricity companies) is based on a 'revenue yield' approach, whereby price changes must be such that the forecasted average revenue-per-unit of output (e.g., per passenger or per therm) in the next year does not increase by more than RPI-X. The necessary forecasts of output are made by the regulated company itself, and the formula involves an additional correction factor to repay or recoup any deviation between prediction and outcome.

The relative incentive effects of each type of formula have been debated and are not unambiguous, although it has been suggested that the revenue yield approach is more open to strategic behaviour by the regulated firm (see Cheong, 1989). Revenue yield may be expected to reduce the risk to the regulated company in two ways: it smooths, over time, the average revenue-per-unit and gives the company (via determination of the forecasts) greater control over the total level of revenue. As with cost pass-through, however, this simply transfers the risks to customers and may reduce the company's incentive to seek a less variable pattern of income. There is also less transparency as the regulatory formula becomes more complex and future price changes less predictable.

In sum, the record on transparency is somewhat mixed. BT's simple RPI-X constraint is still in place, but three of the other utilities make heavy use of cost pass-through, and three have revenue yield constraints based on expectations declared by the regulated companies themselves. Such features reduce transparency and efficiency, though they may protect profits and proceeds or may allow a tougher X on prices. In the absence of transparency, protection for customers has to depend upon faith in the regulatory process rather than upon an explicitly guaranteed outcome. In this respect, cost pass-through and revenue yield are similar to rate-of-return regulation.

3. The Promotion of Competition

The promotion of competition is not traditionally associated with the regulation of utilities in the USA. The regulatory commissions have a long record of resisting entry, and it has been persuasively argued that the real purpose of regulation was to protect incumbents from competition (Stigler, 1971, and Jarrell, 1978). Admittedly, competition issues have loomed increasingly large in telecommunications, especially since the 'above 890'[4] decision in 1969. The FCC has been concerned lately with protecting entrants from various forms of anti-competitive pricing. Nonetheless (and in contrast to anti-trust policy), there is nothing in US utility regulation approaching a statutory duty to promote competition.[5]

The UK regulator's duty to promote competition reflects in part the fact that it is not possible to move from a nationalised monopoly to a competitive industry in a single step. The regulator needs the authority and duty to complete the process of transition (as does the Secretary of State), otherwise obstacles to competition might remain in place.

The emphasis placed on this duty differs greatly between industries, depending upon the scope for entry afforded by the underlying technical and market conditions. At one extreme, potential competition is very limited in water supply, sewage disposal, and airports.[6] The promotion

---

[4] In *Allocation of Frequencies in the Bands Above 890 Mcs*, 27 F.C.C. 359 (1959), the Federal Communications Commission authorised the licensing of private communications systems to give large users an alternative to obtaining service from AT&T. Although this decision had little immediate effect, it set the stage for the introduction of Specialised Common Carriers, such as MCI, which eventually led to the competitive supply of ordinary long-distance telephone service.

[5] The text by Phillips (1969) devotes just 2½ of its 774 pages to the then-novel concept of strengthening the forces of market competition.

[6] Competition for the market, via franchising, has been much discussed (see Vickers and Yarrow (1988); Spulber (1989)), but is beyond the scope of this paper.

of competition has a correspondingly small place in the Airports Act of 1986 and the Water Act of 1989. At the other extreme, the 1984 Telecommunications Act and the associated licences are, to an important extent, addressed to the pace at which competition in telecoms is permitted to develop. The regulator has a potential rôle in the licensing of entrants, specifying the terms on which rivals have access to BT's network and other facilities, and constraining BT's pricing policy (which might encourage or deter entry). Analogous provisions are embodied in the Electricity Act of 1989 and licences. To a lesser extent, this is true of the Gas Act of 1986 and licence, where the rôle of the regulator in promoting competition in gas supply has subsequently been strengthened as a result of the MMC report on that industry.

The duty to promote competition cannot be taken in isolation. The regulator needs to take into account a variety of other economic, social, and political considerations. Specifically, he has duties to secure the financing of licensed activities and protect the interests of consumers. In most situations, different policies will be indicated, depending upon the weight given to each duty. We now give two examples of how regulators have in practice resolved this issue. We then consider the appropriate mode of economic analysis and suggest a direction for future research in order to improve the effectiveness of regulation to promote competition.

An Illustration from Telecommunications

When Mercury wished to interconnect with BT, it was unable to agree on terms, and the regulator, in accordance with BT's licence, was called upon to adjudicate.

One option, stemming primarily from the duty to protect the interests of customers and using traditional welfare economic concepts, was to attempt to calculate levels of interconnect charges which maximised allocative efficiency. This would have required a detailed calculation (for each possible level of interconnect charges) of Mercury's likely outputs in relevant markets, BT's consequent costs and losses in revenue, and the effect of these revenue losses on BT's prices and outputs. Mercury's market share would fall out as a residual from this exercise. However, the approach would beg the question of how to determine Mercury's output reaction function, and Mercury's implied strategy of entry and growth would not necessarily be consistent with promoting competition.

An alternative option was to begin with the duty to promote competition and therefore to examine the impact of the interconnect decision on Mercury's strategy. This would have meant looking at the situation from Mercury's perspective. The margins it could secure were central to its prospects for building up its voice (and other) telephony business. Favourable access to BT's local distribution system meant that Mercury's customers could get not only the benefits of lower prices for calls made over Mercury's long-distance system, but also discounts on virtually all calls delivered by BT. Furthermore, the prospects for future entrants could be expected to depend on the terms achieved for Mercury. Of course, the interconnect charges to be paid by Mercury and others were only part of the story about predicting entry. The effects on BT's costs, revenues, prices, and outputs also needed to be taken into account. Nevertheless, the thrust of this approach is quite different from the allocative efficiency approach, and it would be surprising if its policy implications were the same.

OFTEL's Annual Report for 1985 simply noted that the Director General 'established the prices, based on BT's costs, which should be paid by MCL (Mercury) to BT for use of its network'. No explanation of this cost basis was given, perhaps to avoid any statement that might evoke a test of the decision by the courts. It is widely felt that the phrase 'based on BT's costs' has to be taken with a pinch of salt. There was almost certainly no attempt to run a model of allocative efficiency. The essence of the matter was that the regulator either had to provide sufficient inducement for Mercury to enter the market, or his decision would put at risk a central point of the Government's strategy – that Mercury should become a serious competitor. The regulator's decision does seem to have established a key condition for future effective competition. When it came to the crunch, therefore, the regulator did not let considerations of allocative efficiency stand in the way of a judgement about the promotion of competition, although the precise basis for this judgement was not given.

An Illustration from Gas

The second example is found in the MMC's 1988 report on gas. There had been numerous complaints against BG's policy of discriminating in price, according to whether its customers had access to an alternative fuel (typically oil). These customers, industrial consumers of substantial quantities of gas, lay outside the RPI-X price control basket, but were nevertheless within the regulator's general duty to enable competition. The privatisation Acts empower a regulator to refer any practice to the Monopolies and Mergers Commission. The regulated companies are also subject to general competition law, and it was in fact the Director General of Fair Trading who referred BG to the MMC.

It is well known that, from an allocative point of view, price discrimination may have certain desirable properties. It can lead to

47

greater output and aggregate value of output than a uniform monopoly price. Perfect discrimination yields an output and aggregate value of output precisely equal to that of perfect competition. Nevertheless, the MMC opposed BG's policy of price discrimination, primarily because it would deter new entry.[7] The MMC acknowledged that the prohibition of price discrimination was likely to make some customers worse off, and would limit BG's ability to compete against the oil companies. However, it believed that these disadvantages would be outweighed by the improved prospects for new entry which would be necessary to create 'gas-on-gas' competition, to which the MMC attached great importance.

This conclusion was consistent with the regulator's own view as given in evidence to the Commission. The MMC found BG's policy to be against the public interest and accepted the regulator's suggestion that BG should be required not to discriminate in price. It recommended specific provisions against discrimination to be incorporated in BG's licence. The regulator subsequently negotiated a licence modification of this kind. (Similar non-discrimination provisions have been incorporated into the licences of the electricity companies.)

Economic Analysis of New Entry

The two examples presented above indicate that regulators have taken seriously their duty to promote competition, and that in so doing they have implicitly gone beyond traditional welfare economics. We now consider what the problem of promoting competition involves, and what kinds of economic analysis might be most helpful in that task.

Promoting competition involves facilitating the entry of new competitors, including the entry of existing competitors into new parts of the market. To do this effectively involves three main steps. The first is to assess the likely pattern of entry over the foreseeable future. This will require a prediction of likely changes in technological and market conditions, since these will often provide the necessary opportunities for entry. The second step is to identify decisions that the regulator himself can make in order to change the regulatory framework, and to assess the likely impact of these changes on the future pattern of entry. Examples of these regulatory decisions (in the British system) are the licensing of new entrants, identification and prohibition of anti-competitive practices, determination of interconnect or common carrier (use of

---

[7] 'By relating prices to those of the alternatives available to each customer, it places BG in a position selectively to undercut potential competing gas suppliers; this may be expected to act as a deterrent to new entrants and to inhibit the development of competition in this market.' (MMC (1988), paragraph 8.38 (b).)

system) charges, collection and publication of relevant information, and so on. The third step is to choose which regulatory changes to make. Other things being equal, the preferred changes are those likely to have the greatest positive impact on entry. This is not always an obvious calculation, however, particularly since the whole time-path of entry must be considered. The telecommunications duopoly policy, for example, reflects in part the view that where an entrant has to make a large cost commitment, it is more likely to enter, the less swiftly is a subsequent entrant able to attack the same market (Carsberg, 1987).

The Regulator's Task and the Probability of Entry

In order to promote competition, the regulator's essential task is to assess the relation between his actions (which will include regulatory changes as well as determining disputes and constraining prices) and the probability that entry will actually occur. He will need to consider the scale and time-path of entry and its impact on all the parties involved, as well as on other potential entrants. It will prove impracticable to analyse all the possible avenues and problems of entry simultaneously, however, if only because the regulator's time and resources are necessarily limited. The regulator therefore has to be selective – that is, to take a view about where entry might be most likely, if encouraged, and hence most effective in producing net benefits to consumers and producers, as they will be refined by the impact of entry.

What kind of economic model is most helpful in doing this? It is natural to begin with the same comparative static welfare economic approach that is conventionally used to analyse the problem of price control. This model takes as given (1) the relevant cost and demand functions, and (2) the extent of competition in the market, which essentially depends on the conditions of entry. These assumptions are used to trace the implications for (equilibrium) prices, outputs, profits, number and size of firms, and so on. The question is then asked: What kinds of constraints on the regulated firm will maximise aggregate net surplus subject to securing adequate protection for various classes of consumers? Rate-of-return regulation is set firmly in this world. There is an extensive literature aimed at determining optimal pricing and investment rules that maximise allocative efficiency, taking costs and demands as given.

RPI-X requires the relaxation of the first assumption. It does not assume costs and demands are given or known: indeed, the problem is to provide adequate incentives for the company to discover them. The aim is to stimulate alertness to lower-cost techniques and hitherto unmet demands. The emphasis is on productive rather than allocative efficiency (and even the RPI-X price cap reflects distributional rather than allocative considerations). This is an Austrian world rather than a neo-classical one. ('Austrian' is here defined broadly to include both Leibenstein's familiar X-efficiency on the cost side and the corresponding Y-efficiency on the demand side proposed by Beesley (1973).)

The problem of promoting competition requires the relaxation of the second assumption. Here, the extent of competition and the conditions of entry are not given: the essential regulatory task is to ascertain what they are and how they might be changed. The object is to choose the regulatory policy which will maximise new entry, subject to adequate protection of the interests of producers and present consumers. Nor are costs and demands assumed given or known. Indeed, one of the means of promoting competition is precisely to shift potential entrants' assumptions about the costs and possibilities of serving new markets, and one of the expected benefits of entry is a shift in the incumbents' own assumptions about these parameters.

Substantial recent literature on potential competition and contestable markets analyse the relationship between conditions for entry and price. At least one textbook on regulation (Spulber, 1989) is more concerned with entry and competition than with static welfare analysis of pricing for a protected monopoly. There have also been important developments in the economic analysis of strategic behaviour (Dixit, 1982).

In practice, however, these models are of limited use for the task of promoting competition. Although they analyse the effects of any given entry conditions, they do not help to identify what the entry conditions actually are in any particular situation, nor what the entry conditions would be as a result of any particular regulatory change. Thus, they are of limited assistance to the regulator in assessing how much entry will take place, and where, when, and by whom, as a result of different regulatory policies.

An Alternative Approach – the Potential Entrant

Briefly, an alternative approach would run as follows. In order to identify the entry conditions obtaining at any time, and to predict the consequences of a change in policy, the regulator ought to start from the question: Where and when will entry be profitable? This in turn requires an examination of the situation from the point of view of the potential entrant. Given its assets, knowledge, resources, its ability to buy at current input prices, and the pricing and product policy of the incumbent(s), what parts of the existing market can it profitably develop? What (if any) better contracts with respect to cost, including superior productivity, can it establish? Where have incumbents missed possibilities for adding value or been unable for various reasons to supply? How will incumbents react to its entry? Can it survive their response? In short, what advantages does it have over the incumbents, and how long will these advantages last? The answers to these kinds of questions determine the central calculation for an entrant: the equity that the entrant needs to ante up in order to be a player in the game (that is, its risk capital reflecting its potential sunk costs if unsuccessful), and its potential net revenue stream if successful (the reward for taking the risk).

Admittedly, the models referred to earlier assume profit maximisation, but they do not ask where the profit is coming from. They deal with profit in a purely formal way which does not highlight the need for information about entry and gives little help to the regulator in identifying the relevant factors in practice. Future research might usefully reflect the Austrian insistence on profit as the engine of capitalism and, in particular, on the exploitation of hitherto unforeseen profit opportunities as central to the continuing market process (Schumpeter, 1950; Kirzner, 1973, 1985). Examination of actual rather than hypothetical situations is also necessary, as Coase (1988) has long argued. Applications of the proposed approach (e.g., Beesley (1986) on airlines and Beesley and Laidlaw (1989) on telecommunications) suggest that there is more scope for promoting competition than has hitherto been recognised.

4. Regulatory Effectiveness

We argued in Section 2 that the RPI-X system offers more scope for bargaining, especially on productivity, than rate-of-return regulation. The importance of this depends upon the potential for productivity improvements and on the information available to the regulator to exploit this situation effectively. We also argued that RPI-X offers the company more flexibility in pricing. Whether this is an advantage or disadvantage depends on the need for price changes, on the information available to the regulator, and on the existence of alternative instruments of policy. In Section 3 we noted the UK regulator's explicit duty to promote competition, which in practice has been taken very seriously. Regulatory effectiveness depends upon the scope for new entry and, again, on the information available to the regulator.

In order to carry out his twin tasks of controlling prices and promoting competition, the regulator thus needs to acquire adequate information concerning the scope for cost reductions and the extent and effects of new entry. He will also need to transmit information to incumbents and potential entrants, in order to improve both efficiency and the prospects for entry. The generation and dissemination of information are therefore at the heart of regulatory effectiveness.[8]

Acquisition of Relevant Information

Various devices intended to give companies the incentive to provide the regulator with relevant information have been suggested in the recent economic literature.[9] Typically these devices are set within the context of a given technology and product line: innovation and entry are not encompassed. Once the latter phenomena are admitted, it becomes apparent that the information which the regulator acquired is ephemeral: over time, it gradually becomes obsolete and needs to be replenished. Thus, if the regulator is to succeed in either of his two tasks – controlling prices or promoting competition – he needs to acquire information at a rate faster than that at which it decays. The feasibility of achieving this result depends on two main parameters.

(i) Rate of Change of Technological and Market Conditions

First, there is the rate at which the underlying technological and market conditions change. The slower the change, the more likely the regulator will gradually come to acquire more relevant information and will be in a position to set realistic productivity targets (and, for that matter, performance standards) and determine allocatively efficient price structures for the regulated utility. He will also be able to assess the effects of new entry more accurately. Where the underlying rate of change is slow, new entry is less attractive. In these circumstances, there is likely to be greater pay-off to controlling prices than to promoting competition. Conversely, the faster the underlying rate of change in the industry, the more likely it is that the regulator's knowledge will decay faster than he can replenish it, hence the less likely it is that he will be able to control prices efficiently.[10] However, rapid change provides the

---

[8] Like the market participants, the regulator himself must be alert to hitherto undiscovered opportunities for profit, deriving from both the cost and demand sides. Kirzner (1985) has argued that 'nothing within the regulatory process seems able to simulate, even remotely well, the discovery process that is so integral to the unregulated market'. Our argument is not that the regulatory process is more effective than the competitive market process. (As indicated, the regulator has some advantages and some disadvantages compared with market participants.) Rather, our argument is that an effective regulator needs to be alert in order to promote greater alertness in markets that are not (yet) competitive.

[9] See, for example, the surveys and references in Vickers and Yarrow (1988) and Spulber (1989).

[10] Beesley and Glaister (1983) argued that this is the case in the taxicab industry. Wiseman (1957) has long argued that the very notion of an optimal price is untenable once uncertainty and change are admitted.

very circumstances in which new entry is feasible. Hence, in these circumstances, the regulator's priority should be to promote competition rather than to control price. In the longer term, as the industry becomes more competitive, this in itself will tend to reduce the need for price regulation.

(ii) Multiplicity of Sources of Information

The *second* main possibility of the regulator acquiring information faster than it decays is where there are multiple sources of information. Where there are many companies in an industry, even though they necessarily differ one from another, they may be sufficiently similar that the regulator can use the performance of one as an indication of what another could achieve. This yields a basis for setting efficiency targets in an RPI-X price control scheme. In these circumstances, the regulator's priority is to ensure that the laggards improve to match the (observed) performance of the leaders, while providing sufficient incentive for the leaders to stay ahead and blaze the way for the next round of target setting. The threat of take-over (if either the leaders or the laggards lapse into managerial slack) is an important aid in this endeavour. Conversely, where there is only one company in an industry, the regulator is more dependent upon that company for information, and his effectiveness in bargaining for productivity improvements is thereby reduced.

The prospects for generating information for regulatory purposes should therefore be an important argument in a government's decisions about the structure of the industry and the nature of the regulatory régime. Where the underlying rate of change is slow, there will be information advantages in creating and maintaining many similar firms for purposes of comparison.[11] Of course, it is economically efficient to do this only where the benefits of greater information are expected to outweigh any economies of scale or scope. This is more likely to be the case where a regulated industry is mainly an aggregate of several local monopolies (as with airports and local distribution networks for gas and electricity) than where the natural monopoly element is itself on a national scale (as with bulk transmission grids for gas or electricity).

An Illustration from the United Kingdom

These ideas may be represented in a 2 x 2 matrix. In Tables 1 and 2, the columns represent the underlying rate of change in technology (and market conditions), classified as 'Low' or 'High', while the rows represent the number of regulated companies in the industry, classified

---

11 When dealing with mergers, the Water Act of 1989 embodies instructions to the MMC to this effect.

TABLE 1

PRESENT POSITION

	Rate of Change of Technology	
	Low	*High*
Number of regulated firms		
Many:	Water Electricity Distribution	
One:	Electricity Transmission Gas Transmission and Distribution Airports	Telecoms Electricity Generation Electricity Supply Gas Supply

as 'One' or 'Many'. Each regulated industry, or part thereof, can be located in one of the resulting four cells.

Table 1 shows the matrix as it appears today for the five regulated utilities in the UK. The foregoing analysis indicates a policy of promoting competition in telecoms, gas supply, and electricity generation and supply. Water and electricity distribution provide the most promising conditions for price control. The difficulty of the single regulated utility presents itself in airports, electricity transmission, and gas transmission and distribution.

The structure of those industries characterised by a low rate of technological change could be altered only by government legislation (and clearly many other factors would need to be considered). Where there is a high underlying rate of change, however, the promotion of competition – at its simplest, by licensing new entry – would shift those industries in the one-firm cell into the many-firm cell. With the development of competition, specific industry regulation would become less necessary; whatever needed to be done to help keep competition active might well be performed by the anti-monopoly legislation common to all industries. In other words, deregulation might be indicated.

Table 2 shows the situation that could result in the UK if the policies discussed were put into effect. In telecoms, gas supply, and electricity generation and supply, the regulator's rôle of promoting competition would be paramount, perhaps via general competition policy rather than by specific regulation. In water, airports, and gas and electricity distribution, an emphasis on price control would be indicated, with prospects of success. The problematic areas would be national transmission grids for gas and electricity. Paradoxically, because

TABLE 2
POTENTIAL POSITION

	Rate of Change of Technology	
	Low	*High*
Number of regulated firms		
Many:	Water	Telecoms
	Electricity Distribution	Electricity Generation
	Gas Distribution	Electricity Supply
	Airports	Gas Supply
One:	Electricity Transmission	
	Gas Transmission	

transmission is so crucial to supply, regulatory attention in these natural monopolies would have to focus also on the promotion of competition in upstream and downstream markets via the terms to be set for the use of transmission facilities. So for electricity and gas transmission (and distribution too) the dual rôle of the regulator might be expected to continue in the foreseeable future.

RPI-X versus Rate of Return Revisited

Future research might usefully assess US and UK regulatory systems in terms of the ideas suggested in this section, comparing their abilities to generate and use relevant information, depending upon rate of technological change and number of regulated firms. We may illustrate this by re-examining the initial question of the relative merits of RPI-X and rate-of-return regulation with respect to incentives and efficiency. We argued that RPI-X is indeed different because (*inter alia*) it incorporates a fixed risk period within which gains above the productivity bargain can be kept by the regulated firm(s). These productivity gains are potentially larger at the time of privatisation than subsequently. They are also potentially larger the more rapidly technological conditions are changing, and where there are many different firms, with leaders blazing the way for laggards to follow.

Relating these considerations to the five regulated utilities, it follows that the case for RPI-X price control rather than rate-of-return regulation is strongest in telecoms, gas supply, and electricity supply, where technology is indeed changing. If the aim is to 'hold the fort' until competition arrives, as Beesley and Littlechild (1983) put it, RPI-X will do this with greater potential productivity gains. At the other extreme, where there is less prospect of a shift in technology and only one firm in

55

the industry, as with the electricity and gas transmission grids, there is less scope for bargaining about the potential for improvements in efficiency and no built-in mechanism to give the regulator scope for bargaining via directly relevant comparisons. Here, the grounds for preferring RPI-X are least strong.

In the remaining industries, notably water, gas, and electricity distribution, there is a strong reason for preferring RPI-X initially, given the potential productivity gains on privatisation and the regulator's potential for generating superior information to that available to the companies taken separately. Admittedly, if there is indeed a low underlying rate of change in technology, both the scope for improvement and the discrepancies between companies may be expected to reduce over time, and in practice an RPI-X régime may gradually become indistinguishable from that of rate-of-return regulation. However, a permanently low underlying rate of change cannot be taken for granted. For the present, RPI-X seems to offer advantages.

REFERENCES

Beesley, M. E. (1973): 'Mergers and Economic Welfare', in *Mergers, Takeovers and the Structure of Industry*, IEA Readings No. 10, London: Institute of Economic Affairs, pp. 73-80.

Beesley, M. E., and S. Glaister (1983): 'Information for Regulating: The Case of Taxis', *Economic Journal*, Vol. 93, pp. 594-615.

Beesley, M. E. (1986): 'Commitment, Sunk Costs and Entry to the Airline Industry: Reflections on Experience', *Journal of Transport Economics and Policy*, May, pp. 173-90.

Beesley, M. E., and S. Littlechild (1986): 'Privatization: Principles, Problems and Priorities', in John Kay *et al.* (eds.), *Privatization and Regulation - The UK Experience*, Oxford: Clarendon Press.

Beesley, M. E., P. Gist, and B. H. Laidlaw (1987): 'Prices and Competition on Voice Telephony in the UK', *Telecommunications Policy*, Vol. 11, pp. 230-36.

Beesley, M. E., and B. Laidlaw (1989): *The Future of Telecommunications: An Assessment of the Role of Competition in UK Policy*, Research Monograph No. 42, London: Institute of Economic Affairs.

Besen, S. M. (1989): Statement Submitted by the National Cable

Television Association, in Federal Communications Commission CC Docket No. 87-313, 3 August.

Breyer, S. (1982): *Regulation and Its Reform*, Cambridge, Mass.: Harvard University Press.

Carsberg, B. (1987): 'Regulation of British Telecom', *Telecommunications Policy*, Vol. 11, pp. 237-42.

Cheong, K. (1989): 'The British Experience with Price Cap (RPI-X) Regulation', *Nera Topics*, London: NERA.

Civil Aviation Authority (1988): *Conditions as to Airport Charges in Relation to Manchester Airport under Section 40 (3) of the Act*, CAA Report, London: CAA, 25 February.

Coase, R. H. (1988): *The Firm, The Market and The Law*, Chicago: University of Chicago Press.

Culham, P. G. (1987): 'A Method for Determining the Optimal Balance of Prices for Telephone Services', *Oftel Working Paper*, No. 1, March.

Director General of Telecommunications (1986): *Review of British Telecom's Tariff Charges, November 1986*, London: Oftel, November.

Director General of Telecommunications (1988a): *The Regulation of British Telecom's Prices, A Consultative Document*, London: Oftel, January.

Director General of Telecommunications (1988b): *The Control of British Telecom's Prices*, London: Oftel, July.

Dixit, A. K. (1982): 'Recent Developments in Oligopoly Theory', *American Economic Review*, Vol. 72, pp. 12-17.

Jarrell, G. A. (1978): 'The Demand for State Regulation of the Electric Utility Industry', *Journal of Law and Economics*, Vol. 21, pp. 269-95.

Johnson, L. L. (1989): 'Price Caps in Telecommunications Regulatory Reforms', *RAND Note*, N-2894-MF/RC, January.

Kirzner, I. M. (1973): *Competition and Entrepreneurship*, Chicago: University of Chicago Press.

Kirzner, I. M. (1985): 'The Perils of Regulation – A Market Process Approach', in I. M. Kirzner (ed.), *Discovery and the Capitalist Process*, Chicago: University of Chicago Press, 1985.

Littlechild, S. C. (1983): *Regulation of British Telecommunications' Profitability*, London: Department of Industry.

Monopolies and Mergers Commission (1988): *Gas*, Cm. 500, London: HMSO.

Monopolies and Mergers Commission (1987): *Manchester Airport p.l.c.: A Report on the Economic Regulation of the Airport*, Report MMC 1, London: Civil Aviation Authority, December.

OFTEL, 1986, Report of the Director General of Telecommunications (Annual Report 1985), London: HMSO, June.

Phillips, C. F. (1969): *The Economics of Regulation*, Homewood, Ill.: Richard D. Irwin, Inc., revised edn.

Schumpeter, J. A. (1950): *Capitalism, Socialism and Democracy*, New York: Harper and Row, 3rd edition.

Spulber, D. F. (1989): *Regulation and Markets*, Cambridge, Mass., and London: M.I.T. Press.

Stigler, G. J. (1971): 'The Theory of Economic Regulation', *The Bell Journal of Economics*, Vol. 2, pp. 3-21.

Vickers, J., and G. Yarrow (1988): *Privatization: An Economic Analysis*, Cambridge, Mass.: M.I.T. Press.

Wiseman, J. (1957): 'The Theory of Public Utility Price – An Empty Box', *Oxford Economic Papers*, Vol. 9, pp. 56-74.

3

REGULATORY METHODS: A CASE FOR 'HANDS ACROSS THE ATLANTIC'*

Irwin M. Stelzer

*Resident Fellow and Director
of Regulatory Policy Studies,
American Enterprise Institute*

THE DEVELOPMENT of regulatory techniques in Britain should be studied – and, indeed, is being studied – to see whether it contains lessons for America. This is, in a way, amusing: it was only a few short years ago that fledgling British regulators were touring the United States to learn what they could about regulation there. For the USA had a virtual monopoly on regulatory nous: how to control the prices and quality-of-service of privately owned, government-franchised monopolies. Britain, by virtue of the fact that its gas, electricity, telecommunications and water monopolies were in the public sector, had – until Mrs Thatcher came on the scene – no need for American-style regulation. After all, the British reasoned, publicly owned corporations, free of the greedy imperatives imposed by private shareholders, could be expected to behave in the public interest. And, if they strayed, the elected Minister to whom they putatively reported would quickly bring them into line.

When privatisation first came to Britain, no thought was given to the need for regulatory bodies. After all, the newly privatised oil, steel and automobile companies would be subject to the discipline of international competition. If they attempted to obtain monopoly profits, or produce shoddy products, or in other ways failed to satisfy their customers, those customers could turn elsewhere.

---

* This paper is adapted from a paper published by the American Enterprise Institute in its journal, *The American Enterprise*.

Not so with users of basic utility services. To varying degrees, they were prisoners of their suppliers. So, when the utility industries were scheduled for privatisation, a wave of British economists, accountants, utility executives and sundry policy-makers descended on the USA, seeking guidance from our experience. This provided us with an important new export: regulatory consulting services.

It now seems as if our exported expertise was more a raw material than a finished good. The British took the product, reshaped and reprocessed it, and are now re-exporting it to America, where there seems to be quite a good market for alternatives to the cost-based, rate-of-return regulation that dominated the American scene when the British first came here to study it – and still does, although not as completely.

I think it is fair to say that serious students of regulation on both sides of the Atlantic are hoping that a process of continued intellectual cross-fertilisation is now under way, and that that process will produce ideas that increase the efficiency of regulated enterprises, and public satisfaction with their performance.

For that hope to materialise, it is important that scholars in Britain and in America do not expect too much of each other. For they must understand, at the outset, that both countries approach the job of regulation with certain prejudices – prejudices that often dictate very different conclusions from a similar set of facts.

Conflicting Prejudices

In America, we have a prejudice in favour of competition. This, of course, is not universally shared by all American policy-makers and businessmen: a bit of luggage, owned by an important constituent and lost by an airline, can turn a congressman into a re-regulator. And a customer, 'owned' by an electricity company but lost to an independent power producer, can as quickly turn a free-enterprising utility executive against competition.

US Favours Competition . . .

But, by and large, the thrust of academic scholarship and public policy in this country supports competition where possible, regulation only where necessary to protect consumers from extortion. Deregulation in the transport industries is generally recognised to have produced lower rates, more price/quality options, and improved efficiency.[1] The

---

[1] Forgive these generalisations, necessitated by space limitations. The problems created by a failure to apply sensible anti-trust merger standards to airlines, by continued bottlenecks to entry in that industry, and by the residual market power of railroads in certain commodity markets are, of course, serious. But their solution does not lie in pervasive re-regulation.

injection of more competition into the natural gas and electricity generation businesses is generally considered a good thing, even though the problems created by such moves are only now beginning to be appreciated. And the dismantling of the AT&T vertically integrated monopoly seems to have unleashed efficiencies not previously attainable – again, not without significant transition costs.

... but Britain Prefers Monopoly

The British aversion to competition is best demonstrated by a quick review of structures established for the newly privatised firms. British Gas was sent off into the private sector as a fully integrated monopoly; British Telecom was afflicted with only one competitor, Mercury, when the Government decided to establish a duopoly, at least for a limited period, rather than to permit open competition. After flirting with the establishment of real competition in the electricity business, the Government backed off, settling for a generating duopoly and insulating distribution companies from competition for the next eight years.[2]

US Regulation: Open Hearings and Due Process

Britain and America differ not only in their attitudes towards competition. They differ, too, in their attitudes towards the regulatory process itself, America having a prejudice in favour of open hearings and due process, the British a prejudice in favour of expedition.

America sees the regulatory process as one in which all interested parties should be permitted – nay, encouraged, even paid – to participate. Views are solicited from lawyers and experts representing the regulated firms, customers, competitors and potential competitors, local political bodies, consumer representatives (often self-appointed) and environmentalists and other special-interest groups. Nothing seems to please a regulatory body more than appending a massive list of intervenors to each decision.

The parties are all accorded due process: they file motions, they participate in hearings, they file briefs, and – in the end – some of them appeal the decision to and through the courts.

To the quite proper charge that this process produces huge costs, inefficiencies and delays, its proponents respond: 'True. But these are worth bearing in a democratic society'. Remember: but for the work of environmental intervenors in the famous *Madison Gas & Electric* case,

---

[2] For further details and analysis, see John Vickers and George Yarrow, *Privatisation: An Economic Analysis*, Cambridge, Mass.: The MIT Press, 1988.

the adoption of more efficient pricing of electricity would have been delayed for many years. If academics had not meddled in the legislative process, airline deregulation would have been longer in coming. And if conservationists – many of them strident and some plain daft – had not intruded into the electricity regulation scene, we would not now be groping for better ways to compare the costs of adding supplies with those of reducing demand.

British Approach to Regulation: Closed Negotiation

The British see the regulatory process in an entirely different light. They have no place for what they call 'American-style' regulation. (Regulators should not take offence at the fact that this term is used as a pejorative. 'American-style' is a phrase used in Britain to describe many things that the establishment there finds abhorrent, *viz*.: American-style fast food; American-style television, i.e., consumer-driven programming; American-style *de*regulation, i.e., airline competition; American-style showers, i.e., ones that work. All have one thing in common: consumers love them.) To the British, regulation is a system by which the service provider negotiates with the regulator to decide upon the prices and service offerings that they – the company and the regulator – feel will be in the best interests of consumers, with a passing nod at other affected interests.

True, in some cases a particularly vigorous regulator, such as Sir Bryan Carsberg, successfully 'represents' all the parties absent from the regulatory bargaining process, perhaps by soliciting their views. In others, powerful, disgruntled customers – large users of natural gas are a case in point – can make themselves heard, either directly or by the informal (we would say, *ex parte*) means so clear to the British and so obscure to foreigners. And in still others the voices of all interested parties are in fact heard.

But, by and large, the British process is a closed one, devoid of hearings, intervenors and court appeals. It is, therefore, quicker, cheaper – and less likely to produce results that threaten incumbent firms, either with competitors or with effective demands from customers.

These very different biases – America's in favour of competition, Britain's in favour of managed entry; America's in favour of procedural protection and open hearings, Britain's in favour of closed negotiations – mean that the two countries' approaches to regulation may converge, but will never meet.

Nevertheless, I think it possible to extract the best from both experiences, and synthesise them into one approach which we Americans can properly dub 'regulatory reform'. Let me try.

The American Regulatory Experience

It is important to recognise, at the outset, that much recent talk about the inequities and inefficiencies of the American system of regulation is overblown. For one thing, it ignores the fact that the system worked tolerably well for many years in many of the industries to which it was applied, and still works well under certain conditions. Until approximately the early 1970s, electric utility service was generally deemed to be cheap, safe and reliable. A few mutterings aside, customers were at minimum acquiescent, at maximum satisfied. The utilities themselves grumbled now and then about regulators' insensitivity to their financial needs, but generally earned acceptable returns and kept shareholders happy.

The telephone industry, too, seemed to be functioning quite satisfactorily. A substantial army of generally contented Bell system employees pursued the company's goal of 'universal service' with some success, using the company's monopoly power to cross-subsidise rates in pursuit of its own (at least tacitly accepted) social agenda.

True, there were rumblings from natural gas producers that regulation of their business along utility lines would eventually produce supply and contractual problems, but these malcontents were for the most part Texans, and everyone knew that they could never be satisfied, despite generous depletion allowances and other tax advantages. Regulation of natural gas prices was, after all, 'motivated primarily by income-distributional considerations'[3] – and it was only to be expected that the losers would complain.

The litany of reasons for the closing of the relatively satisfactory period of regulatory history, at least as it concerned the electricity and telephone industries, is now familiar: the OPEC cartel drove up oil prices and with them the cost of oil-based electric power; the Carter inflation exacerbated the cost pressures created by OPEC, and forced regulated utilities to seek large, unpopular rate increases; the success of airline deregulation and the emergence of new technologies caused academics and policy-makers to wonder just how 'natural' some natural monopolies were; the nuclear plant construction programme was mismanaged by both the industry and those responsible for seeing that the regulatory process produced decisions, rather than delay; intervenors proliferated, as did the length of rate cases and other regulatory proceedings.

As a result, the general consensus that regulation produced a

---

[3] Alfred E. Kahn, *The Economics of Regulation: Principles and Institutions*, Cambridge, Mass.: The MIT Press, 1988: 'Introduction: A Postcript, Seventeen Years After', p. xvi, fn. 2.

63

reasonable balance between the interests of shareholders and consumers disappeared. Consumer groups hung utility presidents in effigy (the real thing being understandably reluctant to make himself available); utility presidents threatened to let-the-bastards-freeze-in-the-dark; and regulators no longer saw their appointments as an early step on the ladder to political advancement.

'The Deregulation Revolution'

The calmer among the mounting army of the discontented began to grope for solutions to the problems – although there was little agreement as to just what 'problem' or 'problems' needed solving. One idea seemed to make sense: eliminate regulation in those industries in which competition could be sufficiently effective to permit market forces to allocate resources efficiently. Enter what Alfred Kahn calls 'the deregulation revolution'.[4] Structurally competitive industries such as airlines, trucking, stock exchange brokering, buses and natural gas production were released from the grip of the regulator and entrusted to the invisible hand of the market-place. A flood of entry, innovation and competition generally followed, to wild applause from all in the audience except the trade unions which could no longer pass extortionate wages on to the public, and previously subsidised members of the consuming public.

So far, so good. And easy. For where competition works, regulatory reform is easy to devise: stop regulating.

Restructuring the Telephone Industry

The telephone industry presented a slightly more difficult case than had airlines, but not an impossible one. Technology was obliterating the distinctions between voice and data transmission, making possible cheaper means of delivery than copper wire – and making the telephone and computer industries difficult to distinguish, one from the other, in many instances. But unlike, say, airlines, the telephone industry was dominated by a single, vertically integrated supplier. This meant that a simple repeal of regulation would unleash on consumers a vertically integrated supplier with very substantial monopoly power in many of its markets – much as privatisation of the British gas industry later did.

Regulatory reform in telephony, therefore, had to begin with restructuring and include an element of continued supervision of the resulting entities to constrain their pricing power and their power to impede entry. So we got vertical disintegration, continued State and

---

[4] *Op. cit.*, p. xv.

Federal Communication Commission regulation – and court super-vision of the decree ending the litigation. But we also got a spate of new entry, prices more closely related to costs, increased consumer choice, and the accelerated introduction of cost-reducing, service-enhancing innovations.

All of this was a bit traumatic, particularly for regulators who were suddenly denied the ability to subsidise some consumers by over-charging others (the latter now had competitive alternatives to paying rates in excess of costs), and for consumers who found choice a bewildering experience after decades of monopoly service. But it is not unfair to say that few would turn the clock back to the days of regulated monopoly telephone service.

Electricity Generation

The harder case lies before us: electricity. As with other regulatory reforms, reform in this industry starts with the introduction of competition. Propelled in part by favourable legislation, in part by a reluctance of traditional utilities to commit capital to the care of regulators who showed no reluctance to confiscate it, and in part by technological changes which made small – if not beautiful – at least alluringly attractive, a wave of entrepreneurs entered the business of generating electricity. This seems (one cannot yet be certain of the long-run consequences) to have had the salutary effect of putting downward pressure on costs, as independent producers bid for the custom of utilities and their customers. And it put pressure on other parts of the regulated electricity system to open up to competition. Transmission access, wheeling rights, shopping by customers: all became supplements to regulatory review of rates.

I will not here review, much less attempt to resolve, the many questions raised by the introduction of competition into the still highly regulated electricity industry: Should customers be free to shop, while suppliers remain obliged to serve all-comers, including prodigal sons? Should owners of transmission systems be obliged to provide service to newcomers at rates based on historic costs? Should neighbouring suppliers be allowed to solicit retail customers in some other utility's franchise area?

These are difficult questions. But the very fact that they exist shows that we have come a long way down the road to regulatory reform in the power industry. We have, first, decided to introduce competition at the generating level. Second, we are groping for ways to open up previously inviolate transmission systems. And, third, we are considering weakening local franchise monopolies.

65

But no one is considering abandoning regulation. The Federal Energy Regulatory Commission still sets wholesale prices by determining the rate that interstate sellers can earn on their investments; state commissioners still review retail rates using traditional cost-of-service techniques. And even where this so-called 'traditional' regulation is being *supplemented* by reference to market-based prices, it is not being *replaced*. The invisible hand is being permitted a bit of a rôle in many areas of regulatory activity, but the long arm of regulation still reaches in to set prices, returns and entry conditions in most fields in which regulators retain jurisdiction. Just as reformist economists have been unable to persuade the Russian bureaucrats and the public that *perestroika* will produce efficacious long-run results, economists have been unable to persuade regulators that market forces alone are effective enough to solve all their problems. The first is a pity, the second probably a good thing.

In short, we are stuck with regulation and regulators for a long time to come. So it behoves us to make the system work as efficiently and fairly as possible. Reference to experience in Britain can contribute to that process.

Lessons from British Experience

In the interests of space, I will list five lessons I think we can draw from British experience.

1. Structure Matters

It is fashionable these days for economists to make light of market structure analysis. Anyone citing high concentration ratios is treated, not to a sophisticated Schumpeterian critique - still attractively vigorous, I think – but to that all-purpose excuse for totally ignoring concentrated market power – the theory of contestable markets! Does a firm seem to occupy an entire relevant market? Fear not: a contestant for his position lurks in the wings, or is in training somewhere, or is about to be born. Is a firm shoring up that position by predatory behaviour? Fear not: when it steps over its victims' corpses to collect its ill-gotten gains, some competitive enforcer, oblivious to the fate of his predecessors, will appear on the scene and snatch away any ill-gotten gains. Concentration measures, in short, are held to matter very little - except perhaps to Antitrust Division lawyers who must devise ways around their own merger guidelines.

So too, with vertical integration. In the absence of horizontal market power, there can be no danger in vertical integration, we are told.

I certainly do not mean here to regress to the view that measuring concentration of control and the degree of vertical integration are the end of economic analysis. Clearly, they are not. And, equally clearly, potential competition and the extent of entry barriers must be considered along with concentration measures when reaching conclusions about market power. But, especially in the context of regulation, the structure of an industry remains a relevant consideration in developing proper regulatory policy. Thomas McCraw has put it well in his wonderful study of regulation and regulators:

> 'More than any other single factor, . . . underlying structure of the particular industry being regulated has defined the context in which regulatory agencies have operated.'[5]

This can best be understood by referring to Britain's experience with its gas, electricity and telephone industries. All of these were once state-owned. But each was sent on its way into the private sector in a structurally different condition.

The telephone company was initially required to face only one competitor until 1990; the gas company was sold off as a vertically integrated monopoly; the electricity supply industry was vertically disintegrated, into two generating companies, a monopoly transmission company and 12 local distribution monopolies (all references exclude Scotland).

Despite these structural differences, all of the industries are regulated pursuant to the now-standard British formula known as RPI-X: average prices may rise at the same rate as the retail price index, less something ('X') to account for technological change and improved productivity.[6]

That structure matters is demonstrated by the fact that RPI-X has worked reasonably well in the telephone business, and very poorly in the still-integrated monopoly gas business.[7] (This also proves that, in the regulation business, people matter, a point to which I will return shortly.) It does not do too much violence to the facts, many of them provided to me by Carsberg, to say that, in the case of telephony, real prices have come down; individual rates are now more closely aligned with the costs of rendering individual services and competition is being introduced into some aspects of the business. I reserve for later comment the question of service quality.

---

[5] Thomas McCraw, *Prophets of Regulation*, Cambridge, Mass.: The Belknap Press of Harvard University Press, 1984, p. 305.

[6] There are, of course, various nuances in each application. In the case of electricity, for example, the nuclear plants will remain in the public sector. For some details relating to telephony, see my 'Regulating Telecommunications in Britain: A New Alternative to the US Approach', *Telematics*, Vol. 3, No. 9, September 1986, pp. 7ff.

[7] We do not yet know how it will work in the electricity business.

Gas is a different story. Because the Government chose a monopoly structure for the industry, and perhaps because technology is not the driving force for change that it is in telecommunications, regulation of British Gas has proved less satisfactory than has regulation of British Telecom. British Gas retained and used monopsony power, to the consternation of gas producers; it discriminated secretly among its customers; it resisted the regulator's efforts to obtain rudimentary cost information. In short, it behaved like the vertically integrated monopoly that it is.

Not surprisingly, the RPI-X regulatory formula did not work as well in the gas industry as it had in telecommunications, where at least some competition was available to assist the regulator in achieving his goals. In the end, the gas industry's overseer had to order a *de facto* restructuring of the gas industry, assigning a portion of all new gas discoveries to British Gas's competitors, and forcing British Gas to transport those supplies at reasonable rates to any customers the new, competitive suppliers can round up.

So structure matters. So does competition.

2. Competition Matters

It may be saying the same thing to point out that competition also matters. If so, the repetition is worthwhile. In Britain, even the limited competition in the telephone business has, I think it is fair to say, made the regulator's life easier. It has provided him with a means of extracting more dynamic performance from the dominant supplier: unhappy with the state of repair of public call boxes, for example, he expressed his displeasure by inviting competitors into that part of the business.

But competition within a regulated environment has also created problems – just as it has in America. For the dominant firms were unenthusiastic about interconnecting, or about providing access to such bottleneck facilities as they control. British Telecom attempted to deny reasonable access to key facilities to its one competitor, forcing the regulator to set reasonable terms for such access. British Gas was no more eager to cede its monopoly position, eventually forcing its regulator to order certain rate structure revisions, contractual reporting changes and, in the end, changes in the structure of the industry. The hope is that the injection of some competition into the gas industry will make regulation work better.

3. People Matter

In the regulatory game, people matter. While regulators are limited by the economic forces at work at any time – in deflationary periods entry barriers become more attractive, in inflationary periods the public favours freer entry – their biases, intellects and perseverance can affect the regulatory process in important ways. In America, Alfred Kahn's penchant for economically sensible prices was a powerful force for rate restructuring in the electricity business, and his preference for competition hastened the demise of airline regulation. In Britain, Sir Bryan Carsberg rose above his training as an accountant to adopt an economist's attitude towards such concepts as cost. And, like Kahn, he brought to the game a bias in favour of competitive solutions: 'I believe that a presumption exists in favour of competition', he announced in his agency's first annual report. This 'presumption' was, I believe, one of the factors that impelled him to force British Telecom to grant access to its competitor on what he hopes will prove to be reasonable terms. To cite Thomas McCraw again: '[P]olicy remains a work of man. . . . [I]ndividual persons and particular ideas have mattered a great deal in regulatory history.'[8]

4. Procedure Matters

It is also true that procedure matters. As I noted earlier, our British friends think we are quite mad to allow lawyers and intervenors to stretch hearings over years, perhaps decades. We, in turn, think they are quite undemocratic to rely on closed negotiations between the regulator and the regulated, to deny many parties an opportunity to be heard, and effectively to deny all parties the right to appeal decisions of the regulator – a single Director, not even a commission.

There is some merit in both views. There is no question, for example, that intervenors in US nuclear plant cases know that their ability to delay a decision enables them to kill most projects, regardless of the merit of their arguments. Intervenors know, in short, that process dominates substance. But neither is there any doubt that the failure of environmentalists and opponents of nuclear power to find a forum until very recently deprived British policy-makers of an important point of view concerning nuclear power. A quiet chat between a Minister and the Chairman of the Central Electricity Generating Board did not prove to be the ideal forum for reasoned consideration of the advantages and disadvantages of the nuclear option.

5. Profits Matter

The British experience gives us still another clue to the shape regulatory reform might take in America. From the outset, the British were

---

8 McCraw, *op. cit.*, pp. viii and 303.

determined to avoid cost-of-service, rate-of-return regulation. They gave and still give several reasons. First, they see such regulation as expensive, necessarily involving detailed auditing and the protracted hearings they so loathe. Regulation of prices, rather than profits, 'is much less costly to administer than rate-of-return regulation', according to Carsberg.

Second, the British are repelled by the cost-plus nature of rate-based regulation. They feel that it reduces incentives to efficiency:

'. . . a rule that operates directly on prices – like the RPI-3 rule – is greatly to be preferred over the main alternative method used to control the prices of monopolies – rate of return regulation. Rate of return regulation gives a monopoly business too little incentive to operate efficiently because, in practice, it too readily allows businesses to pass their actual costs on to customers; by linking prices to the general level of inflation, the RPI-3 rule gives a good incentive for efficiency: it creates a situation in which the incurring of excessive costs will detract from profits while improved efficiency will increase profits.'[9]

Yet, determined as they were to regulate prices rather than profits, the British were before very long driven to pay attention to earnings – witness recent expressions of outrage over BT and British Gas profits. Carsberg knew all along that this would happen, but it is not unfair to say that he was more or less alone in that wisdom. In the case of British Telecom, price increases perfectly consistent with the price ceiling formula began to produce equity returns approximating 20 per cent. OFTEL revealed in its second annual report that 'the rate of return on capital employed was probably a little above the minimum acceptable in competitive capital markets . . .,' but not so excessive as to warrant abandoning price cap regulation. But the regulator did warn that if British Telecom's 'rate of return on capital employed was significantly above the minimum acceptable level', some modification or replacement of the price control rule would be recommended. In short, profits matter, even in a regulatory scheme specifically designed to avoid examining them by concentrating on prices.

As I noted earlier, the British experience, combined with our own, provides some hints as to the direction in which we might move regulatory systems to increase their efficiency. For there is little doubt that America now has a regulatory régime that fails to discourage protracted proceedings; creates uncertainties possibly sufficient to increase the cost of capital; creates a bias in favour of expense-intensive (read, fuel-intensive, in the case of electricity companies), capital-starved

---

[9] OFTEL, second annual report.

capacity; does not always attract to it the most able people; and may not encourage efficient performance.

Five-point Review: Towards a Transatlantic Merger

Let us review each of the things that British experience suggests matter – structure, competition, people, procedure and profits – to see what lessons we can extract.

1. *Structure*: The British experience suggests that a vertically integrated monopoly is the most difficult of all beasts to regulate. In the case of most industries subject to regulation, these integrated companies can use the natural monopoly of their transmission grids – gas pipelines, electricity transmission lines, the telephone network – to deter entry into other strata of the business. Having learned this lesson in the gas and telephone businesses, in both of which the regulators finally had to mandate access, the British Government decided to privatise its electricity business only after separating the generation, transmission and distribution sectors.

This would suggest that those concerned with improving the efficiency of the American electric utility industry must give serious consideration to one of two courses of action. First, they must improve the rules governing access. Such improvement should include rules creating economic incentives to owners of these facilities to make them available, and to endure the pain of constructing additional lines.

Alternatively, we can decide that the regulatory game is not worth the candle, and vertically disintegrate the industry, converting the transmission systems into separately owned, highly regulated entities. It will be interesting to see whether Carsberg's efforts to overcome the access hurdle *sans* vertical disintegration bear fruit; if they do, control of access prices might prove a feasible alternative to disintegration. Since such surgery would undoubtedly entail high costs, at least in the transition phase, and very possibly in the long run, we can only hope that regulators can work out efficient access terms, and avoid more draconian solutions.

2. *Competition*: British experience also teaches that competition can be a valuable ally of the regulator. In gas, the poor fellow asked to control the rapacity of British Gas was deprived of such help; in telecoms, the regulator was granted at least one competitor by the Government and several others by technology.

The lesson is clear, but not easy to follow: competition should be encouraged. The difficulty lies in setting the rules of the game so that we get the efficiency gains of competition, rather than a mere proliferation of players. Let me explain, with reference to electricity generation.

Clearly, the development of alternatives to utility-owned generation is providing regulators with a valuable tool with which to lower power costs to competitive levels: bidding. This process will tell us more surely than even the most stringent review of costs in a prudence hearing whether customers are paying a reasonable price, and whether capacity is being added in an efficient way. But it will not do so if (a) the bidding process is tilted in favour of one or another of the bidders, and (b) the regulators, having satisfied themselves that the *process* is competitive, then second-guess the *results* it produces in a new round of *ex post* prudence reviews.

How might we avoid tilting the process? First, utilities should not be forced to acquire capacity they do not need, merely to give a fillip to the no-longer infant independent power industry. Second, utilities should not be permitted to bid to meet their own requirements. They can, of course, offer to build plant at a stated price, and be allowed to go forward if no independent can match that price. But in many circumstances that would be a silly business strategy, involving the commitment of capital to the tender mercies of the regulatory process – capital which might be used to build unregulated facilities in the service territories of others.

Bidding is not the only aspect of the regulatory process that requires a set of pro-competitive rules. Again, the touchstone should be some kind of symmetry. If customers are permitted to shop for supplies, suppliers should be relieved of an obligation to serve them on other than mutually agreed contractual terms; if competitors are free to enter, incumbents should be permitted to respond, although not in a predatory manner.

Throughout, the beacon through the haze of uncertainty should be competition: when in doubt, decide in favour of more rather than less competition.

3. *People*: The British have, somehow, managed to find a set of quite able, fair-minded regulators. In part, of course, it is easier for them to be fair-minded than it is for their American counterparts, because they are less subject to the political pressures associated with our wide-open hearings. And in part the British can find good regulators because they need so few of them! But, that said, we might still learn something from Britain's ability to attract generally able people to the demanding, often thankless business of regulation.

The first is that it is easier to attract a good person if he has clear authority. That may mean that the job of being a sole regulator is more attractive than that of being a member of a multi-person commission.

The second lesson might be that our selection process, which often puts little premium on training or experience, needs revision. No British government would dare appoint to an important regulatory position someone with no training in the relevant discipline. Perhaps we should consider adopting some variant of our judicial appointment system: have the relevant professional association review economists, accountants and lawyers – perhaps even engineers, if we get desperate – to determine whether they have certain minimum qualifications for office.

The dangers of this procedure are obvious. For one thing, the back-scratching that now seeps into judicial appointments might infect the review procedure I am suggesting we consider. For another, the lay populists who often bring a novel and important point of view to the regulatory process would be excluded. And, finally, we would be excluding from consideration many intelligent people, quite capable of absorbing on-the-job training.

But we might, by combining this selection procedure with single commissionerships, attract more skilled men and women to the regulatory ranks.

4. *Procedure*: This is one area in which there isn't very much we can learn from our British friends. Their closed proceedings would be quite unacceptable here, and properly so. Expedition at the expense of a full presentation of all viewpoints would be too dearly bought.

But we might borrow one legal wrinkle from Britain. Would it be possible to force parties who frivolously protract proceedings to bear the costs of such delays, just as some commissions now compensate parties who contribute to decisions in some important way? A few fines would certainly focus the parties' minds on the need for relevance and speed.

Again, this would have dangers, especially in the hands of highly opinionated and/or highly political regulators. But surely it is worth experimenting with some method of ending the now endless proceedings in which we often find ourselves.

5. *Profits*: On the question of regulating prices instead of profits, I would be inclined to give two cheers for the British system, rather than the usual three. I make this modest deduction of one cheer for four reasons.

First, the idea is not original to Britain. The decoupling of an enterprise's costs from the prices it charges has long been the goal of economists trying to provide regulated firms with incentives to increased efficiency. Kahn has pointed out that within the framework of rate-based, rate-of-return regulation, regulatory lag[10] provides just such an incentive. If costs rise, for whatever reason, failure to adjust rates upward, instantly, places part of the burden on shareholders. And managements have some incentive to drive costs down: for a while, at least, they can retain 'excessive' earnings for their shareholders.

A *second* reason for withholding the third cheer is that price regulation solves some of the problems created by cost-based regulation, but creates another. Given a ceiling on prices but not on profits, a company is tempted to derogate from the quality of service. A penny saved is a penny earned, even if the saved penny means longer waits for repairs, or more frequent busy circuits.

Decline in Service After Privatisation

In Britain, just such a decline in service occurred in the early years of privatisation, and may still be going on, if the record number of consumer complaints is any guide. The regulator's response – and here we might learn a lesson – was threefold. First, where possible (call boxes), he invited competitors to enter, both to provide consumers with an alternative supplier and to goad British Telecom into providing better service. Second, he imposed a series of fines for late repairs and other service failures. Finally, he insisted on the publication of service-quality statistics. None of these, of course, is a perfect offset to the service-derogating incentive intrinsic in price regulation. But in combination, they are useful supplements to such regulation.

A *third* reason for less than whole-hearted enthusiasm for the British formula is that it envisions a permanent decoupling of prices and costs – or at least does so in the hands of others than Carsberg. Such a decoupling gives no weight to the impossibility of rationally determining 'X' – the amount by which rate increases shall be kept below increases in inflation. If 'X' is taken for what it in practice is – a wild guess at the rate of improvement in productivity – it can be used only as an interim device, one to permit regulators to regulate on the basis of price for a reasonable period, subject to periodic tests of the reasonableness of the resultant level of profits – but with no *ex post* seizure of any 'excessive' profits. And, fortunately, that seems to be the direction in which regulation in this country, at least in the telephone industry, is heading. If these experiments succeed, we might just get the incentives to efficiency produced by price regulation combined with the benefits of profit regulation.

---

[10] Defined by Kahn as 'the inevitable delay that regulation imposes in the downward adjustment of rate levels that produce excessive rates of return and in the upward adjustments ordinarily called for if profits are too low'. (Kahn, *op. cit.*, Vol. II, p. 48.)

Fourthly, regulation based on price alone cannot assure the public that it is not being gouged, subjected to prices so high and/or service so poor that the regulated company earns extortionate profits. Without such assurance, public support for the regulatory process wanes, cynicism replaces confidence in the process, and talk of renationalisation is heard in the land.

So what is needed here is an international merger. Perhaps if Britain's regulators borrow some aspect of rate-base regulation from America, and American regulators accept the use of some index external to regulated companies as an interim rate guideline, both countries will achieve minimisation of monopoly profits and maximisation of incentives to efficiency. Or at least they might come as close to those goals as regulation, the imperfect substitute for competition, permits.

PART TWO
THE REGULATORS

4

ENTER THE REGULATORS

Sir Alan Peacock

Executive Director, The David Hume Institute

1. The Rationale of Regulation to Promote Competition

THE INSTITUTE OF ECONOMIC AFFAIRS has been in the forefront of discussion of the problems associated with trying to develop a sensible system of regulation of certain sectors of the economy which accords with the preservation of the impetus to make all sectors of the economy as competitive as possible.[1]

At first sight, regulation may be the antithesis to competition. If the private firms are to be allowed to compete with one another, why need there be regulation at all? Intervention by government to control their operations simply diverts scarce resources which have more important alternative uses and encourages business leaders to spend their time cultivating the regulatory authorities rather than concentrating on the job of satisfying customers. So the argument goes, and there is ample evidence that regulation of business activities can produce these undesirable side-effects.[2] There are, nevertheless, circumstances in which, in principle at least, regulation has a positive part to play in preserving and extending the competitive process, and this provides the

---

[1] Representative publications are *Privatisation and Competition: A Market Prospectus* (edited by Cento Veljanovski), IEA Hobart Paperback 28, 1989; *Financial Regulation – or Over-Regulation?* (edited by Arthur Seldon), IEA Readings 27, 1988.

[2] See Alan Peacock *et al.*, *The Regulation Game*, Oxford: Basil Blackwell, 1983.

79

principal rationale for the activities of the regulators who have kindly agreed to contribute to this volume. A rehearsal of the arguments for regulation as a means for creating competition may be useful.

Those who consider that regulation is necessary in order to promote competition, with the ultimate objective of maximising the sovereignty of the consumer, must hold to the proposition that the market economy, left to itself, will not achieve this objective, or even produce an approximation in which monopolies would only be temporary phenomena. In a European context, the most important contribution to this doctrine was probably made by the German 'social market economists' or *'Ordokreis'*. Their earliest Manifesto in 1936, which was a brave attack on the corporatist philosophy of the Nazis, put particular emphasis on 'workable' competition. Today their efforts are crowned with success in the special attention paid to competition policy in the economic clauses of the German constitution and ultimately in the firm commitment to a European competition policy.[3]

Not only does Ordo thinking and German practice pre-date Thatcherism but it emphasises that much more is at stake in controlling single monopolies or cartels with a view to preserving competition. While Thatcherites are inclined to see the political dangers of monopoly as lying in the threat posed by trade union power, there is a strong Galbraithian flavour in Ordo thinking, where the emphasis is on big business. The Ordo-liberals differ from Galbraith in seeking solutions to the problems of reducing the political influence of business not by neutralising private monopoly by state monopoly – countervailing power – but by making competition policy an integral part of general economic policy. Although no German economist is likely to claim that German competition policy is an unparalleled success, there can be no doubt that this integrated approach has done much to achieve consistency in policy-making. This is an issue which is bound to arise in contemplating the extension of our regulatory system by the establishment of separate regulatory bodies for each privatised sector of the economy.

2. Privatisation and Competition

The extent to which regulation is necessary might be considered to be a function of the size of the public sector itself. The dilemma posed by Galbraith and recognised by the Ordo-liberals could be avoided, so it

---

[3] See the important essay by Werhard Möschel, 'Competition from an Ordo Point of View', in Alan Peacock and Hans Willgerodt (eds.), *German Neo-Liberals and the Social Market Economy*, London: Macmillan for Trade Policy Research Centre, 1989.

would seem, by placing all those services provided by the public sector which technically could be provided by private enterprise firmly in the private sector. When the economic history of the UK for the latter half of the 20th century comes to be written in, say, 50 years time, it is likely that historians will point to the privatisation programme as the most revolutionary part of the Thatcherite economic programme. Here we have a unique merging of theory and practice. The 'competition ethos' associated with the 1980s, which is recognised world-wide, is not always traceable to precise actions by either governments or businesses. In the case of privatisation of public utilities, however, we can point to a clear link between the Government's views on political economy in general and its manifestation in particular, radical measures.

A rough measure of the magnitude of change is provided by the reduction of employment in public corporations from 2,065,000 in 1979 to 844,000 in 1989. There was a comparable fall in public corporation investment as a proportion of gross domestic fixed capital formation from 17 per cent (1979) to 5 per cent (1989).

However, to equate privatisation with increase in the operation of competitive forces is a naïve error. In the British case, indeed, there is a somewhat paradoxical situation. Broadly speaking, privatisation has not been extended to important activities in which market forces could become more potent. Thus in large segments of the provision of education and health, it would be technically possible to operate competitive market systems. However, politicians fight shy of privatisation arrangements which will not be politically acceptable even if final consumers – schoolchildren, students and patients – were to receive compensatory income support alongside the introduction of payment for services rendered. Furthermore, the incumbent producers of such services are perceived to have neither the commercial skills nor the incentive to acquire them which would be necessary for them to compete successfully. In contrast, public utilities already selling services in the market-place, and which are privatised, do not encounter these difficulties, but hardly fit with the competitive ethos if one is simply substituting a private 'natural' monopoly for some public version.

It is true that there is an important change in property rights which, in principle at least, means that privatised concerns can become subject to the discipline of the capital market. How effective that discipline will be is open to question. Certainly the present Government, rightly in my opinion, does not believe that the forces of competition, even when we achieve the EC single market, will be sufficient to force major privatised concerns covering fuel and power, telecommunications, etc., to conform to the chief aim of promoting consumer sovereignty.

Hence the recourse to a major extension in the use of regulatory agencies.

3. Economic Analysis and the Regulatory Problem

The conventional textbook approach to the use of regulatory techniques is to begin with the identification of circumstances where the free market leads to 'market failure'. Our textbooks are filled with static equilibrium models of various market forms which explain the nature of 'market failure' through the presence of monopolies and external effects of market activities that defeat the objective of maximising the sovereignty of the consumer. At least the more sophisticated versions, particularly those using the economics of the environment as an example, examine the relative merits of eradication of market failure by comparing regulation of private including privatised concerns with the use of fiscal measures or nationalisation. The problem with this analysis is that it normally stops short of the interesting point where formulation of actual measures is made.[4] Martin Shubik pokes fun at the economist pontificating on policy measures by his story of the 'wise' owl. The owl is consulted by a centipede suffering from sore feet. The owl ponders over the matter and announces gravely: 'Your condition will be cured if you move the pressure on your feet by hovering a few inches above the ground.' The centipede looks puzzled and asks: 'How do I do that?' The owl replies: 'I have solved your conceptual problems: do not bother me with the trivia concerning implementation.'[5] Much of welfare economics adopts an owl-like stance!

Those with practical experience of government or who have researched its workings in depth know that the simple prescriptions of welfare economics assume an omnicompetent government whereas inherent in the actual relationships between government and industry there is 'government failure' as the counterpart of 'market failure'. Neither the incentives nor the opportunities may exist which make it possible for government to conform to the norms displayed in textbook diagrams. A positive economic analysis of regulation soon shows how simplistic the prescriptions of welfare economics really are. However, the opportunity cost of studying regulatory practice is high. It entails knowledge of the workings of government which is often difficult to obtain and skills in its interpretation which are not normally taught in

---

[4] An honourable exception amongst recent textbooks is Michael Parkin's *Economics*, New York: Addison Wesley Publishing Company, 1990, Part 7.

[5] Martin Shubik, *A Game-Theoretic Approach to Political Economy*, Cambridge, Mass.: MIT Press, 1984, p. 615.

our economics graduate schools with their pronounced emphasis on the elegant mathematical expression of economic ideas rather than on studying its subject matter.

The essence of this positive analysis lies in the acceptance of the uncomfortable fact that when the government is the 'principal' determining the policy and an industry, firm, or consumer is the 'agent' through which the policy is meant to be carried out, their relationship cannot be as clear-cut as the simple mathematics of price theory suggest. Even if we assume that regulators are determined to adopt a 'public interest' stance and are not dismissed as 'rent seekers', as they frequently are in public choice literature, they will hardly find themselves in the position depicted in economic diagrams in which it is assumed that regulated producers are passive adjusters to 'levers' controlled by regulators.

For example, it is easy to draw a diagram indicating how the price of electricity might be controlled and what effect controls would have on profits and output in the short run. However, the diagram assumes that the regulator has complete information on the production functions and costs of the regulated concern. Such information has to be supplied from the regulated concern and this presents obvious difficulties. Can the concern be trusted to supply accurate information given that its interests are affected by what information is supplied and acted upon? Information relates to planning magnitudes which cannot be known for certainty. Will the concern's estimates of these uncertainties be unbiased? The regulator has to devise means of checking whether the estimates are 'reasonable' and this requires scarce professional resources, not only embodying a thorough knowledge of the economic characteristics of the concern but also negotiating skills. In short, having to resolve disagreements about the status of the information supplied, which is only one example of interface problems between regulator and regulated, implies a bargaining relationship between them. The regulated concern is not a Pavlovian dog reacting to stimuli supplied by the regulator.

4. Enter the Regulators

Great interest, therefore, attaches to how our regulators see their task and to the criteria which they would select as indicative of their degree of success in carrying out their functions. They are aware, I am sure, that the most famous analysis of the economics of regulation, which contributed to the award of the Nobel Prize in Economics to George Stigler, suggests that their efforts could be doomed to failure! About 20 years ago, he advanced the proposition that 'as a rule regulation is acquired by the industry and is designed and operated primarily for its benefit'[6] – the so-called theory of regulatory capture. There are many subtle twists in the exposition of his theory but, shorn of some qualifications, he holds that irrespective of whether an industry seeks regulation or has it thrust upon it, the advantage over consumers in organising lobbies and bargaining with government authorities frequently results in situations where producers influence the formulation of regulations so that they redound to their benefit – for example, by limiting entry into the market. In characteristic Chicago fashion, Stigler sets about providing systematic statistical evidence to support his claim. Some of our regulators will sense that I am trailing my coat, because they know that I know that they are sympathetic to both the philosophy and methodology of the Chicago School, and am implying that one indicator of their success should be their ability to prove Stigler wrong!

However, I would not want to make the Stigler thesis the focus of discussion of the regulators' activities. For one thing, the origin of the activities of most of the regulators writing in this volume lies firmly in the reduction in the activities of the public sector and in the concomitant need to ensure that the consumer benefits from the process. As evidence of this, regulation of privatised activities does not merely mean that regulators have to seek to simulate competition, but, where possible, have to encourage new entrants. For another, it may be that in the case of privatised services which are of direct interest to consumers, such as telephones, fuel and power, not to speak of airlines, there is a much more potent incentive for consumers to organise themselves to monitor the pricing of services and the improvement in their quality. In any case, it would be grossly unfair to make even a preliminary judgement of the activities of those of our regulators who have hardly had time to prepare the menu, far less to translate it into dishes meant to satisfy the consumer.

In short, it would be churlish not to express goodwill towards those regulators who have so readily come forward to explain their objectives and *modus operandi*, and to outline the problems that they expect to encounter. It is a safe prediction that their contributions will be regarded not only as authoritative, as they must be, but also of compelling interest.

---

[6] George Stigler, 'The Theory of Economic Regulation', reproduced in his *The Citizen and the State*, Chicago: University of Chicago Press, 1975, p. 114.

5

OFFICE OF FAIR TRADING: REFLECTIONS ON REGULATION

Sir Gordon Borrie
Director General of Fair Trading

THE MOST OBVIOUS CONTRAST between my rôle as a regulator and the rôle of the other regulators represented in this collection of papers is that they each have a specific industry to regulate and they operate under specific statutory powers which were purpose-built for that industry. My rôle embraces industry and commerce generally and I operate under a variety of statutory powers derived in part from general legislation (most obviously the Fair Trading Act 1973, which established my Office) and in part from specific legislation concerned with a particular industry, like the Estate Agents Act 1979 or the Broadcasting Act 1990. Broadly, my activities are twofold – one is concerned with the promotion of competition and the other with the protection of the consumer. But both these activities range over the supply of all goods and services, with limited exceptions.

But there is another respect in which my work is different from that of the industry-specific regulator. Much of my work is not primarily the work of a regulator at all. It is true that, in the interests of consumer protection, I am a regulator of the consumer credit industry. Everyone in that industry – lenders, brokers, debt collectors, etc. – has to have a licence from my Office and I have the power to refuse or revoke such licences if I consider the applicant or licensee unfitted to hold one. Under the Estate Agents Act, although there is no requirement that estate agents obtain a licence before they can do business, I do have the power to issue warning and prohibition orders against estate agents whom I consider are unfit to carry on business. But a lot of my Office's consumer protection work is not regulatory at all: it includes the provision of information and advice to consumers and examining what policy changes and legislative changes may be required in the future. Examples are our 1990 Reports on Timeshare and on Trading Malpractices.

Promoting Competition to Avoid Regulation

And as for the responsibility of my Office to help promote competition in UK industry and commerce, that function too is not primarily a regulatory one. Indeed I would say that, on the contrary, it is intended to try and ensure the maintenance and improvement of competition so that regulation by state authorities (or at any rate continuous regulation) is not needed. Whether I am pursuing into court companies who have engaged in secret price cartels or questioning the desirability of a merger between firms in the same product market because it may result in a dominant company, or asking the Monopolies and Mergers Commission (MMC) to investigate industry-wide vertical restraints, such as the tied-house system in the beer market, I am not so much seeking to regulate the industry as intervening at a particular moment of time in order to promote conditions in which the 'invisible hand' of market forces, driven by competition, will ensure that an industry performs efficiently and in the interests of consumers. It seems to me there is a considerable distinction between a one-off intervention by government authorities such as an inquiry into and prohibition of a merger between, say, Kingfisher and Dixons, or a Court Order prohibiting a cartel in the building materials industry, and the on-going regulation of a private monopoly or duopoly such as may be created by the privatisation and partial liberalisation of a public monopoly.

Of course I do admit that sometimes, in some industries with which I get involved, on-going monitoring is needed and as recent history of the beer industry shows very well, more than one intervention may be desirable. Moreover, sometimes initiatives I take may lead to Orders against, or undertakings given by, firms by which their behaviour is subsequently regulated by my Office on a continuous basis. The most obvious example of this is where the MMC, having investigated a market at my request, concludes that a dominant firm in that market has behaved against the public interest in respect of the prices it has charged, and the MMC recommends that the firm's prices be subsequently regulated by the Office of Fair Trading (OFT). There have been a number of such cases over the years, the most recent examples concerning salt (where two firms dominate the market in the UK), and opium derivatives (where the leading firm has over 80 per cent of the market).

These regulatory outcomes of monopoly investigations are similar in kind, if less extensive in scope, to the regulation by OFTEL and other special agencies of the privatised public utilities. Competition policy will only lead to so specific a form of regulation of business behaviour where the MMC is confronted with a case of market failure, resulting from a situation of natural monopoly or, at least, other high-entry barriers which cannot easily be removed. In salt, for instance, the two firms controlled the available sources of brine and, in the MMC's view, had little reason to fear competition from new entrants. But regulation is a last resort. Wherever possible, the instruments of competition policy aim to remove restrictions on the effective working of competition.

Externalities

Market power supported by high entry barriers is not, of course, the only cause of market failure; there are other reasons why leaving firms free to make their own decisions may not lead to a socially acceptable outcome, even if those firms are genuinely in competition with each other. One such reason is where an economic activity has effects on parties other than those who are directly involved in that activity – externalities. The traditional example is the adverse effects on other businesses (or households) of pollution from a neighbouring factory. But regulation may be justified because of more subtle kinds of externality than a belching chimney. In financial markets, for example, the prospect that the failure of one financial institution could, through loss of confidence in the whole system, put the survival of all such institutions at risk is an externality which can justify regulation. Another cause of market failure which justifies regulation is in-adequacies of information available to (usually) the customer for any good or service, leaving him/her ill-equipped to make intelligent decisions as between competing offerings.

Most recent discussion about regulation in the UK has centred on the regulation of the privatised public utilities. This is hardly surprising. The privatisation of publicly owned enterprises has been one of the more striking policies of the last 12 years, and also one of the more controversial – certainly where the enterprises have been dominant in their markets, as in telecommunications, gas, electricity and, in the local context, water (and not forgetting airports).

87

Problems of Regulating a Monopoly Supplier

It is not for me to anticipate in any way what the star-studded cast of special regulators who will follow me are likely to say about their particular regulatory tasks. I do want to offer a few general observations. I would say, first, that I am sure it was right of the Government to establish *special* régimes at the outset for the regulation of the privatised enterprises where the privatisation was not accompanied by, or could not be accompanied by, structural changes which would have created a competitive market structure. There was the option of privatising and relying on the general competition legislation administered by my Office to investigate and control any abuse of market power that subsequently manifested itself. While I would not go so far as to say that this would be akin to leaving the stable door open until the horse had bolted, it would be putting temptation in the way of the horse and, to strain the metaphor, it could take some time – using the competition legislation – to get him back into the stable. When the gas industry was privatised, the Government *did* rely on the general competition legislation in relation to the contract (largely industrial and commercial) sector of the market.

The regulatory régime set up by the Gas Act 1986 distinguished between the tariff (largely domestic) and the contract sectors of the market. British Gas's charges to *tariff* customers are subject to a special regulatory régime, which imposes considerable restraint on BG's pricing policy as shown by the revised price-cap formula recently announced by Mr McKinnon. But, in the contract sector, where it was assumed BG faced competition from other forms of energy, BG were left free to negotiate their prices with their customers, with the general competition legislation as the only safeguard. Complaints to the OFT about the level and structure of BG's charges led me to make an early monopoly reference to the MMC. In its report, published in October 1988, the MMC concluded that BG's pricing policy had operated against the public interest, and the Commission made a number of recommendations bearing on that policy. But, more importantly, the MMC made recommendations aimed at reducing BG's dominance of the market, in particular, that they should not contract for more than 90 per cent of deliveries from any new gas field within the UK Continental Shelf, and that they should publish details of their 'common carriage' terms – that is, their charges for transporting gas through BG pipelines. British Gas gave the Secretary of State appropriate undertakings but the whole process of investigation was a protracted one.

Of course, I do not underestimate the difficulties of creating a competitive market structure at the outset, indeed, the impossibility of doing so where a genuine, natural monopoly is involved. But, with electricity privatisation, the Government have, clearly, made a bigger effort (I assume influenced by the example of gas) to improve the chances of competition within the industry, both by separating out the natural monopoly element (the national grid) and by creating a number of generating businesses as well as by allowing a phased freedom to customers to contract with different suppliers. And, with water privatisation, the regulatory régime designed for the several local, natural monopolies incorporated the novel notion of yardstick competition as a surrogate for real competition in the market-place.

Deregulation in the Bus Industry

When the bus industry was deregulated, it was brought fully within the scope of the general competition legislation and it was not thought necessary to create an OFBUS. Competition was being encouraged from the outset, primarily by privatisation and the breaking up of the National Bus Company (NBC), and it was thought that there was no need for special regulation. Predictably, the structure proved to be unstable, and there have been many subsequent mergers resulting in some quite large, if geographically spread, new-style operators. Several mergers have been referred on my advice to the MMC and divestment ordered following adverse reports from the MMC; but challenge in the courts has made the future of this application of competition policy uncertain.

Further, the established local operators have exploited the many advantages they have over potential, usually small-scale entrants, which advantages reduce in practice the contestability of the bus market. One advantage is control of an essential facility, such as a bus station. It is an anomaly, perhaps, that whereas the 1985 Act requires that the operator of a publicly owned bus station shall make that facility available to all operators on a non-discriminatory basis, there is no such provision for privately owned bus stations. In 1986, acting under the Competition Act 1980, I did rule as anti-competitive the refusal by Southern Vectis, the dominant bus operator on the Isle of Wight, to allow a small competitor to use its bus station at Newport because of the lack of any alternative, reasonably comparable, facility. I accepted an undertaking from Southern Vectis to allow competitors access on payment of a non-discriminatory cost-related fee.

Predatory Behaviour in the Bus Market

Another feature of the bus market since deregulation, which may also be of wider relevance, is strategic predatory behaviour – usually the use of predatory prices – designed to eliminate competitors and deter subsequent new entrants. In one writer's phrase: there is nothing like some 'corpses on the lawn' for discouraging new entry. Up to the end of 1990 we have had 105 complaints of predatory behaviour by established bus operators against (usually small) new entrants.

The dividing line between predatory and aggressive, but wholly legitimate, competitive behaviour is a notoriously difficult one to define and apply and, generally, I believe that competition authorities (and regulators) should err on the side of caution before taking action in response to allegations of predation. But where the market structure and characteristics of the firms involved suggest that predation could well be a profitable strategy in the long-run sense, then intervention may well be justified.

The investigation of predatory behaviour may lead to the overt regulation of the pricing (or other) policies of a firm by my Office in the same way as can an investigation into allegedly excessive prices of a dominant firm. But my main point here is that any authority or regulator concerned to encourage competition to a dominant firm needs to be on the look-out for those policies which can be deployed strategically to make life impossible for putative competitors. He also needs, of course, adequate instruments for dealing with such tactics when they occur.

It is commonplace to say that competition and regulation are alternatives. When competition works effectively, there will be no need for business behaviour to be regulated. When competition fails to work, and cannot be made to work, then regulation (by some means or another) is called for. But I have already mentioned that regulation may be justified for other reasons than monopoly power, in particular by the existence of externalities, and by information inadequacies.

Regulation of Financial Services
Although the privatised public utilities have attracted the greatest political and academic attention in the last decade of regulatory reform (to use the phrase of Kay and Vickers), there have also been some important developments in the regulatory arrangements of other sectors, notably, financial services, certain of the professions – particularly auditing, conveyancing and other legal services – and, most recently, broadcasting, where the rationale for regulation would include externalities and information problems. In some cases the extent of regulation has been increased, not diminished. This is certainly so for financial services under the Financial Services Act 1986.

The purpose of this Act is, of course, to improve investor protection. The Securities and Investments Board (SIB) and the subsidiary self-regulatory organisations (SROs) responsible for particular forms of investment business (which are broadly defined by the Act) are charged with regulating the industry by prescribing business conduct and other rules which must be complied with by those authorised to engage in the relevant branch of investment business. These rules are almost bound to restrict competition to some degree by limiting the means by which practitioners may compete with each other, by restricting entry to newcomers, for example by capital adequacy requirements, or by restricting competition from the providers of different, but substitutable, services or financial products. And with a system of self-regulation, even self-regulation backed by statute, there is a risk that the rules may be drawn up as much to protect the interests of practitioners as to protect the interests of users of their services – investors. The Financial Services Act exempted the financial services sector from the general competition legislation. Instead, I had to report to the Secretary of State on the rules and practices of the SIB and the SROs before they were recognised by the Secretary of State for the purpose of regulating the sector (this meant before 29 April 1988 – so-called 'A-Day') and, subsequently, on any rule changes or practices that may give cause for concern, and on the rules of any further regulatory body seeking recognition. In my reports I must say whether any of the rules, practices, or whatever, are likely significantly to prevent, restrict or distort competition. If I so report, it is for the Secretary of State to consider whether the adverse effects on competition outweigh any benefits to investor protection; if so, he can require the regulatory body to change its rules.

The Financial Services Act has been a far from popular measure. It imposes considerable compliance and other costs, costs that businesses which have always been run fairly and properly resent having to pay. But I have been concerned that regulation intended to protect investors may be counter-productive. In particular, I have been concerned about the burden of regulatory costs and how they bear on the diminishing number of independent financial advisers whom I regard as a crucial source of information and advice to investors, and a vital element in the competition between life offices. Fortunately, steps are now being taken to simplify the various rule-books. I have no doubt that the hitherto heavily legalistic, and often opaque, rule-books have not only added to costs but, by their complexity, may have created uncertainty about what was and was not allowed, thereby perversely providing a lesser degree of investor protection.

My own rôle under the Financial Services Act is a narrow one. The OFT does not act as a regulator. Instead we may intervene and seek to influence the decision-making process of the regulators. This rôle obliges us to become knowledgeable about a variety of financial markets and about many forms of investment business. In this respect, our work is the nearest we get to that of the special regulatory agencies such as OFTEL, OFGAS, and others represented in this collection of papers. The problem facing any regulator is that he cannot be as well-informed as the business(es) he is regulating. The same goes for my Office in our rôle of surveillance over the financial services regulators. My Office does not require a high degree of expertise on particular industries in administering the general competition legislation, because our function is, essentially, to initiate in-depth investigations when we think there is good reason to do so. But in financial services, we must have a higher level of expertise. Under the Companies Act 1989 and the Courts and Legal Services Act 1990, we are given a similar interventionist but non-regulatory rôle concerning auditors and certain legal services. We have to report on the effects on competition of various rules of professional bodies. Similarly, we have a special rôle in assessing the competition effects of networking agreements among the would-be Channel 3 television broadcasters, under the Broadcasting Act 1990. Thus, my Office is having to spawn a number of small, specialised units within the Competition Policy Division of the Office.

I am glad that the value of competition is recognised in these recent statutes. In general I believe it is a necessary condition, albeit not always a sufficient condition for economic welfare. Regulation is sometimes necessary as a surrogate for competition. I believe that the promotion and protection of competition should be given greater prominence as a policy objective. I believe that competition policy would especially be more effective if cartels were prohibited as in Article 85 of the Treaty of Rome, and that UK law included the investigatory powers and sanctions that EC law has. We find quite often that blatantly anti-competitive agreements are made in secret and, while the restrictions are void and unenforceable in law, there is no penalty for failing to register. Almost as bad, my Office has severely constrained powers to investigate suspected secret, and therefore unlawful, agreements. I have therefore welcomed the Government's plans, announced in a White Paper of July 1989, to reform our law broadly on the lines of the European Community law.[1] Unfortunately, as yet there is no sign of any legislation to give effect to the White Paper proposals or any other reforms.

'A Patchwork of Regulatory Agencies and Instruments'

As a final remark, I would say that the pace of regulatory reform over the last 12 years has left us with something of a patchwork of agencies

---

[1] *Opening Markets: New Policy on Restrictive Trade Practices*, Cm. 727, London: HMSO, 1989.

and regulatory instruments. No doubt, a case can be made for competition between regulators – but my guess is that the time will come when the regulation 'industry' has itself to be rationalised. In some industries, the most desirable outcome may be that the regulator works himself out of a job by enabling competition to thrive to such an extent that regulation and a specialised regulatory agency are no longer required, only the more general watchfulness and general competition powers of the OFT. That may be some way off, and for other industries, specialised regulatory bodies may be required on an indefinite basis.

6

OFFICE OF GAS SUPPLY: REGULATION OF THE GAS SECTOR

James McKinnon
Director General of Gas Supply

Introduction

THE PRIVATISATION of The British Gas Corporation in 1986 as a single entity conferred PLC status on the enterprise and set the stage for the type of interaction between the newly created Office of Gas Supply (OFGAS) and the 100 per cent monopolist.

At the time of privatisation, media commentators and business analysts alike concluded that the regulatory régime was weak and that British Gas PLC would continue to operate in the same way as had BGC prior to privatisation. This view was shared by the top management of the day at British Gas which made pronouncements to the effect that existing policies would continue to be pursued by the same management team which had created the policies. Thus it was clear that BG had absorbed the media content of 1986 – or perhaps it had been responsible for it. A careful reading of the Gas Act 1986 and the Authorisation leads to a different conclusion from the one reached by the media, analysts and British Gas.

The small team at OFGAS saw matters in a somewhat different light. It was convinced that change was required by the various pieces of legislation and was clear as to what was expected of it. We believed that the introduction of competition was the key to securing change. We were assured by all that it would be impossible to generate competitive activity in any aspect of the market. With such friendly advice as that being available, who needed enemies!

OFGAS not only believed it to be possible to create real competition in the industrial segment of the gas supply market but that it was also possible to enhance value for money in the tariff segment by means of surrogate competition. This was the challenge that faced the 23-strong, or in the minds of commentators, the 23-weak team at OFGAS.

The OFGAS Approach

We took as our starting point that where competition existed there was no need for a regulatory régime. It seemed clear to us that the sub-sets of the environment existed which would enable real competition to develop in the industrial market segment. It was a question of mobilising the various elements to obtain the desired result. The MMC story on gas supply has been well documented but it has to be remembered that the opening chapters were written by the Gas Consumers Council and the Office of Fair Trading. The final chapter was compiled by the Department of Trade and Industry. The sequel has been in the hands of OFGAS and we have just about reached the half-way mark in our efforts to write competition sufficiently large before turning the concept over to where it belongs – the market-place.

The above shows two main aspects. The first is that it is inaccurate to think of OFGAS as the regulatory body in the gas supply industry. GCC, OFT, MMC and several government departments are substantially involved as well. The second and basic feature is that whilst regulation can give a kick-start to competition, such activity can be sustained only if the players in the game see that long-term profitability will be available to them through participation in the market-place.

In a matter of months it is likely that industrial users of gas will recognise that an embryo market exists. That market will grow and as more and more customers obtain benefits from its existence the need for price schedules will diminish to the point at which they can be removed. Competition will replace regulation and a further OFGAS objective will have been achieved. We have already attained the desired status in the area of common carriage. In this case grave doubts had been expressed that potential competitors would ever be able to gain access to the BG pipeline system. It was not easy but it was ultimately possible for OFGAS to cause BG to accept the rules of the game. BG now trades profitably in the pipeline business and competitors have a viable means by which they can deliver gas to their customers newly weaned away from BG. And not a regulator in sight.

The concept of surrogate competition by definition means that the regulator must retain an active participation in the market segment. However, if he judges matters properly he can 'incentivise' the monopoly to accept that its commercial interest is best served by providing value for money to the users in the market segment concerned. That is the approach that OFGAS has followed in the case of the tariff segment of the gas supply market. We would hope that the value provided to tariff customers and the efficiency achieved by the gas supplier will combine in the future to cause the level of intervention by OFGAS to be reduced to a minimum. It should be emphasised that constant vigilance will be exercised by OFGAS at all times, notwith-standing the apparent calmness of the water in the tariff market.

The Requirement for Information

It seems to be too obvious for words that a regulator will need to have sufficient information about the area with which he is concerned in order to do his job properly. No one, save perhaps the company being regulated, would deny this. Even such a company may come to the conclusion that a regulator should be given the facts so that fair solutions may be reached. At the outset of our relationship with BG the company showed a natural reluctance to share information with us. We, as regulators, have meticulously respected the information we have been given by all parties and we have been careful to exercise the highest level of security at all times. In regard to our extensive review of the tariff price formula we are pleased to record that BG has made available information of the most sensitive kind, of the type which it would never have considered providing five years ago.

At a fairly early stage it became clear to us that we should work with BG to disaggregate the financial position of the tariff market. This was a time-consuming task and took over two years to bring to a satisfactory conclusion. The benefits which flowed from this project were con-siderable and enabled OFGAS to take a consistent position on a number of issues. We were able to use the output to develop a financial model of BG's pipeline system at the time of formulating our ideas on an appropriate common-carriage pricing system. Furthermore, the data developed were invaluable to us as we moved to a consideration of the future cost patterns of BG over the years to 1997 in regard to the tariff review work.

It would be a mistake to think that financial information is the only type which will benefit a regulator. Perhaps the most valuable project we have undertaken at OFGAS is the tariff customer outreach programme. When we came into being we were conscious of the fact that as we were totally unknown our ability to be helpful to customers was minimal and the fact that we did not operate regional offices did not help matters.

We embarked on a series of regional meetings at which we met with local caring agencies, local authority social services, DHSS as it was then styled, working in close liason with our colleagues of the GCC. We were astonished and gratified at the response to our initiative. What had begun as our effort to tell people what we could do for them quickly developed into a series of lasting partnerships which we believe have been of great value to a very large number of tariff customers over the past five years. The volume of information we are able to generate about the level of service which is being provided by BG throughout Britain is enormous. The flow of data which comes to us through the outreach programme has enabled us to operate a 'top down bottom up' procedure on level-of-service questions. When we agree a revised procedure with BG we make the content known to our wide range of regional contacts and arrange for feedback as to how the procedures are being implemented by BG at local level.

As part of our range of duties we monitor developments in other parts of the world. In particular we try to keep abreast of events in Continental Europe as we move closer to the single market. Of course it works the other way also and there is a high degree of overseas interest in what we have managed to achieve in Britain. This interaction provides us with valuable material with particular reference to research and development progress; here we have been particularly fortunate to have the assistance of good friends in the USA and Japan.

Progress to Date

In April 1991 we announced that BG had agreed to accept the revised package of proposals which we had prepared in respect of the tariff formula review.

We believe that BG will be able to perform well in the face of the challenge posed by these proposals. The tariff customer in Britain will be served as well as any customer of any utility in the world if BG is successful in meeting the new challenge. In that sense one of the major objectives of the gas privatisation will have been achieved. The gas customer in the tariff sector will receive enhanced value for money and BG will have become more efficient whilst retaining the opportunity to improve its profitability.

As the level of competitive activity in the industrial sector grows so will customer choice become wider. This process will bring advantages in terms of price and quality of service to the customers and additional efficiency to the operations of suppliers. As if this were not enough, there will be the added bonus of the disappearance of the regulator.

7

OFFICE OF TELECOMMUNICATIONS: COMPETITION AND THE DUOPOLY REVIEW

Sir Bryan Carsberg
Director General, Office of Telecommunications

THE OFFICE OF TELECOMMUNICATIONS – widely known as OFTEL – was the first of the specialised bodies established to regulate an industry which had previously been dominated by a nationalised body, with extensive monopoly power. OFTEL commenced operations in mid-1984, a few months before the privatisation of its main regulatee, British Telecom (BT). At the start, the Government was tentatively thinking of staffing levels of around 50 but when we demonstrated a need for more, we had strong ministerial support and were able to increase our numbers steadily to the present level of about 130.

The Scope of OFTEL's Work

The main focus of regulation is on 'telecommunications systems' – that is, the telecommunication networks, or apparatus connected to those networks. Licences are required to operate these systems and regulation is given effect through conditions in the licences. The licences are issued by the Secretary of State for Trade and Industry, after considering my advice. I have the function of enforcing the licence rules, some of which depend on my judgement for their application, and I also have the function of amending the rules. If I think a change is required, I can either proceed by agreement with the licensee or, if this is not possible, by making a reference to the Monopolies and Mergers Commission and obtaining its broad support. In either case, I must give public notice of the proposed amendment, allow at least 28 days for representations to be made to me about it, and consider those representations, before finalising the modification.

Although BT is the biggest of the firms which I regulate, and the most demanding of resources because of its continuing monopoly power, the number of firms covered by OFTEL's functions is actually surprisingly large. Licences are held by Mercury Communications, the fixed-link national competitor to BT, and Kingston Communications (Hull), the original operator of the local telephone service in the City of Hull. Numerous radio-based systems are included, notably the first two mobile cellular telephone companies, Racal-Vodafone and Cellnet, the three new mobile operators, known as Personal Communications Networks (PCNs), several operators of satellite uplinks, radiopaging networks, and regional and national private mobile radio (PMR) systems. Over 130 cable television licences have been issued or are about to be issued, and, as from the beginning of 1991, we added National Transcommunications, the transmission system formerly operated by the Independent Broadcasting Authority, as well as the transmission system of the BBC, to the list. In addition, a number of special individual licences exist which cover extensive private networks such as those operated by British Rail and companies in the fuel and power industries; and if one adds in class licences, covering the operation of apparatus attached to public networks, the number of people operating under telecommunications licences increases to a figure in the region of 25 million.

It seems to me that most important regulatory activity falls into two main categories: the promotion of competition and the development of incentive regulation. Naturally, we have a great deal of routine business which does not easily fit into these categories – for example, the approval of apparatus for connection to public networks – but I have always thought that a sound way to confront a regulatory problem is by considering two lines of attack as the first focus. First, I ask whether the best way to find a solution may be to promote competition. If this is not practicable or insufficient, the next line is to ask whether some form of incentive regulation is appropriate.

Incentive Regulation

We have obtained a great deal of experience with incentive regulation in the seven years since we opened our doors at OFTEL. Control of prices by price caps is the best known example. BT's first price control rule of RPI-3 was established by the Government before privatisation. However, we undertook a major review in 1988, as a result of which the controls were extended and the main cap was tightened to RPI-4½; and we took the process further recently when BT accepted the inclusion of international call prices in the controlled 'basket' and a further tightening of the cap to RPI-6¼. Price cap regulation is a form of incentive regulation because it works by setting a ceiling on prices for a number of years, thereby giving the regulatee the opportunity to make a higher profit by exceeding the efficiency target implied in the price cap.

An even more striking example of incentive regulation is BT's Customer Guarantee Scheme. After I became concerned about BT's performance in repairing faults and providing new service on time, I persuaded the company to agree to a compensation plan under which it would guarantee to provide a firm date for providing an exchange line – previously it had given only an estimate that could not be taken seriously – and guarantee to meet that date within two working days and also to repair faults within two working days. If it failed to reach these targets, it would pay compensation to the customer concerned of a minimum of £5 per day and a larger sum, up to a maximum of £5,000 in the case of a business customer, if financial loss could be demonstrated.

I might include the publication of information as a further example of incentive regulation. The publication of the results of my survey of the state of BT's public call boxes produced a public reaction which was, perhaps, the main factor in encouraging the remarkable improvement that has taken place in this part of the service over the last three years.

Promoting Competition

My colleagues in the other regulatory agencies will also have had a good deal to say about price control, quality of service and such matters. One of the most distinctive features of the telecommunications industry is the progress we have already made with the promotion of competition and the widely held view that much more competition is likely to be feasible over the next few years. Because of the interest of our experience in this area, I shall focus on the promotion of competition for the rest of my paper.

The first important message about competition, perhaps, is that it is a 'regulatory weapon'. A regulator does not need to wait, hoping that it will occur, but can take active steps to encourage it; and it may be the most effective way of bringing about improvements in value for money for the customer.

The Benefits of Competition

The general advantages of competition are well known. Competition encourages efficient operation because only efficient firms prosper in competitive markets. Competition encourages the development of innovative services, and it also encourages energetic realisation of the potential provided by technological developments. A monopolist can afford to make its customers wait for the application of new technology; in a competitive market a firm cannot take the risk that a competitor will get there first. Competition will find out what is possible and what is economic in these matters and do so more surely than regulatory assessment.

More specifically, competitive markets provide better-informed judgement about the trade-offs that have to be made in economic activity. Consider, for example, price and quality of service. Given efficient operation, increasing quality of service involves higher costs and higher prices. It is not obvious that customers want to pay for the highest quality of service attainable. In competitive markets, customers are likely to be given a choice and the markets should allow different customers to obtain their different preferred combinations of price and quality. Developments of this kind can be undertaken by regulated monopolists, and have been, but I am struck by the observation that BT made virtually no progress in this direction before privatisation and the introduction of the threat of competition.

I could give many other examples of how a regulator's life can be made easier by competition. I foresee that companies might compete to assure customers that they have quality assurance to minimise the danger of billing errors. Or firms might advertise that customers should 'come to us and we will help you to prevent unauthorised use of your telephone' – including unauthorised use on the telephone company's side of the network termination point. Companies might vie with each other to help customers avoid the receipt of nuisance calls – telephone selling, or threatening and abusive calls – or perhaps even to help customers ensure that their children do not telephone pornographic services, instead of accepting the proceeds of these calls with gratitude. In all these cases – and many others – the optimal solution is unsure but guidance of the market is likely to be preferable to judgement of the regulator.

Effective Competition

I now turn to consider some of the issues involved in making competition effective. Perhaps the first point to make is that competition can take place at various levels. In particular, for example, we can seek competition in the use of networks, regardless of whether we have competition in the operation of networks. I take the view that, where there is no threat to competition from the abuse of unregulated monopoly power, no reason exists to curtail competition in the provision of services over networks operated by others. This view has been accepted in the complete liberalisation of the use of networks within the United Kingdom. We have been unable to apply this principle to international networks, without limit, because we would be unable to control the approach taken in the parts of the network that are in other countries and because the monopoly operators in those countries might be in a position to distort competition.

The Reasons for a Duopoly

Some of the most interesting questions arise in relation to competition for the operation of networks. The issues can be considered in the context of the developments that have taken place in the UK. Our first step was to consider a duopoly by encouraging the establishment of a competitor to BT in operating fixed-link networks. We decided to consider allowing just one competitor partly, no doubt, because of the feeling in the 1980s that the establishment of competition in network operation was very much of an experiment and some degree of caution was appropriate. However, people also thought that establishing one competitor would avoid a diffusion of the competitive effort and that one competitor would have a better chance of success than any one of many competitors.

In deciding on the introduction of a competitor, the issue in people's minds was whether or not this was likely to improve value for money for customers. It would not necessarily do so because the operation of telecommunications networks involves substantial economies of scale and some of these would be lost if the market was divided between two operators. However, the establishment of competition was likely to produce strong benefits in the form of improvements in efficiency and an incentive to provide innovative services, and the benefits were judged likely to outweigh the costs. Evidently this judgement depended in part on the assessment of the existing state of efficiency of the UK telephone network.

Purists might argue that it should not be necessary to make a subjective cost-benefit assessment of the type I have outlined. They would say that the worthwhileness of competition should be left to the market to decide. Competition should be permitted. It would succeed if it improved value for money for the customer; otherwise it would deservedly fail. However, it seemed to me that at least two reasons existed for not relying on this *laissez-faire* view in telecommunications. First, the immediate prospect was for the establishment of a duopoly. Duopolies may not engage in vigorous price competition: they may effectively set their prices by tacit agreement – the new entrant may simply adopt a slightly lower price than the incumbent at a level where it is not worth the while of the incumbent to respond – and this behaviour may make it possible to pass on higher costs in the form of higher prices. In other words, in a duopoly one cannot be sure that market forces will allow competition to survive only if it improves value for money.

Entry Assistance in a Duopoly System

The second reason for not relying totally on market forces in our situation concerned the need for entry assistance. In an industry like telecommunications, where one starts with a complete monopolist, entry is difficult. Establishment of a network requires a high investment and takes a long time. Furthermore, the new entrant will lack economies of scale in the early years and will therefore have to accept low margins initially. Competition may be beneficial and may be viable once the entrant reaches a certain point in its development but competition may not take place without some entry assistance. It would be better to manage without this entry assistance but it is worth giving if it is necessary to the establishment of competition.

Our financial modelling suggested that entry assistance was necessary in the UK, and it was given in two ways. At the start of competition BT was contributing to some of the costs of its local network through the prices for long-distance calls. It was required to continue this practice by a limit on increases in local prices. Mercury, the new entrant, was allowed to interconnect with BT's network without making an equivalent contribution to BT's local costs, equivalent to the one BT was implicitly required to make. This advantage helped Mercury to offset its disadvantage from its lack of economies of scale in pricing its long-distance calls.

Furthermore, BT was practically constrained to charge uniform tariffs. Its regulations contain a prohibition on undue preference and this could have been used to prohibit some differential tariffs, but not all. However, in practice the main influence was BT's own billing system which did not have the capability of operating differential tariffs. This meant that any such tariffs would have to be put into effect by some special arrangement and this would have been economic only for a small number of customers. This meant that Mercury could concentrate its efforts on the routes and the areas with the densest telephone traffic, where it would experience lower-than-average unit costs, with a limited ability on the part of BT to respond.

These forms of entry assistance represent a kind of interference with market forces and are another reason why it would not have been valid to rely wholly on the market to determine the sustainability of competition.

Cable Television

During the period of the duopoly, the UK did allow one other very important class of entrants into the market for fixed-link telephony: the cable television companies. These were extremely important in bringing the prospect of competition at the local level. However, they were required to operate in telecommunications through an agreement with either BT or Mercury and they were, therefore, in effect part of the duopoly policy.

The 'Duopoly Review'

The Government decided to limit competition in operating fixed networks to a duopoly for seven years from November 1983 and it stated that it would review the policy at the end of that time. The main part of that review was completed in March 1991. The decisions were made by the Secretary of State for Trade and Industry, after considering my advice. We both wanted more competition. We wanted it for the benefits I have described above, benefits which have been partly achieved by the duopoly policy but not, we thought, to the maximum possible extent. We thought that a particular potential existed for more competition at the local level. Indeed, the opportunities for competition may be even greater at the local level than they are at the long-distance level.

Modelling work carried out at OFTEL indicates that economies of scale at the local level, for many areas of the country, are no bigger than at the long-distance level. Large resources are used at the local level and local operations are generally regarded as being less efficient than long-distance operations; and it is at the local level that scope for innovative service and customer friendly service is at its greatest. The decision was therefore made to open the operation of telecommunications networks to widespread competition, except in the case of international networks where the lack of willingness of other countries to adopt similar arrangements is a constraint. Within the UK, in the area of fixed networks, would-be entrants can apply for licences knowing that there will be a general presumption in favour of their being granted them.

Entry Assistance after the Duopoly Review

This approach made it necessary to review the provision of entry assistance. It was evidently not appropriate to extend the kind of entry assistance I have outlined above to all new entrants, without limit on their number or the extent of the assistance. If entry assistance were continued without limit, uneconomic entry might result and value for money to the customer might diminish, because the loss of economies of scale might become excessive and because some new entrants might survive even though their operations were inefficient. At some point, we would have to allow BT to exercise more pricing flexibility or require BT's competitors to pay a contribution out of call charges to BT's costs of providing exchange lines, on the same scale as effectively provided by BT. Such contributions levied on BT's competitors can be called 'access charges'.

I decided to pursue both options. I established a framework for levying access charges on BT's competitors, through the interconnection arrangements; and I introduced a plan for allowing BT to introduce quantity discounts to a limited but increasing extent over a period of five years. BT would still have to limit its price increases for exchange line rentals but it would continue to be permitted to increase these relative to call charges. These proposals were incorporated in proposed licence modifications which I advertised for public comment on 7 March 1991.

The proposals I advertised have naturally been the focus of vigorous debate. BT's competitors have objected to the concept of access charges and the proposed scale of the charges. I am currently considering these objections and I may well conclude that the detailed arrangements require some modification. However, I believe that the concept is correct even if the point of application needs to be varied. Mercury is now a very large business and it will progressively move to a position in which it is able to compete with BT on equal terms. The cable television companies have yet to get started in any significant way in tele-communications but the structural arrangements already give some entry assistance in that they have the special privilege of integrating television and telecommunications services. They have also been able to choose the geographic areas in which they are to operate as being those with above-average density of population.

Prices and the Consumer

As a final comment on my experience in promoting competition in telecommunications, I would draw your attention to the tensions between this and consumer protection. Consumer protection calls for a strict control on prices to prevent the possibility of the earning of monopoly profits. If prices are not controlled strictly, customers are likely to complain loudly. However, the lower the prices and the lower the profits of the dominant company, the less competitors are likely to be encouraged to enter the market, and competition may well be in the best interests of customers in the longer term. Similar pressures apply to the balance of individual prices. At present, local prices are uneconomically low and long-distance prices are economically high. Altering the balance of these prices would increase the encouragement given to competition at the local level. However, such a change would also affect residential customers detrimentally, and vociferous objections would be likely to ensue.

Future Prospects

In spite of these difficulties, however, the prospects for increasing competition now appear to be very favourable. Mercury is gaining in strength and several other companies have expressed an interest in entering the long-distance market. Many cable companies are poised to develop local networks and various radio-based services are likely to become available. We have five mobile operators with nation-wide licences and the three new ones are likely to commence operations before the end of 1992. Mobile operators are poised to compete head-on with fixed operators. I do not know which companies will be the most successful telecommunications operators over the next 10 years. However, I am convinced the ability to ask this question is the most important development that has occurred over the last 10 years.

8

OFFICE OF ELECTRICITY REGULATION: THE NEW REGULATORY FRAMEWORK FOR ELECTRICITY

S. C. Littlechild
Director General of Electricity Supply

1. Introduction

AS THE 'NEW BOY' in the regulatory game, whose full statutory powers and responsibilities were conferred barely a year ago, I am in no position to produce a long list of strengths and weaknesses of regulation in the electricity industry, much less to pronounce on the strengths and weaknesses of regulation in the other industries. My experience of the practice of regulation (as opposed to the theory of regulation) is strictly limited. The most sensible approach for me is therefore to set out what are my statutory duties and functions, to illustrate with half-a-dozen examples how I have exercised my powers during the last year, and to finish by assessing whether, in my limited experience to date, the powers which I have are adequate or excessive.

2. Statutory Duties

My statutory duty is to exercise my functions in the manner I consider best calculated

(a) to secure that all reasonable demands for electricity are satisfied;

(b) to secure that licence holders are able to finance their authorised activities; and

(c) to promote competition in the generation and supply of electricity.

In addition to these three primary duties, there are a number of subsidiary duties which require me to protect the interests of electricity consumers with respect to prices, quality and continuity of supply; to promote efficiency on the part of licensees and the efficient use of electricity supplied to consumers; to promote research and development; to protect the public from dangers arising from electricity; to secure machinery for promoting the health and safety of employees in the industry; and to take into account the effect on the environment, the protection of the interests of rural consumers and the interests of those who are disabled or of pensionable age.

If one had to summarise all these duties in a few words it would probably be protection of customers and promotion of competition. To a greater or lesser extent, this theme runs throughout all the regulatory bodies.

My job is to promote competition where it is feasible and sensible to do so, bearing in mind that it was not possible at the time of privatisation to move in a single step from a state-owned monopoly to a privately owned, fully competitive industry. My task in part is therefore to help to complete this transition: not merely to monitor competition but actively to promote it.

At the same time the regulatory framework recognised that there are certain parts of the industry where competition is not viable, or not viable yet, or only viable to a limited extent. In these areas my job is to protect customers against monopoly power, and ensure that customers' complaints are given a fair hearing.

3. Balancing Objectives

I am sometimes asked whether there is not a conflict between all these objectives, and if so how I go about resolving it. Which of all these duties has priority? I answer that I do not see it that way at present. In my experience so far, there has not been a conflict between these objectives. This is not to say that the duties are irrelevant: far from it. Rather, the more immediate problems so far have been to trace through the full implications of the available actions for the statutory duties, and to assess what types of arrangements would be relevant in a competitive market. Let me illustrate with two examples.

(a) Direct Sales Limits

The licences of each of the two main generating companies contain a condition limiting their sales in each of the public electricity supply areas to 15 per cent of these markets. However, there is provision for me to relax these limits if the generators apply for this and if I think it appropriate to do so. Shortly after I had been appointed, the two generators did so apply. I decided to allow increases in four areas but not in the others. A year later they applied for further relaxations, which I did not grant.

In considering these applications, it was certainly appropriate to have regard to a number of the statutory duties. The duty to secure that licensees could finance their licensed activities was relevant since on the first occasion the PESs had entered into contracts which assumed that they would have a larger unopposed market than they would do if I granted these requests. The duty to protect customers was clearly important also, since relaxing these limits could be expected to lead to lower prices being offered, at least in the short term. Relaxing the limits would also be consistent with the duty to promote competition in supply. At the same time, it was argued that relaxing these limits would have an adverse effect on entry of new generators and hence on competition in generation. Such an outcome would be against the longer-term interests of customers.

Overlaying all this was the importance of achieving a stable transition from a nationalised monopoly industry to a privatised competitive one, an aim which was not spelled out as an explicit statutory duty but nonetheless is consistent with achieving most if not all of them. Finally, one is conscious that the media inevitably tend to simplify any decision. Is the regulator attempting to upset the régime and defy the Secretary of State? Is he siding with the generators or the distributors? Does he really believe in competition? Has he been captured? What signals is he giving about his future regulatory style?

In announcing my decisions on the two sets of applications, I explained in some detail my thinking, so there is no need to repeat that here. The point I would make in this paper is that the main task for me was to assess precisely what effects refusing or accepting these requests would have on the development of competition, especially in generation, so that I could balance the short- and long-term interests of customers. The 'problem', to the extent that there was one, was not one of a conflict between objectives but one of assessing the likely implications for the future of a given decision.

(b) Connection Agreements

In another type of decision, again involving the statutory duties, the main question has been: What type of arrangements would be most consistent with a competitive market?

To illustrate, British Oxygen decided to take its supplies of electricity from a second-tier supplier and needed to sign a connection agreement with Yorkshire Electricity for use of the local distribution system. The two companies were unable to agree terms and the matter was referred to me to determine. One of the issues in dispute was the extent of liability that each party should assume. Yorkshire had proposed £100,000; British Oxygen proposed £5 million. I determined that £1 million would be appropriate. In a subsequent dispute over a connection agreement between Allied Lyons and Eastern Electricity, the question at issue was whether liability should apply only to plant and equipment, or more generally to economic loss (loss of profit). Allied Lyons argued for a broad definition, Eastern for a narrow one. I decided in favour of the narrow decision: the parties should not be liable for economic loss.

Here again, my reasoning has been set out in the decisions on these two cases. As before, an important task was to trace through the implications of any decision. For example, it might be thought that it was simply a matter of deciding between the benefit to the company and the benefit to the customer, but insofar as a higher exposure to liability increased the costs of the electricity company, one would expect this ultimately to be reflected in higher prices to the customer. So even focussing on the customer or company separately, it was not immediately clear what the effects of any decision would be.

In approaching this determination, I found it useful to ask what were the practices in other competitive industries. Do companies engaged in negotiation where there are competitive pressures find it appropriate to assume liability for economic loss? I found that they did not. Of course, experience and practice in other industries will not always be directly applicable in the electricity industry, which has its own peculiarities, and some of the licensees have statutory and licence responsibilities which need to be taken into account. Nonetheless, looking at what arrangements apply in competitive industries can be a useful guide to determining certain disputes in the electricity industry.

4. Legal Interpretation in Premises Disputes

A third and somewhat different type of decision is illustrated by the various disputes over the meaning of the term 'single premises'. Customers whose demand exceeds one megawatt are eligible to take competitive supplies, but this one megawatt must be taken at what the licence refers to as a 'single premises'. The licence does not explicitly define this term. In about two dozen cases, a customer and its potential second-tier supplier have argued that the customer's site and the buildings thereon do indeed constitute a single premises, whereas the regional electricity company has argued that it is not, typically saying that it is an aggregation of several different premises, each under one megawatt. In many cases, the regional companies have argued that whether or not a site is to be considered single premises depends on whether or not there is a single meter there.

The first such example involved the York District Health Authority, which had a site containing two hospitals and a nurses' home. These were supplied by electricity from Northern Electric via two separate meters. York District Health Authority wanted to take its supply from Yorkshire Electricity and argued that this was a single site. Northern challenged this. I determined that it was in fact a single site so that YDHA was eligible to take supply from Yorkshire Electricity, although in the event Northern Electric responded by making a better offer and YDHA stayed with their former supplier.

It might be thought that this was a simple decision between the interests of two or three parties. Or again, many people perceived this as a choice about the importance of competition. Would the regulator seize this opportunity to break the franchise, or at least promote its erosion? However, from a statutory point of view, this was a different type of decision from the two decisions described above. The statutory duties could not be brought to bear in the same way. The decision had to be made on the basis of ascertaining the legal interpretation of the words 'single premises'. I had to ask myself: How would a court interpret this term? I concluded that if the Secretary of State had intended that the criterion of single premises should be the number of electricity meters on the site, it would have said so explicitly. I had to have regard to a wide variety of other factors concerning the purpose and use of the site and the component parts thereof. These considerations led me to the view that this was a single premises, and nothing in my statutory duties led me to change this view.

5. Speed of Decision-Making

I have just returned from a trip to the United States, discussing the nature of regulation in the US electricity industry. Regulation has been well established there for over 40 years, and there are many procedures which protect both customers and utilities. It does seem, however, that decisions can be a long time in the making. They talk in terms of years rather than weeks or months. I was told that one case was recently set aside by the judge, after 25 years, on the grounds that it had 'gone stale'. This makes me more comfortable with the speed of my own decision-making.

In the case of the direct sales limits, a decision has to be made within

28 days of a request if that request is not simply to fail by default. In the other two cases mentioned there is no explicit time limit, although one is very conscious that the parties need a decision in order to get on with their business, and that, for the customer at least, a delayed decision may mean a delayed opportunity to obtain electricity at a more favourable rate.

Bearing in mind that we are making a great variety of new decisions for the first time, in circumstances where the parties involved as well as ourselves are still familiarising ourselves with the new shape of the industry and trying to work out the implications of various alternatives, and where the procedures for decision-making are themselves in the course of being established, I hope that we are moving along at a reasonable rate. Nonetheless, there are occasions on which it is more appropriate not to be rushed into a quick decision, but to stand back and allow time for further thought and further experience. Let me give two examples.

(a) NGC Transmission Charges

One of my early tasks, just before vesting, was to approve the form of charges that the National Grid Co. (NGC) proposed to make for use of its transmission system. NGC was a newly created organisation, the like of which had never been seen in Britain before. Indeed, nowhere else in the world is there a separate transmission system of this kind, set in a competitive industry with respect to generation and supply, and having the NGC's statutory duties to operate efficiently and to facilitate competition. In the limited time available, NGC gave thought to how to structure its charges. I did not find the analysis fully convincing but it was clear that the theoretical underpinnings for a full analysis were not then available – neither engineers nor economists had given much thought to these issues before – nor had the data to support a different kind of scheme then been collected. Meanwhile, the show had to get on the road unless privatisation was to be brought to a halt. The solution was to accept, with some modifications, the proposed structure of transmission charges *pro tem*, on the understanding that NGC would carry out a thorough analysis in association with my office. A revised set of charges would begin to be implemented at the time of the scheduled review of NGC's charges three years after vesting.

That review is just beginning. It will give us a chance to take into account the experience to date (for example, with respect to potential entrants needing to assure themselves that transmission capacity will be available in future), and also to take advantage of the wide variety of ideas and suggestions which will undoubtedly be put forward which there was not previously time to explore. For instance, during my recent trip to the USA, it became apparent that access to transmission and the terms of access were becoming a major issue as competition in generation developed, and many different proposals were under discussion there.

One of the important tasks this summer is to appraise proposals for transmission charges in the context of the British electricity industry. I hope that it will be possible to find a structure of charges which more closely reflects costs, which facilitates competition, and which provides appropriate incentives to NGC itself.

(b) Metering

It soon became apparent to me that metering was going to be a crucial issue in the future electricity industry. Customers who wished to take supply of electricity from a competitive supplier needed to have a meter capable of measuring usage on a half-hourly basis. Before vesting, virtually no customers in the country had such meters. Nor indeed were more than a negligible supply of such meters available and such meters as existed were very expensive. The very largest customers found it worthwhile to acquire and install such meters. However, in order that the benefits of competition are extended to all customers, as provided for in the privatisation, this raised important questions about the types and costs of meters to be installed, and the rate at which an installation programme could take place.

In considering this problem it soon became clear that more sophisticated metering and associated two-way communications offered many additional benefits for customers. For example, companies could offer a wider range of tariffs from which customers could choose; in particular, there could be greater reflection of costs of electricity at different times of day or year. Some customers, particularly larger industrial ones, could respond to fluctuating prices in 'real time'. Other customers could programme their meters to cut off supplies to certain appliances when the price was particularly high. In aggregate terms, demand would become much more responsive to market conditions. There would be more efficient use of plant and less need for a large reserve capacity.

Furthermore, metering technology was changing rapidly. In fact, after I called a seminar to promote thinking about metering, there was a significant move on the part of meter manufacturers to equip themselves with technologies likely to be more viable in the new competitive market-place. There could also be opportunities for cost savings and benefit sharing between the utilities: if there are facilities for two-way communication of information on electricity, that could also be available in gas and water as well, and could no doubt be linked with telecommunications, cable television, the provision of banking services and other marketing services. The appropriate course of action was therefore to promote further thinking about the benefits of metering, while acquiring more information about the appropriate technologies and ways of proceeding.

During the course of the last year an important additional benefit of more sophisticated metering has become apparent. As my second Annual Report explains, the single major source of customer complaints in the electricity industry concerns disputed bills, and the main reason for this is estimated billing. The customer whose bill has been estimated on the low side for two or three quarters will receive a particularly large bill when the actual reading takes place. This causes problems for a large number of customers. These problems could be avoided by meters capable of giving an accurate reading by remote access whenever required.

The potential benefits of modern metering are high, but so are the potential costs. For this reason, it seemed inappropriate to rush into a quick decision, and to gather more information. Thus another task this summer is to give further consideration to what policy I should adopt towards metering, bearing in mind the commitment I have made to work to ensure the introduction of meters to the appropriate standard so as to make the benefits of advanced meters a reality in line with the Government's timetable for moving to full competition.

6. Does the DGES Have Adequate Power?

The first question asked by most media presenters is whether a regulator has teeth. There is no doubt that all the regulators do. But at a more serious level, are the powers of the Director General of Electricity Supply (DGES) fully adequate to regulate the electricity industry successfully?

As yet these are early days to form a judgement, but for the present my answer is 'yes'. The nature and scope of the powers provided in the Act and in the licences reflect a learning experience on the part of government. For example, there are more extensive and more explicit powers for the DGES to obtain information from licensees than there are for some other Directors. I suspect there has also been a learning experience on the part of the industry.

The DGES has more extensive powers than some of the other regulators in other respects. For example, the whole of the consumer protection arrangements lie within the ambit of the Office of Electricity Regulation (OFFER). The 14 Consumers' Committees advise the Director General, and are able to exercise greater authority as a result of the statutory powers which the DGES possesses. This is not the case in the gas industry.

A third area of greater power is with respect to determinations of disputes. I understand that the Director General of Telecommunications has no formal power to determine disputes between customers and licensees. He can advise and warn, but ultimately he does not have the power to determine a dispute. In contrast, the DGES does have that power, and it covers a wide range of disputes involving both domestic customers and large industrial customers. It also covers disputes between licensees.

An incidental consequence of this power, together with the fact there were no less than 19 initial major licensees in the electricity industry, means that my job is to a greater extent than that of the other regulators a matter of refereeing a contest between companies within the industry, rather than of fighting a battle against one dominant company. I once remarked that in electricity it was not a case of David against Goliath, but the reply was that it was more like David against 19 Goliaths. I can only remark that I do not see it that way: despite the relatively small size of OFFER, the powers that I have mean that we are every bit as powerful in legal terms as any of the licensees.

7. Are the Powers of the DGES Excessive?

Some commentators have expressed concern that the powers of the regulators may be excessive. I must say this fear has never yet kept me awake at night. There seem to me several very substantial constraints on the power that I have.

o *First*, I do not have unconstrained power to act or to use the resources at my disposal in any way whatsoever to pursue my statutory duties. For example, I could not build a small generating station at OFFER to promote competition, improve the environment or encourage research and development. I can only take into account my statutory duties when pursuing one of my statutory functions. These include the monitoring, enforcement and (where appropriate) amending of the licences; issuing of new licences; determining disputes between licensees or between customers and licensees; offering advice to the Secretary of State; and so on. These statutory functions are fairly closely defined.

o   *Second*, there are a number of significant areas of the electricity industry where regulation is effected by agencies other than OFFER. The Health and Safety Commission is responsible for health and safety. The Nuclear Inspectorate is responsible for all aspects of nuclear safety. The Department of the Environment and local planning organisations determine environmental policy and (subject to the specific powers of the Secretary of State for Energy in respect of overhead lines and larger generating stations) can prevent the construction of transmission and distribution lines or generating stations in particular areas. Responsibility for referring mergers to the MMC lies with the Secretary of State for Trade and Industry, advised by the Director General of Fair Trading; a merger can be prevented only if the MMC authorises this, and responsibility for action lies with the DTI and the OFT. Finally, the European Commission is taking an increasingly active rôle in the whole of British industry, not least in electricity. The recent transit directive is a notable example, and there have already been cases of appeal to the European Commission. Government policy towards the industry is itself constrained by EC considerations.

o   *Third*, the Secretaries of State for Energy and for Scotland have extensive functions in the electricity industry upon which I can advise but which are ultimately for their decision. Examples include the initiation of endurance régimes and the laying of non-fossil fuel orders to encourage the development of renewable energy.

o   *Fourth*, although I have power to change the licences by agreement with the licensees concerned, I cannot unilaterally dictate a change in these licences. For example, I do not have 'the power to control prices' in such an explicit form. I need to appeal to the MMC for permission to change a licence. Only if the MMC finds that there is something against the public interest which could be remedied by a licence change do I have the authority to make a licence change consistent with its recommendation. Furthermore, any proposed licence change, whether by agreement or following an MMC recommendation, must be publicly advertised and any representations must be duly considered.

o   *Fifth*, in important respects the power that I have derives from or is constrained by the Secretary of State. My power to issue licences to new entrants derives from a general authority granted by the Secretary of State the terms of which were a matter for him. My present general authority requires me to include certain clauses in all generation and second-tier licences – for example, that licensees in England and Wales should be members of the Pool. The general authority does not allow me to issue second-tier licences in breach of the franchise, or to issue transmission licences or public electricity supply licences without the consent of the Secretary of State. Furthermore, the Secretary of State has the power to prevent my making licence changes by agreement, to prevent my making certain references to the MMC, and to prevent my carrying out certain recommendations of the MMC. This constraint is more extensive in the case of electricity than for telecoms, where such detailed powers can be exercised only where national security is involved.

o   *Sixth*, all my actions are subject to judicial review. I need to be able to establish in court that I have followed correct procedures (for example, that in determining a dispute I have given the parties concerned an opportunity to see all the evidence and to make representations to me). I also need to be able to prove that the decision I have come to is a reasonable one – or, more accurately, that it is not a decision that no reasonable person could have come to.

o   *Finally*, like any other regulator or indeed any other public figure, I am constantly being judged by public opinion and by the media. A regulator who is widely perceived to be biased, or inconsistent, or vacillating, or acting unfairly, inevitably loses a great deal of authority. It is worth mentioning also that any one term of office for a regulator cannot exceed five years.

For all these reasons, it seems to me that there are significant and substantial checks upon the extent of the power enjoyed by any regulator, not least in the British electricity industry.

8. Summary and Conclusions

The arguments of my paper may be summarised briefly as follows.

First, the Director General of Electricity Supply has a wide variety of statutory duties which have to be taken into account in exercising his statutory functions. In practice I have not yet found a problem of conflict between these objectives. Rather, the task has been to trace through the implications of the alternative courses of action available. As an economist, I see scope here for further development of economic analysis and empirical modelling.

Second, the kinds of decision that I have had to take vary in character. Some, as just noted, primarily involve predicting the consequences of particular actions; others involve asking what arrangements would apply in a competitive industry; yet others involve ascertaining the precise legal meaning of a particular term. In one way or another, however, all contribute to the stable transition of the industry from a nationalised monopoly to a private competitive industry.

Third, there are important cases in which it is better to allow time for further analysis, and acquisition of data and learning from experience, than it is to make immediate binding decisions. This inevitably means a degree of uncertainty for licensees and market participants, but I believe that this disadvantage is more than outweighed by the advantage of the better decisions that should result.

Finally, I believe that the powers of the DGES are sufficient to cope with the problems he faces without being excessive. I have therefore every confidence that it will be possible to fulfil my statutory duties, and to promote a stable transition to a fully competitive electricity industry in Britain.

9

OFFICE OF WATER SERVICES: REGULATION OF WATER AND SEWERAGE

I. C. R. Byatt
Director General, Office of Water Services

The Start of a New Regime

IN MY HUME LECTURE, given in May 1990, I described the threefold regulation of the industry – regulation of the quality of drinking water by the Drinking Water Inspectorate (DWI), regulation of discharges of waste water by the National Rivers Authority (NRA), and economic regulation by the Office of Water Services (OFWAT). I also drew attention to the rôles of the Secretary of State for the Environment (DoE) in relation to environmental policy, that of the Secretary of State for Trade and Industry (DTI) in relation to competition and consumer policy, the appellate rôle of the Monopolies and Mergers Commission (MMC), the concern of the Secretary of State for Social Services (DSS) with low-income water customers, and the ubiquitous rôle of the European Community (EC). Although privatised, water and sewerage companies are still closely entangled with the traditional concerns of the public sector.

This time I want to consider how the régime has developed and to discuss the issues which have arisen. In doing so it may be useful to bear in mind the distinction between the framework of rules – the structure of the regulatory régime – and the operation of this régime. This is akin to the traditional distinction between rules and discretion. 'Discretion' includes the response of the regulated as well as the regulator to unexpected events.

It is important to keep the framework as set out in the Licence up to date – that is, to incorporate changes in the rules as and when they arise. Stability is an important virtue in any regulatory régime. But it would not be realistic to operate as though the initial document was not capable of improvement in the light of experience.

Since the inception of the régime, there has been one amendment to the Licence – concerning the administration of infrastructure charges. The methods of calculating the charges for first-time connection to the system were changed so that they are now more closely related to the likely demand for water. Also, some amalgamation of Licences is planned, first to deal with the Three Valleys merger and, secondly, to deal with cases where jointly owned but hitherto separately managed companies are amalgamating their managements.

I am now proposing a further change, to ensure that any diversification into other activities does not damage the core water and sewerage business.

The way of operating the régime has developed from a paper plan to a working system. This has involved:

o developing reporting arrangements, mainly concerned with the costs and financial and non-financial performance of the companies, and developing a basis for comparative competition;

o developing a style of doing business with a fairly large number of companies and with the other regulators of the industry;

o setting up a network of Customer Service Committees, which are there to serve the interests of the customers in 10 regions of England and Wales and ensuring that the work of these committees is closely related to the work of OFWAT headquarters in Birmingham.

The work of the first year of operation has also involved two major policy issues, one concerning the economic consequences of environmental and quality improvements and the other concerning how water and sewerage should be paid for – both charging systems and tariff structures. A third, which has emerged as an issue over the last 6-9 months, is the diversification of water companies and the need to ensure the protection of the core business. I shall turn to them later in this paper.

The Importance of the Consumer

First, however, let us look at the present position of the consumer. A major rôle for an economic regulator is to promote the interests of the consumer. This includes encouraging competition and promoting the development of markets. Where this is difficult or inadequate, the regulator must act directly to prevent the exploitation of a monopoly position. Such exploitation may be manifested in overcharging or poor service or general neglect of the wishes of customers.

Consumer sovereignty is a far cry from the water industry. The provision of water and sewerage services is a statutory, and water distribution is a natural, monopoly. The scope for direct competition is presently limited to greenfield sites more than 30 metres from a main. Unlike telecoms, gas and electricity, there is no national network to act as a common carrier for competing suppliers. It may be possible to develop such competition, but, in the absence of structural change, only in the longer term.

It remains to the regulator to provide such surrogate market forces as are possible. Fortunately there are a fairly large number of water companies – 34 independently managed water companies and 10 independently managed sewerage companies. So it is possible for the regulator to make comparisons of company costs and performance.

Water is in a special position compared with the other utilities. The usual supply and demand relationships are attenuated on the demand side. Although most water for business use is metered – or soon will be – the payments for most water used for domestic purposes are not related to the amount of water consumed. Most domestic customers are effectively charged for being connected – and remaining connected – to the system and pay a zero marginal price for the water itself. They have no scope for reducing their bills. Domestic customers can opt for a meter, but few have availed themselves of it. Where customers do not pay for the amount of water they use, companies do not have a financial incentive to supply what the customers want.

The product itself is subject to extensive regulation. The quality of water, which is not naturally homogeneous, is not determined by market forces but by administrative decision. The quality of drinking water is controlled by statutory regulations following an EC Directive. The quality of waste water is controlled in part by EC Directives and in part by national law.

Customers have little influence on the product they get – or what they pay for it.

In the present régime much power is in the hands of the professionals. They have the major influence on the costs incurred and the prices paid. Their positions can lead naturally to situations which push up costs. The experts on water quality may want to play safe and set high standards. Some of them have, indeed, elevated this into the precautionary principle. These standards are translated into costs by

121

another set of professionals, engineers. They do not want to risk failing to provide enough equipment. Experts on corporate finance then translate these costs into prices which are sufficient to finance the costs of new equipment and tighter operating standards. They will not want to risk failure of share and bond issues by recommending returns which may be too tight. When the new standards are put into effect, compliance is monitored by a further set of professionals whose prime concern is to ensure that these standards are met in all conceivable conditions.

The consumer is left to pick up the bill.

It may be that some thought should be given to customer preferences and to incorporating their views on price increases into the régime. Metering may have a rôle to play here, but it is only part of the story. As a way of getting into this issue, OFWAT is planning surveys of consumer perspectives, preferences and expectations. This work may have implications for the regulatory régime – implications which would be structural and be as much the concern of the political arm of government as of the economic regulator.

These considerations all point to the need for the regulator to be prepared to take up cudgels on behalf of the consumer. The regulator has to act as a surrogate for the market and try to prevent monopolistic abuse by the companies. The regulator may also need to try to prevent the consumer from being exploited by any imperfections in the process of setting and implementing standards.

The regulator also needs to ensure that consumers (and outside commentators) are provided with information. We want to operate an open system. One example is our contribution to the water industry statistics being published by the Centre for Regulated Industries. Another is consultation on policy issues, for example, *Paying for Water.*[1]

Customer Service Committees

The position of the consumer is strengthened by the close links with the Customer Service Committees (CSCs). The regulator is responsible for appointing Chairmen and members. It puts us automatically closer to the concerns of customers than we might otherwise be. We get valuable intelligence from the regions. I meet the Chairmen regularly and find them a very useful source of advice.

The CSCs have a statutory responsibility to look after the interest of the customers of the companies allocated to them. They deal with complaints which the companies have not resolved. They have

---

[1] Birmingham: OFWAT, 1990.

encouraged companies to make *ex gratia* payments to customers who get a particularly bad service.

The CSCs have also looked at problem areas, such as debt and disconnections, where, together with them we are beginning to draw up a Code of Practice. This is a sensitive issue at a time when water bills are rising sharply in real terms. The new obligation to take customers to court before disconnecting them is not always satisfactory; it can simply result in adding another £30 to the unpaid bill. Better practices by companies in dealing with those who have problems in paying offer a better pay-off.

Medium-Term Framework

Turning to the mechanics of utility regulation, I want to emphasise the importance of a medium-term approach, which links incentives to companies with protection for consumers.

o The RPI + K system, like RPI - X, provides the firms with incentives to act efficiently and reduce costs below what was assumed when K was fixed. There will be no retrospective clawing back of the benefits to shareholders of gains made by innovations.

o I would like to see as much stability as possible in Ks between periodic reviews. (It would be prudent to plan for a periodic review which could affect price caps from April 1995.) The periodic review provides the ideal opportunity for looking at all the obligations placed at one point of time – at a time when companies will be producing an asset management plan.

o The Licence allows for interim adjustments of K between periodic reviews. The interim adjustment machinery was scarcely designed for incorporating major new obligations into K. Such adjustments may well be necessary where the Secretary of State makes changes in environmental standards. Subject to that, however, OFWAT will try to avoid the 'cost pass-through trap', where each year there would be adjustments, up and down, as part of an annual cycle of bargaining which would resemble the Investment and Financing Review of the former nationalised industry régime. That would scarcely be good for incentives, nor, I suspect, for profitability.

o The industry's very large investment plan – amounting to some £28 billion or more over a 10-year period – will be best managed in a medium-term way. We have recognised this in our monitoring procedures and in our proposals for a staged approach to new obligations. New obligations can be agreed in principle as eligible for an interim adjustment to K and provision can be made for design and development work, before estimating the full cost of new developments.

Regulatory Information

It has been one of our key objectives to establish a regulatory régime based on good information. Good, accurate and consistent information will provide the basis of effective regulation and useful comparisons.

A reasonably defined and stable reporting régime has now been established. Stability in the reporting cycle and avoidance of *ad hoc* requests should assist those planning and managing the industry. It should also facilitate the integration of information systems for both internal and external reporting.

A number of expert working groups has been set up to advise us on the information needed for regulation. Membership has been drawn from the industry, the other regulators, the independent certifiers and the CSCs.

To emphasise the importance of reliable data and to provide quality assurance without breaching our aim of arm's length regulation, we have taken full advantage of the facility for independent certification in the Licence. (This is an extension of the appointment of auditors, where the regulator has access to the auditor.) For the generality of information coming to us we have required companies to appoint external consultants to oversee the information to be submitted and to confirm its adequacy, accuracy and integrity. We believe that this approach to quality assurance is a major strength of the régime.

This rolling technical and financial audit is, we believe, a necessary discipline. It is an innovation in regulatory reporting. We intend to develop a Code of Practice in this area. Audit involves costs but, given the nature of the industry, we do not think that these are excessive.

Because of the weakness of market mechanisms, and because of the drive to higher standards, we hope to create a comprehensive series of output measures which are good surrogates for improvements in performance and efficiency. In time they should provide a means of determining the success of the company in meeting its externally imposed targets and obligations.

At present we do not have sufficient of these measures for operational purposes. Our monitoring of the very large capital expenditure programme has to rely on progress on capital expenditure compared with the figures which underlay the determination of K. Customers are paying for the programme; it is up to us to ensure that it is carried out. Otherwise Ks should be reduced. I want, however, to emphasise that we are not monitoring by project and are concerned to preserve incentives to efficiency.

Guidelines for Current Cost Accounts

We have also been innovating on the accounting side. The Licence requires the provision of current cost accounts. We are rather proud of the guidelines we have developed for this purpose. An early decision was to concentrate on measuring profit after making provision for the maintenance of financial capital as the basis for current cost accounts. This fits well with the duty on the regulator to ensure that companies can finance their functions, leaving other monitoring tools – particularly the annual return on capital expenditure – to confirm that companies are maintaining their operating capability. In developing current cost asset valuations it seemed to us to be important to link accounts to the engineering information now available in asset management plans.

We will be using information from the regulatory accounts for two main purposes:

o   comparisons of the total cost of supply and the effectiveness of asset use by different companies;

o   monitoring the real rate of return on the utility business. (This does *not* imply that Ks will be set to yield a specific return in current cost terms.)

The information is also relevant to some tariff issues; the avoidance of undue discrimination and undue preference presupposes a proper allocation of costs, including capital costs, between services and to particular groups of customer.

Mergers and Comparative Competition

The existence of a significant number of companies enables the regulator to compare costs and performance. This 'comparative competition' is inferior to market competition, but it is considerably better than nothing. The power of such competition derives in part from the quality of the monitoring information available and in part from the ability of the regulator to identify and measure exogenous reasons for differences in performance, such as the proportion of water abstracted from wells or rivers and the density of population in the supply area.

The operational rules for the preservation of a sufficient number of comparators have been established during the first year of operation. The Water Act contained special provisions with respect to water mergers. In three cases which went to the MMC, notably the Three

Valleys case, it was established that mergers which prejudiced OFWAT's ability to make comparisons were against the public interest unless there were significant advantages, usually in the form of price reductions, to consumers in the area affected.

The Three Valleys merger was allowed on the basis that the price cap would be reduced by 10 per cent. Subsequently, OFWAT has agreed to the joint management of two groups of small, contiguous and jointly owned companies in North-East and South-East England. In both cases there were reductions in the price caps.

OFWAT's own work on comparative competition will build on the work carried out for the DoE at the time of privatisation. Our comparisons will be wider and will cover capital cost and performance measures as well as operating costs. We shall need to identify a manageable number of exogenous factors. Some of the information which we require, for example, the amount of water delivered to customers, is not yet all available. Good measures of the water delivered to customers' taps will be crucial in comparisons of performance and efficiency.

We need to have built up good comparative studies by the time of a first periodic review. We hope to be publishing early results before then – but probably not until we have information from the regulatory accounts and the annual (July) return on capital expenditure and performance for the year 1991-92.

Cost of Capital

The Water Act tells the regulator to 'secure that companies holding appointments ... are able (in particular by securing reasonable returns on their capital) to finance the proper carrying out of ... [their] functions'. The scale of the investment programme puts considerable emphasis on this cost of capital.

When setting the initial K factors, the Secretaries of State, after taking advice from the City, made certain assumptions. Two key ones were:

o   a 7 per cent real cost of capital for the water and sewerage companies (raised to 8 per cent for the water only companies because of their small scale of operations); and

o   interest cover of four times, and an average dividend yield of 8 per cent covered 2·5 times by net earnings, with annual dividend growth of up to 5 per cent real.

Some people think that these assumptions look unduly generous today. I have therefore been examining the evidence which financial markets are revealing on this matter.

126

As far as borrowing is concerned, water companies have been able to borrow extensively at low rates. Much finance has been raised through the European Investment Bank (EIB) on terms only fractionally above gilt-edged rates. One company has issued an indexed bond which is yielding only half to three-quarters of a percentage point above a comparably dated indexed gilt. There has also been extensive leasing, which may prove to be even cheaper.

As far as equity is concerned, market sentiment has changed since 1989, when the Water Authorities were floated. The dividend yield of around 8 per cent at flotation has settled down at around 6 per cent. Expectations of real dividend growth in the economy as a whole are now more modest than in the late 1980s and, indeed, are rather closer to the longer-term trends of the past.

I propose to issue a discussion document on these issues in the near future so that they can be adequately exposed before further determinations of the cost of capital are required. In the meantime I take some comfort from the Licence which requires me to look at non-equity methods of finance in the first five years. The assessment of the cost of debt should be rather easier than full examination of the weighted cost of capital.

I now turn to the two big policy issues.

New Quality and Environmental Objectives

One of the important issues which has arisen during the course of the year is the financing of improvements to water quality and to the environment.

Much of the capital programme for the 1990s is to improve the quality of water – both drinking water and waste water. The large K factors, leading to increases in price of 50 per cent or more in the next 10 years, result in large part from these quality and environmental improvements.

Despite the attempt to set out and to cost all the obligations falling on the water industry at the time of privatisation, not everything was included in K; there is a slightly untidy pile of notified items to be dealt with. Also, new obligations are appearing – often on a short time-scale. Not long after privatisation the Secretary of State announced that the dumping of sewage sludge at sea should be phased out and that the UK would be adopting the EC municipal waste water directive. Shortly afterwards the National Rivers Authority (NRA) published a consultation document proposing much tighter consent limits for the discharge of treated sewage. A few months later progress on the EC Bathing Waters directive was accelerated.

New obligations can have major implications for customers' bills.

(Capital investment sounds fine, of course, until you come to pay for it.) I am, therefore, concerned on behalf of the customer that all initiatives should be properly costed before decisions are made. It would make a mockery of the regulatory régime if costs only appeared on the scene when the hapless regulator received costings from the companies justifying substantial increase in their K factors to meet their new obligations.

I must emphasise that I am not arguing against new obligations; only that they should be properly costed and that those taking the decisions should be fully aware of the likely increase in customers' bills before they are imposed. I feel that consumers expect the regulator to show this concern on their behalf. There could be a danger that quality regulators – in Brussels and in national capitals – could use the regulatory régime to spend other people's money without full consultation with them.

There has been a useful clarification of responsibilities. It is established that decisions on quality and environmental improvement are for Ministers and not for regulators, and Ministers have undertaken to take full account of costs when making these decisions. As David Trippier, the Minister for the Environment and Countryside, put it:

> '... we have made it clear ... that wherever possible, the costs of environmental improvements should be identified; and that additional improvements which will further increase charges need to be considered in the light of a sober and realistic assessment of their costs and benefits – both by the regulators themselves and by those who have to meet the standards.'

I doubt if these will be the last words spoken on this subject.

Paying for Water

In contrast to the situation in most other countries, domestic consumers in England and Wales are charged according to the rateable value of their property, not according to how much water they use. Rateable values cannot be used for water bills beyond the year 2000. New domestic properties are generally being metered and most non-domestic customers are either metered or likely to be metered in the not-too-distant future. A big question-mark still hangs over the large number of existing domestic customers. How should they pay in the future?

Any discussion of charging methods should be linked with a discussion of tariff structures. Such analysis of tariff structures as has taken place has been rather primitive, certainly when compared with the analysis which has been done on electricity tariffs. Such work as has been done on water has usually come to the conclusion, convenient for the company if not for the consumer, that most (90 per cent?) costs are 'fixed' and that charges should contain a very high standing charge element.

The distinction between fixed and variable costs leads into the wider, and more economically relevant area of short-run versus long-run marginal cost pricing. The water industry cries out for work in this area; in doing it I think it is important to link the analysis of costs closely with the analysis of demand. Prices are signals. Little is to be gained from rapid changes in price signals for a commodity whose use is linked with life styles and with decisions on specific water-using capital equipment.

Analyses of the costs of water must also recognise that, as in other resource-based industries, costs rise as the facilities which are easy to exploit begin to run out. This is evident in the South and East of England, although not yet in other parts of the country. This is closely linked with the costs of using the environment. There is a strong case for integrating these costs into the costs of water for the final user and the NRA and OFWAT are examining ways in which this could be done.

Consumer choice is an important objective of pricing policy. The opportunity to economise on an increasingly expensive commodity is going to be of growing significance, especially for people on small incomes. (OFWAT is commissioning a study, jointly with the DOE, in the areas covered by the metering trials, to explore the extent to which metering can cause hardship.) It is also important for those who wish to use a lot of water without restrictions and are prepared to pay the cost of supply.

In OFWAT's view, the broad thrust of these arguments points towards tariffs where the bulk of the costs are covered by the volumetric element of the charge, and where the standing charge is relatively low. Many customers also hold this view.

Much work also needs to be done to improve the basis for tariffs based on the allocation of costs. The allocation of costs to the provision of clean water and the disposal of waste water is fairly straightforward. The allocation of waste water costs to domestic sewerage and to trade effluent and to foul sewerage and to surface drainage is more difficult because of the extent of shared facilities.

In this important area of consumer choice, the regulator of a monopoly must take some position. Regulation is not just about average prices.

Because we thought it was important to involve the public, we have consulted widely by issuing a consultation paper, organising CSC meetings, conducting a random opinion poll and by asking the companies to distribute 17 million questionnaires. We shall be setting out our response later this year.

The Water Act gives the companies the ultimate power to draw up charging schemes, under the supervision of the regulator. I am glad to say that the companies have welcomed this initiative.

Diversification and Ring Fencing

A third policy issue which is giving me some concern at the moment is the possible impact of diversification of the water companies on the core utility business. At the time of privatisation Ministers judged that it was desirable to allow diversification into other areas.

OFWAT was set up, not to regulate all the activities of the water companies, but only the core utility business.

Diversification can complicate life for the regulator. But as I interpret the task currently given to me, it is to ensure that the core business is fully protected. OFWAT will ensure that the core business carries out obligations placed on it at the time K was set (in particular carrying out its investment programme within the price limits set), without any further recourse to customers. Any losses in any diversified business, and any adverse effect such losses might have on the cost of capital for the Group as a whole, must be met by the shareholders of the PLC and not by the customers of the core business.

Conclusion

I have tried to convey the flavour of the job of regulating the water industry. Privatisation has not opened up the industry to competition and to market forces. Perhaps this was not possible.

Privatisation has, however, led to a much more explicit regulatory régime and to a more medium-term approach. The more explicit nature of the régime, and the establishment of different regulators for different purposes, have pointed to the necessity of developing working relations between the regulators.

The regulators and the companies are learning to live together. The companies have accepted the need for regulation and while relations with OFWAT are not cosy, neither are they confrontational. The emphasis on good information is an important one, and should be robust to whatever changes in régime the future may bring.

Finally, the 18 months since privatisation have seen the opening up of some important policy issues. First, there has been worthwhile debate on the whole relationship between the benefits of environmental and quality improvement and the financing of those benefits. Secondly, the whole area of how customers pay for water – charging systems and tariff structures – has been opened up to public consultation.

A high profile for water and sewerage is not always comfortable for those involved. But I believe that it is in the public interest.

10

AVIATION REGULATION: WHAT THE FUTURE HOLDS

Sir Christopher Tugendhat
Chairman, Civil Aviation Authority

I WOULD LIKE to begin my short paper by congratulating the IEA on holding this seminar. As a result of privatisation, the conduct and practice of regulation has become of central importance to the economy. Yet it is still a subject about which comparatively little is known outside the organisations gathered here today, the industries they regulate and the Government departments concerned. All of us – even those that have been going as long as the Office of Fair Trading (OFT) and the Civil Aviation Authority (CAA) – are, I think, conscious of continually breaking new ground and establishing precedents. By bringing us together in this way, the IEA enables us not only to learn from each other, but also to provide the basis for a comparative study from which others may draw some general principles.

General Principles

For my part, I find it hard to say what those general principles should be. Indeed, I suspect that each of us will vary the emphasis somewhat – and perhaps more than that – in the light of personal and industrial experience. The industries we regulate are so different that it would be remarkable if that were not so. I therefore proffer my own thoughts on the nature of regulation, generally with a good deal more hesitation than my remarks about current issues within my Authority's fields of responsibility.

In essence I would say that the purpose of regulation is to establish and maintain the framework within which the provision of a product or service is conducted, on the basis of laws passed by Parliament and guiding principles laid down by government. Within the limits of those laws and guiding principles, the regulator must act in a completely independent manner in order to promote and safeguard the public interest. If, on the basis of experience or because of changing circumstances, he comes to believe that those laws and guiding principles run counter in any degree to the public interest, he should try to get them changed. But, until they are, he must either operate within them – or resign.

He must also ensure that his work is characterised by openness and the consistent application of known principles. This means that should the necessity for it arise, he must resist any attempt by government to bend those laws or guidelines in such a way as in fact to bring about a change of practice without Parliament being aware of what is happening or being able to debate and, where appropriate, decide on the matter.

In defining the public interest he should, in general, equate it with the consumer rather than the producer. But he should also bear in mind that the ultimate consumer interest is that the provision of the goods or services in question should continue to be supplied at a reasonable price. This means that the producers must be enabled to do that – and not in practice prevented from doing so. I use the plural producers advisedly. In almost all cases – and certainly in aviation – the encouragement of competition between producers is, in itself, one of the most effective ways of promoting the interests of consumers.

Safety Regulation

Now to specifics. At the Civil Aviation Authority we engage in two forms of regulation: safety and economic. I will deal with safety first because in aviation this must be the overriding consideration, but I will do so briefly because I feel that as this paper is for the Institute of Economic Affairs you would wish me to focus primarily on the economic side of our work.

The CAA has responsibility for the safety of all users of UK airspace and for ensuring that UK air safety standards are maintained and, where possible, improved. We aim to achieve that objective without impeding progress towards a more liberal economic régime and to achieve the harmonisation of air safety regulation internationally.

Fundamentally, we set standards and satisfy ourselves that those standards are met by the designers and manufacturers of aircraft, airlines, aerodromes, flight crew, aircraft engineers and air traffic services. And we try to do this in an efficient and cost-effective manner. We employ about 350 professional staff to undertake this task.

Essentially, all aircraft on the UK register are required to have a Certificate of Airworthiness and are required to conform to an approved Type design; airfields used for public transport or by flying schools are required to be licensed; pilots, air traffic controllers and engineers are licensed, and manufacturers and maintenance organisations are approved. We also require airlines to be certificated, and require them to conform to specified standards of operation. Their operations are regularly monitored by CAA inspectors.

Cost Recovery

We try to regulate with a light touch, but do not hesitate to ground either aircraft or flight crew when there is a problem which will take time to resolve. All the costs of this work are fully recovered and a specified return on capital is achieved. Although the charges are made on manufacturers, aerodromes, airlines, pilots and so on, a high proportion, roughly 80 per cent, is passed on to the airlines who recover the cost from the price of a passenger's ticket. This means an annual cost to airlines, for safety regulation, of £40 million which, when related to their turnover of £7,000 million, amounts to less than 0·6 per cent. As there are about 60 million passengers carried by the UK airlines each year, this amounts to an average of 66 pence on the cost of a single ticket; hence this work finances itself and there is no recourse to public funds.

In the sphere of international co-operation and harmonisation of safety standards we have made good progress which has economic benefits for manufacturers and airlines by reducing the need for, and the financial burden of, multiple certification and differing standards. Eighteen European countries are currently working together on this. They have achieved a great deal and are now expanding their work from aircraft certification to cover aircraft maintenance and operational safety requirements. All this work is to maintain and wherever possible improve already high safety standards. Encouragingly, in the last 15 years the UK's jet airliner fatal accident rate has been brought down from 0·8 per cent to 0·2 per cent fatal accidents per million revenue hours – a fourfold improvement, but one that spurs us on to do even better.

Economic Regulation

I now turn to economic regulation. Our economic regulatory duties derive from two pieces of legislation – the Civil Aviation Act of 1982 and the Airports Act of 1986.

(a) Airports

So far as airports are concerned, the underlying problem is that they all enjoy at least some degree of local monopoly. For this reason every UK airport of any significance is subject to economic regulation. The Civil Aviation Authority is thus empowered to intervene if it believes that certain specified courses of conduct by airport operators discriminate amongst or significantly disadvantage the users of the airport – who are, principally, airlines and other suppliers rather than the passengers. In practice, despite the degree of local monopoly, there is significant competition between operators of regional airports in this country because of the predominance of charter travel in their business, and we have not yet had a formal complaint about the trading practices of any airport outside the big four, namely, Heathrow, Gatwick, Stansted and Manchester.

The Big Four

In respect of those four, we have additional duties because they have been designated for our attention by the Secretary of State for Transport. As a consequence, we have the oversight over their trading practices and are required to control their airport charges – specifically their charges for bringing aircraft into and out of the airport. The Act requires us to regulate charges on a five-yearly basis, and points us towards, but does not insist on, a formula. The first quinquennial formula was fixed for the three London area airports by the Secretary of State with effect from April 1987 and is therefore due for renewal next year. We have begun this process by making a reference to the MMC, and its report is awaited. Manchester follows a year later, and we expect to refer the charges at Manchester, as part of a general reference of that airport, within the next six months. In these matters I must emphasise that the MMC's rôle is an advisory one. It is the CAA that will take the final decisions.

While all airports enjoy at least a degree of local monopoly, in practice this has not become a problem with the generality of them. However, this is emphatically not so in the case of the four major airports. Heathrow has a long history. It has a breadth and depth of international services which is probably the best of any airport in the world. These factors, plus the interlocking nature of those services, have all served to give Heathrow an appeal to passengers which far outweighs that of any other airport in this country. This is confirmed both by theory and by historical study. Our figures suggest that, all things being equal, a passenger has a preference four times as high for Heathrow as for Gatwick – and Gatwick is the next preferred airport in Britain.

Because Heathrow is *de facto* full, this has given Gatwick a major rôle as a complementary and overspill airport for those who wish to serve the London and South East market but cannot get into Heathrow. When we conducted our studies on where a new runway might best be sited from an economic point of view, our conclusion was very clear. Heathrow was much preferred, and if a new runway were built there, most of the traffic now at Gatwick would want to move to it. Failing that, a new runway at Gatwick was the firm choice. These facts of the market give Heathrow and Gatwick, both at or near capacity, substantial monopoly power, though they will not be the only points the Government will take into account when eventually deciding on where the new runway should be.

We should not overlook Manchester in all this. That in turn has built up a substantial monopoly for traffic in the northern half of this country. It has a throughput three times as high as the next busiest airport (which is Glasgow), and has a range of international scheduled services, in particular, which is far superior to any airport other than Heathrow and Gatwick. It too has established a significant degree of local monopoly. Unlike Heathrow and Gatwick it is not yet near capacity, but at current rates of growth it may be expected to fill up rapidly and will need to consider another runway for shortly after the turn of the century.

In none of these cases is there any real likelihood of future competition, because of the huge social and environmental difficulties inherent in building a new runway. What makes them attractive to passengers is the range of services, interlining possibilities, and so on. It is not because they are cheap, although airport charges per passenger are low at Heathrow and Gatwick over the year as a whole compared with most other UK airports. The costs perceived by the passenger – for example, car parking – are often ferociously high. Yet their attraction remains. Our rôle in airport regulation is therefore simply that of the regulation of conduct.

Trading Practices and Charges – the Five-Year Formulae

The work we have had to do on airport regulation so far has been relatively straightforward, but I fear this honeymoon is coming to an end. So far we have dealt with a number of complaints about trading practices at Heathrow and Manchester. The outcomes have, in general, been straightforward in the sense that the issues are sharply defined and the answer has narrowed down to one of a small number of possibilities.

Where life becomes much more difficult is of course in setting the five-year formulae, to which we have to address ourselves in respect of the London area airports in the next few months. Here again the basic issue is straightforward. If we decide to stick with the formula, be it revenue yield or tariff basket, the critical issue is the value of X. This is straightforward in concept if not in determining the 'right' number. The difficulty arises because of the impact of the charging formula on competition in the airline industry.

I suppose the biggest single issue will be the charging formula as it relates to larger aircraft and to small. There is an argument that access to Heathrow and Gatwick should be sold by auction or by some other method of market-clearing pricing. That is not my concern here: if that were established, the relevant parts of the Airports Act 1986 would have to be repealed, or amended so radically as to be tantamount to repeal. Given that there will be a price cap, the issue is whether Heathrow should be allowed to rebalance its charges in such a way that, over the medium to longer term, small aircraft are squeezed out. It is the superficially rational answer at an airport which is runway capacity constrained, but not – subject to planning permission – terminal capacity constrained, that the price régime should be designed to force out small and/or less profitable operations.

The airport charges revenue we are concerned with comes from a landing charge; a per passenger charge; and parking charges. The last of these is becoming relatively less important in the scheme of things. The landing charge was initially weight-based, but in peak hours is now a flat charge. The per passenger charge distinguishes between domestic and international passengers (on the grounds that international passengers give rise to higher costs because of extra baggage, customs and immigration, and so on), but otherwise it is a charge per passenger. At both Heathrow and Gatwick in the last few years the weight discrimination for the runway charge in peak hours has been eliminated and parking charges reduced. Because parking charges were mainly paid by large long-haul aircraft, the effect of these changes has been to raise the cost of using Heathrow by small aircraft relatively to large aircraft.

Rebalancing of Charges at Heathrow

There is no doubt that, within any foreseeable overall price cap, Heathrow could, by pricing, squeeze out a high proportion of current domestic scheduled services unless there were further constraints on their pricing freedom. For the regulator, the issues are not straightforward. Rights at Heathrow were gained by historical accident in an environment constrained by regulation. Market forces played no part in this process. If now we were to allow Heathrow to operate pseudo-market pricing in this way, it would mean the elimination of services between a number of regional airports and Heathrow – and indeed possibly Gatwick – and perhaps the elimination of the airlines operating them. This has implications for airline competition. Domestic scheduled services account for a high proportion of the output of British Midland but a low proportion of the output of British Airways. In any rebalancing of charges between long- and short-haul operations, British Airways is likely to gain as much as it loses. That is emphatically not so with British Midland. In addition, there are social issues. The existence of effective domestic scheduled services to London, and particularly Heathrow, has implications for regional development and regional employment. These are real issues, principally for the Government rather than the Civil Aviation Authority.

(b) Airlines

I turn now to airline regulation. Here our approach is well-known – it is to pursue a multi-airline policy. By that we mean one in which Britain does not have to rely on British Airways as a national champion. I admire BA very much and feel sure that it will be the principal provider of British-owned air services for as far ahead as I can see. But not only is the concept of national champions a discredited relic of the 1970s, it is also against the consumer and, I believe, the national interest.

The fact that British airlines compete against each other, as well as against foreign carriers, means that air travellers to and from Britain have a wider choice of carrier than is the case with any other European country. As a result, fares for UK originating flights are, in general, lower than in other European countries. The combined British share of the traffic on those international routes on which more than one British airline competes is also larger than on those where there is only one British and one foreign carrier.

Encouraging Competition at Heathrow

These are factors that were very much in our minds when we recently advised the Secretary of State for Transport to cancel most of the so-called Traffic Distribution Rules that, *inter alia*, limited access to Heathrow only to those airlines that had been flying into the airport in 1977. We did not advocate taking anything away from BA but we did advocate giving the others the opportunity to compete with it at the airport that is most people's first choice. I am glad to say that Malcolm Rifkind accepted our advice.

It was also to encourage competition that, after BA's take-over of BCal, we refused BA the right to operate Gatwick-Brussels, Gatwick-Paris and Gatwick-Nice, which were old BCal routes, in order to give other airlines a chance to compete with the services that BA was already running from Heathrow. But we do not always come down on the side of the smaller airlines. When British Midland asked us to put a cap on BA's services between London and Glasgow with which British Midland was having difficulty competing, we refused. We did so on the grounds that we should not intervene to tilt the balance one way or the other once the competitive environment had been established, unless the larger airline's activities were manifestly unfair and anti-competitive.

There are those who say the collapse of Air Europe, coming after the take-over of BCal some years ago and the failure of Laker before that, invalidates the multi-airline concept. I find this logic difficult to understand since those who propound it do not argue that corporate collapses in, say, the retail, financial services or manufacturing sectors mean that we should rely henceforth on only one British-owned company in each field of activity. Moreover, it is striking how, when an airline goes bust, even in difficult times, let alone good ones, there are always others who wish to take its place.

Then there are those who say that British-owned competition is unnecessary because there are plenty of foreigners to do the job. Again I do not agree and certainly not in Europe.

International Aviation: History of Collusion

The history of international aviation has not been one of competition. To the contrary, it has been one of collusion and parallel behaviour. Scheduled airlines' main source of profit has always been carrying businessmen on international scheduled services. It is a price-insensitive market and so competition was always going to appear in the form of scheduling and service standards and not price-cutting. It was, of course, for this reason that IATA for so long tried to suppress competition through regulating service standards, while governments got together to force their only too willing airlines into capacity-sharing agreements and revenue-sharing pools.

There are some who hope that things have now changed, that in a liberalised market in the Community, for example, these old airlines which for so long have collaborated at the expense of the user have learned new tricks. I wish I could share this hope, but I cannot. If the ownership of all the airlines were vested in the private sector, with managers judged harshly on results and broad social considerations set on one side as matters for government legislation rather than behind-the-scenes pressure, things might indeed be different – although even then there would be no guarantee. But governments will continue to play a significant part in the ownership, financing and running of these airlines. The decisions management take will be affected accordingly. I do not believe this is a prescription for a truly competitive market.

So it must be up to the regulators both here and, I would argue, throughout Europe to right the balance. That could be done by having one central regulator in Brussels but I believe the most effective method would be to have individual national regulators operating on the basis of a set of common Community rules – just as individual national customs services co-exist with a common European external trade policy and tariff régime.

Lessons for Aviation from Oil and Banking

I will conclude with some lateral thinking linking aviation to my experience and study of two other industries with which, at various times, I have been involved – oil and banking.

As you will recall, international oil was for long dominated by the so-called Seven Sisters and UK domestic banking by the Big Four. In both cases the traditions and cost structures of the companies concerned were broadly similar and they had a long experience of working together in formal and informal cartels. They did compete but each management knew that any initiative it might take in the market-place could be matched or bettered by its rivals and profits thereby affected. To break out of this situation would have involved radical change to the nature of one's company and this no-one was anxious to undertake.

The Seven Sisters' grip on international oil was basically broken by the discovery of new sources of crude outside the Middle East by new companies. Thereafter the Middle East governments finished the job by nationalising production and enabling new companies to enter the transportation and distribution functions. The grip of the Big Four banks was broken by deregulation enabling others, notably building societies and foreign banks, to compete and the banks themselves to enter markets previously reserved to others, again notably the building societies.

The problem with aviation is that runway and other infrastructure shortages enormously re-inforce the entrenched positions of the former state airlines. Ideally the mould would be broken by some fundamental change in the operating environment, as happened in oil and banking. My view is that because of infrastructure shortages and the close links that exist between the former state airlines and their governments, this will not happen. So licensing provides the only available (and therefore least-worst) means of keeping the door open for potential newcomers, enabling those who pass through it to gain a foothold and providing those who achieve that with an alternative to becoming mere clients of their bigger rivals.

11

INDEPENDENT TELEVISION COMMISSION: THE REFORM OF BROADCASTING REGULATION

David Glencross

Chief Executive,
Independent Television Commission

I SUPPOSE it is well known that the new regulatory régime ushered in by the 1990 Broadcasting Act is a lighter touch régime. And to ensure this result, Parliament has put on the statute book an Act which has 204 Sections and 22 Schedules. It has 291 pages, excluding the table of contents. The 1981 Act which it replaces has 66 Sections, 9 Schedules and 81 pages, excluding the table of contents. So perhaps it is not a lighter touch after all. In fact, when David Mellor was piloting the Bill through Parliament he said that the Bill 'deregulates in some matters, but where it regulates it does so firmly'.

Generally speaking, for a Bill of such importance its Parliamentary progress was relatively uncontentious, save for last-minute flurries in the Lords over impartiality and religion. So it was not surprising to hear Baroness Birk, speaking for the Opposition more in sorrow than in anger, say that 'The only area in which I found the Minister lacking was his great reluctance to accept any amendments that we put forward'. But, contentious or not, it was a piece of legislation which will without doubt have a major impact on UK broadcasting and the style and practice of regulation.

As a representative and product of the old duopoly I venture into a seminar organised by the Institute of Economic Affairs with some degree of nervousness. I am slightly better prepared than the GCSE candidate who wrote that Madame Smith was one of the leading economists of the 18th century, but I feel that if Adam Smith were alive today he would regard Independent Television and the BBC much as he regarded the University of Oxford, as 'a sanctuary in which exploded systems and obsolete prejudices find shelter and protection'. I am sure that the great Scotsman would relish the picture of the two broadcasting institutions embodying, as their critics allege, ancient values and ossified class structures, whilst simultaneously being accused of engaging in moral and political subversion. In the great scheme of things this is perhaps one of the lesser intellectual paradoxes of our time.

The Principles of Regulation

Now the case for regulation in broadcasting is no different in principle from the case for regulation in other public utilities. Regulation by statutory bodies set up for the purpose is intended to protect the public interest, prevent the abuse of monopoly power where monopoly exists, and to do so at arm's length from government in its day-to-day operations.

In the case of broadcasting, first in radio and then in television, the desirability of regulation has from its beginnings in the 1920s been re-inforced by the scarcity of frequencies, which has restricted entry to the market. Along with this has been a fear that the monopoly and subsequent duopoly could be exploited not only unfairly in commercial terms but in terms of possible influence on the population at large. The BBC started in 1922 as a private company, the British Broadcasting Company, essentially owned by the radio manufacturing industry, anxious to capitalise on the equipment and expertise in radio communication that it had built up in the First World War. Only after the first of many commissions and inquiries into broadcasting did the government of the day decide that the private BBC should be turned into a public corporation.

Once the BBC had obtained its Royal Charter accompanied by its licence agreement the pattern was set for broadcasting in the UK to be a regulated monopoly for 30 years. That changed only with the introduction of ITV in the mid-1950s. The concept of broadcasting as a public service, and not as an economic activity, went virtually unchallenged. The Second World War and the BBC's rôle in that, both for the home and overseas audience, only strengthened the attachment to the principles of public service. How very different from the experience of the USA where radio was seen essentially as a commercial activity serving markets, with any public benefits along the way as a kind of uncovenanted bonus. There was of course regulation. It is a great fallacy to think of the USA as a place of no regulation, but it was and is regulation of a very different kind designed to establish some order in the use of frequencies and to prevent excessive (however that may be defined) concentrations of media ownership.

Meanwhile, in Britain the assumptions that broadcasting existed to serve the public lay behind all subsequent legislation and commissions of inquiry. If broadcasting was too important to be left to the market it was also too important to be left either to the politicians or broadcasters alone. Hence the BBC was not and is not a department of government. It is not funded out of general tax revenue, save for the External Services, but out of a household levy, the licence fee.

The Arrival of Competition

When ITV came along in the mid-1950s it was from the beginning subject to regulation by a public authority, the ITA. But the ITA itself, and its successors down to the present ITC, was not a part of the civil service and not funded out of taxation. Although a creation of Parliament, the ITA was wholly financed from the commercial activities of the contractors it appointed.

The establishment of the ITA owed much to the deep suspicion of commercial broadcasting as practised in the USA, plus an old-fashioned and snobbish disdain for trade. There were certainly fears that the coming of commercially financed television would lead to a rapid and terminal collapse of civilised values, but in practice the existence of a public authority was able, over the years and not without difficulty, to exercise a positive and beneficial influence on the programme service.

That public authority worked on the assumption that the service would, so far as possible, be available to everyone who wanted to receive it, and that it would cater for a wide variety of tastes and interests, including minority interests.

But even to work on such assumptions was to mix institutional structures with value-judgements about society and about programmes. To cater for a variety of tastes and interests, to cater for minorities is to make a value-judgement that these tastes are worth catering for. To provide geographic universality is to make a further value-judgement about the costs and benefits involved in bringing signals to remote areas. You are recognising obligations comparable to those of the national postal service. Everyone has the right to send and receive letters at a common price within a country, or even as now within the European Community. The same principle does not apply to telephone charges or railway fares which are proportional (very broadly) to distance. Yet the television system has worked.

Even Sir Alan Peacock – why do I say even? – stated in his Report[1] that

'the BBC and the regulated ITV system have done far better in mimicking the effects of a true consumer market, than any purely *laissez-faire* system financed by advertising could have done under conditions of spectrum shortage'.

In broadcasting, in other words, a combination of advertising priorities for audiences and spectrum shortage would not deliver the range and quality of a regulated commercial system. In particular, because the market for programmes, and therefore choice in programmes, has been constrained artificially by shortage of distribution outlets, market forces cannot work normally. In these circumstances the regulated duopoly has outperformed what a constrained market system would have provided.

Now spectrum shortage is a relative term, or perhaps a term of art. In the 1960s it was widely believed that it was impossible to put local radio on to AM (medium wave) transmission. Until the mid-1980s it was not thought feasible to have a fifth terrestrial UHF channel. The Astra satellite services demonstrated very conclusively, much to the chagrin of BSB, that it was possible to use medium-powered telecommunications satellites to transmit a direct-to-home broadcasting service. It was therefore on the basis of upsetting the old orthodoxies that the whole thrust of the 1988 Broadcasting White Paper and the subsequent legislation was founded. It was not surprising that the first word in the title of the White Paper was 'competition', or that the opening paragraph on the duties of the new ITC said that

'the main requirements of a regulatory body are flexibility; the ability to look at the television system as a whole to ensure that the various enterprises are able to compete on equal terms'.[2]

The logic of that process, leading to the possibility of many more programme providers, was that the relationship between the regulator and the regulated would change dramatically. The ITC is at the moment in a transitional phase until the end of 1992, since it remains the publisher of ITV and Channel 4 until the new Channel 3 licences begin on 1 January 1993. At that point Channel 4 becomes a self-standing public corporation. Channel 4 will no longer be a wholly-owned subsidiary of the ITC, as of course it was of the old IBA.

---

[1] Home Office, *Report of the Committee on Financing the BBC* (the Peacock Report), Cmnd. 9824, London: HMSO, 1986, p. 131.

[2] Home Office, *Broadcasting in the '90s: Competition, Choice and Quality*, Cm. 517, London: HMSO, 1988, p. 44.

The New Approach

The ITC's approach to regulation will spring from its different status from the bodies it has replaced, the IBA and the Cable Authority.

The ITC will not itself be a broadcaster as the IBA was, nor will it have a duty to promote a particular technology as the Cable Authority had. As broadcaster and publisher of its contractors' programmes the IBA has sometimes been hard put to distinguish between the rôle of manager and the rôle of regulator. There has also been a sense in which it has been the advocate both of the system and of its contractors. By contrast, the ITC will be a regulator of some hundreds of licensees competing for viewers and for revenue. It will be a licensing body operating at arm's length from its licensees. This does *not* mean that it will not have a powerful influence in shaping the system in the 1990s or that it cannot exercise a generous influence in favour of good rather than mediocre broadcasting; or that it cannot adopt different procedures in respect of particular groups of licensees. It *does* mean that the ITC has had to and will continue to have to set out its requirements (whether they apply to all or only to particular groups of licensees) clearly in its licences, codes and guidelines, and that these documents and its procedures generally are founded on the provisions of the new Act. Provided that they conform with the licences, codes and guidelines, the licensees will be free to make their own decisions.

To a considerable extent the system will be one of self-regulation by the licensees within a clear framework of obligations and codes of practice. The ITC will need to have an effective information system to allow it to take prompt action when problems arise. For their part the licensees will have to have their own internal procedures to ensure that they meet the requirements and standards of their licence. It will be for the licensees, for example, to make proper arrangements for the handling of complaints from the public about programmes, scheduling, advertising and technical operations standards. But there is another element of regulation by the ITC which is a departure from the old system and that is to do with competition.

Competition Policy

In respect of competition policy there are two references in the Act and the contrast between them could hardly be greater. One is as brief and general as the other is lengthy and specific. The *first* in Section 2 of the Act deals with the functions of the ITC generally. It says:

'It shall be the duty of the Commission –
   (a) to discharge their functions ... in the manner which they consider is best calculated –

(i) to ensure that a wide range of such services is available throughout the United Kingdom, and,

(ii) to ensure fair and effective competition in the provision of such services and services connected with them.'

The services referred to are television programmes and additional services such as teletext.

The *second* deals with programme networking on Channel 3 and consists of Section 39, which itself runs to two and a half pages, plus Schedule 4, which adds another five pages.

The ITC (and the IBA before it) did not claim that independent television was so different from any other industry, or so complex, that UK and European competition law should not be applied, or that all competition regulation should be undertaken by the ITC. What the IBA sought for the ITC was a rôle which would allow it to act quickly, and from a position of considerable knowledge of the industry, in order to ensure that the pace of progress towards a more competitive system was not delayed or frustrated. In a setting where the losers could so easily be small, newly formed and vulnerable firms, rapid response will frequently be of the essence.

There were three main areas in which the ITC anticipated that problems could arise – advertising, independent programme production and networking access, and networking arrangements between Channel 3 licensees.

(i) Advertising

In advertising, the issue arises in large part from the virtual monopoly which exists in the sale of television advertising. There are, of course, many forms of advertising. However, the behaviour of advertisers over the years shows that they believe, in relation to a wide range of products, that television advertising is particularly valuable, and that other forms of advertising do not provide close substitutes.

The ITV contractors sell the advertising on both ITV and the Fourth Channel, and currently, this accounts for about 98 per cent of all UK television advertising. During the 1990s there will be greater competition, with the fourth channel being sold separately, a new fifth terrestrial channel, and growing opportunities for cable and satellite. But ITV is not a single entity. It is organised largely on a regional basis, and consists of 16 separate contractors with important elements of competition between them. The analysis of monopoly in independent television is not therefore straightforward. There are other questions too.

One issue here is the extent to which it would be acceptable for independent sales houses to sell the advertising of several Channel 3 licensees, or of more than one channel. Another is whether it would be reasonable for Channel 3 licensees (the market leader) to refuse to take advertising which promotes the television services of rival channels.

(ii) Networking

Networking is a particularly complicated issue in relation to Channel 3, because although Channel 3 will be a regional system, many programmes will be networked, in the sense of being broadcast nationally and simultaneously. This necessarily involves collective decisions on the part of the regional licensees.

Against this background, the IBA argued that the ITC and the OFT should have concurrent powers in relation to competition, of the kind which have been introduced in other areas, such as civil aviation and telecommunications. This was rejected by the Government, but looking at the terms of the Act which have now emerged, the final outcome may not be very different.

Insofar as present ITV practice provides a guide to the future, Channel 3 network programmes will account for about 70 per cent of the Channel 3 audience and 70 per cent of the advertising revenue. Each of the 15 licensees involved is bound to feel uncomfortable about a situation in which it does not have direct control over such a large slice of its output and the revenue that it generates, but must instead rely on collective decisions entered into with 14 other firms. Bearing in mind that the 15 regional Channel 3 licences will consist of large and small ones, the ITC believed there to be an unacceptable risk that – left to themselves – larger licensees would seek to dominate the network arrangements in order to limit or eliminate the collective decision-taking which, as independent firms, they would find unpalatable. Although a single network might emerge, in due course there could well be a lengthy period of damaging conflict involving high costs and low programme quality as two or more rival networks struggled to dominate the system.

The Government accepted the need for a network but sought to ensure that the network arrangements satisfied another aspect of its policy. This was that there should be open competition for the supply of network programmes between those programmes made and offered to the network by individual Channel 3 licensees – whether large or small – and those made and offered by independent programme makers.

It has long been the case that ITV companies are involved in two businesses rather than one. *First*, they are involved, as broadcasters, with the supply of programme services to viewers (in and around which there are the advertisements which generate the system's income). *Secondly*, however, the ITV companies are all, to a greater or lesser extent, in the business of making and supplying programmes. Until the early 1980s there was a relatively small independent programme production sector in the UK. Nearly all programmes made specifically for ITV were made by the ITV companies themselves (or by ITN which is owned by the ITV companies). As a result, the ITV system did not traditionally draw a clear and complete distinction between the two types of business. Although the network arrangements worked very effectively indeed (in terms of the range and quality of the service delivered to viewers), the supply and exchange of programmes rested not so much on a series of transactions entered into at negotiated arm's length prices between buyers and sellers, but more on a rather complicated set of barter arrangements with guarantees of production to the five major companies and guarantees of programme supply to the rest.

(iii) Independent Programme Production and the Network

The introduction of the Fourth Channel in 1982 led to a substantial independent production sector and in relation to the Channel 3 networking arrangements the Broadcasting Act requires there to be an evenhanded competition for network programme supply between licensees and independent programme makers. As a matter of regulation this is to be achieved by the application of a competition test, which is set out in Schedule 4 of the Act. The test takes the familiar form of ruling out arrangements which would restrict, distort or prevent competition.

Readers of Section 39 and Schedule 4 of the Act will see a carefully articulated sharing of regulatory responsibilities between the ITC, the OFT and the MMC. No doubt, left to their own devices the ITC and the OFT would each have drafted this part of the legislation differently, but those who predicted regulatory clash have been disappointed. The relationship so far is proving a constructive one, very much in keeping with the concurrent powers approach which had been sought at the outset.

Wider Competition Powers

Turning to the other reference to competition, in Section 2 of the Act, its very brevity raises questions of intention and interpretation.

We see the requirement to ensure effective competition as a requirement to avoid unacceptable degrees of monopoly or of dominant positions in the market-place. We would therefore see our task very much in terms of the competition test in Schedule 4 of the Act, that is, a duty in relation to arrangements which would restrict, prevent or distort competition.

It would follow from this approach that once the ITC was satisfied that, within reasonable minimum limits competition was not being restricted, prevented or distorted, then we would see our task as complete. That is to say, we would not seek to put any wider construction on the word 'competition' so that it related to the normal trading or interaction of buyers and sellers within a competitive market-place. In this respect the significance of the word 'fair' in Section 2 of the Act is not easy to assess. We do not believe, however, that it requires the ITC to consider and seek to resolve any case in which, however legitimately, a person or firm has a sense of grievance about the way in which they have been treated in their business dealings with one or more ITC licensees. Section 2 does not make the ITC an ombudsman for independent television.

A further issue is the scope of Section 2 in terms of how wide a range of activities and firms are affected. The provision of television programme services provided by ITC licensees (and what the Act calls additional services - that is, teletext) is certainly caught, but what are 'services connected with them'? We do not doubt that the activities of ITC licensees in relation to television advertising, the sponsorship of programmes and subscription television are within the scope of Section 2. We would also regard the provision to ITC licensees of their main inputs, such as programmes supplied by independent producers, or the provision of scripts, music or production facilities, as being caught in principle, but always within the confines of the sort of competition test outlined earlier.

Responsibilities and Penalties

Once the licensees have been granted their licences and when they have agreed networking arrangements amongst themselves subject to the guidance the ITC has given, the licensees will really be in business.

Within their licence requirements Channel 3 licensees will be free after 1992 to decide the schedules. The old IBA requirement to schedule mandated programmes in peak time, save for national news as specified in the Act (and, intriguingly, Gaelic programmes in Scotland), will no longer exist.

This will provide some nice choices for the companies. Should they, as publishers in this brave new world with no IBA to shelter behind, take a controversial programme from another company? Of course, they will indemnify each other, as now, against actions for defamation, but programmes of political controversy do not only or mainly involve questions of defamation. Much wider political questions arise. It will not be a matter for ITC intervention, though I think it only fair to say that a

149

company which chose not to take a network current affairs or documentary would have to show how it would maintain its overall tally of such programming in its schedule. It would not be sufficient to substitute repeats of soap operas.

The ITC has considerable sanctions that it can impose on licence defaulters and transgressors. These include, on an ascending scale, verbal and written warnings, directions to broadcast apologies and corrections, directions not to repeat a programme or advertisement, fines, the shortening of a licence, and finally the revocation of a licence.

This all sounds like a punitive régime. The ITC has the power to make it so. But its principal interest, and I hope that of its licensees, will be to see that programme services are of a high quality and do serve a wide range of tastes and interests. That will not come about if broadcasters are terrified to make the slightest move for fear of ITC sanctions cracking down on their heads. Quality in broadcasting is a sensitive plant. It should neither be over-indulged nor starved of affection.

Regulatory Confusion

One of the complicating factors for licensees is the proliferation of statutory bodies, all with a finger in the broadcasting pie. I have already mentioned the OFT. OFTEL too has an important rôle both in the setting of the transmission tariff and more widely as a result of the recent duopoly review of telecommunications.

Then there are our old friends at the Broadcasting Complaints Commission and our newer friends at the Broadcasting Standards Council. Neither of these bodies lays claim to be a regulator and their powers are limited to investigating complaints and obliging the broadcasters to publish their adjudications. But it is not surprising that members of the public believe that these bodies can force programmes off the air, and if they do not then the hopes of those who lobbied hard for their creation will be disappointed. I am not arguing that the BCC or BSC should be given regulatory powers, merely that their existence and the possibility of overlap between them in certain kinds of complaints does not present a clear picture to the public at large of where regulatory responsibility lies.

There is a comparable difficulty in regard to television advertising. I do not refer to the Advertising Standards Authority. There is, I believe, a general understanding that the ASA's functions do not overlap with the ITC's advertising regulation. There is, however, an increasing tendency both in the UK and in Europe to impose or seek to impose increasingly detailed and complex disclosure requirements on advertisers. This is particularly the case in investment and credit advertising and also in pharmaceuticals. The motive for protecting the public interest is impeccable. No-one wants the public to put their money into fly-by-night conmen or to over-extend their financial commitments, still less to prejudice their health by lapping up quack remedies.

But is it really necessary or desirable for a building society TV commercial advertising mortgage facilities to include two lengthy separate warnings as the Government has recently proposed making a legal requirement. The Consumer Credit Act regulations *already* require a detailed warning about the risk of repossession for default on repayments; it is now proposed to add an additional separate warning inviting viewers to reflect on whether they can afford the mortgage. There are practical difficulties in incorporating all this information on a TV commercial at a length and in a size of lettering which makes it readable. The ITC has intervened with the television companies to insist that warnings of this kind should be held on screen longer, and we have commissioned research on the issue. But there is a real risk that in trying to tell viewers too much in a short space of time the exercise in consumer protection will be self-defeating.

The Limits of Television

What will characterise the 1990s, however, is not simply an expansion of television services but a much greater selectivity by the public in exercising choice. The programme planning of cable and satellite has already moved from the broad-based menus of the four existing terrestrial services. There are losses as well as gains in this. If you can pre-select your menu you may miss the surprise dish which excites your palate in ways you never thought possible. With a fragmented audience the importance of any single programme is proportionately diminished. But that in itself may be no bad thing. The proposition that a single television programme is phenomenally important or influential is rarely sustainable. Television is only one factor in people's lives, only one piece of everyone's experience which helps to shape opinion.

It can influence, it can entertain, inform and educate, occasionally all at once, occasionally not at all. In regulating this singular means of communication the ITC will look first to its positive virtues and to its potential for excellence and quality. That is an aspiration which regulators of all industries might feel able to share.

12

CURRENT THEMES IN REGULATION

M. E. Beesley
London Business School

ANY ATTEMPT at a summary of such an intensive but wide-ranging set of papers must be arbitrary. In being selective, it seems best to concentrate on four issues which emerged from the proceedings. These are likely to be significant for the future development of regulation. They arise naturally from the unique coverage of the conference, representing themes common to shaping all the regulators' tasks.

Regulation to Strengthen Consumer Sovereignty

As the day progressed, it was revealed that the reforms of the middle and late 1980s in one sense represented a determined effort to strengthen consumer sovereignty at the grass roots. This, it was pointed out, was not always necessarily in the consumers' own interests, as in the reservations expressed about the position of financial advisers after the 1986 Act. But it was recognised that the utility regulators are building vigorously on the network of consumer representation they have inherited, in an attempt to make the consumer's voice more comprehensive and direct. This implies a corresponding focus on accountability and regulatory response.

The relation between price control and service quality poses a major challenge for the regulators. The question arises of how to develop mechanisms, originally largely conceived of as channels of complaint for nationalised industries, which will become active inputs to the regulators' decisions, and specifically in assessing the value of alternative levels of service quality. There is, for example, scope for using quite sophisticated consumer survey techniques in which the new consumer activists, encouraged by the regulators, could be directly involved.

Balance Between Specialists and Generalists

A second recurring theme was the appropriate division of labour between, on the one hand, the general competition authorities, OFT and MMC, and on the other, the specialist regulators. It was noted that the privatising Acts are not uniform in their treatment of this division. For example, the Telecoms and Electricity Acts conferred a high degree of responsibility for curbing large firm power on the specialist regulator. In gas and airports, much more was left to the general authorities. In television and financial services the arrangements call for the development of specialist expertise within OFT itself. The conference took several points bearing on the question of change – should there be further integration in the specialists' operations, or more delegation to the generalists. Integration has the advantage that price control can be made an argument in winning concessions from incumbents which ease entry, as recently done in Telecoms. On the other hand, OFGAS has used the independence of MMC effectively, both directly to ease entry in gas supply in the industrial market, and as a credible threat to curb price increases in the controlled sector.

How these varying arrangements perform in helping the emergence and preservation of competition will be tested more rigorously as the incumbents feel more threatened by regulators' early successes. Change in both the specialists' and generalists' spheres may well be required. The question arose of whether competition will ultimately require further separation in ownership. It was also noted that the question of strengthening UK competition law, in limbo since the White Paper of 1989, will have to be settled. And the White Paper leaves open the question of how far the specialist regulators' pro-active rôle in dealing with large firm power in their jurisdictions should, or could, be adopted more widely.

Regulatory Power, Competition and Natural Monopoly

The conference was left in no doubt that the specialist regulators were becoming formidable powers in their respective industries, whatever legislative hand they were dealt on privatisation. This raises the third issue. The Acts were careful to protect the new regulators from judicial review. With respect to their pro-competitive duties, it may be that when full competition does develop, they will be wise enough to immolate themselves, leaving the field to the (hopefully strengthened) general competition law. This is to ask a lot of them, both in terms of judging when sufficient competition has arrived, and in terms of relinquishing power. But the more important longer-term issue concerns the remaining natural monopoly elements in the regulators' industries. These can be identified as water and sewage, the electricity and gas distribution grids, and the monopoly power BAA derives from location, which was well illustrated in CAA's paper. The regulatory innovation dealing with this is the regulators' ability to use cross-sectional comparisons in bargaining with the industry, sometimes referred to as 'comparative competition'; it was referred to approvingly during the conference.

The expectation would be that, over time, the regulators' ability to build a balance of information favourable to themselves will increase. In most cases, the referee between the industry and the regulator, in case of dispute, is the MMC. However, in price control this safeguard is effectively missing in the case of airports, where the MMC's rôle is essentially as advisor to the CAA, itself the final arbiter. Even in the other cases, the very success of a regulator and his increasingly favourable position *vis-à-vis* the industry may erode the value of the safeguard. In each case, there is a question about how the basic deal between the Government and the industry, encapsulated in each Act, can be challenged. And, quite generally, the UK regulatory system is much less open to independent intellectual challenge than, say, the American. Regulators' reasoning is disclosed at their choice. The conference considered the view that there should be a greater adversarial element in the UK proceedings, but came to no conclusions about how to introduce it.

Economic Foundations of Regulation

Besides listening, and reacting, to highly practical accounts of how regulators conduct their affairs, the conference was an occasion which raised the fourth question, namely the intellectual foundations for their decisions. Within the framework set by their respective Acts, the regulators have been delegated by the wider society the duty of conducting a series of cost-benefit analyses, leading to decisions about industry conduct. Their willingness, indeed eagerness, to shoulder this task was manifest in the presentations and in the regulators' own styles, different as these are. Whether the necessary distinctions are made in the economic analysis they command to help perform the tasks is to me, at least, less clear. The two basic regulatory tasks – of more or less permanent utility regulation, and of managing the emergence of competition – basically call for differing economic approaches. The first is the natural domain of neo-classically-inspired arguments about utility pricing. The second calls for profit-oriented analysis, especially of entry, which is much more Austrian in starting point and assumptions.[1]

We heard little to indicate a general recognition that there were in analytic terms such horses for courses. Reflection on the proceedings suggests there are at least two kinds of reason for this. First, there is the inherited framework. This discourages engagement with economic debates. RPI-X price control concentrates on setting up a viable means to strike reasonably stable bargains with the industry about the level of prices; it does not seek to define price structures as indicated in the neo-classical utility pricing literature. Secondly, neo-classical and Austrian ideas make very uncomfortable intellectual bed-fellows for most economists. So long as regulatory decisions remain largely unexplained, so long can possible shortcomings in judgements about what is, or is not, applicable economic analysis be avoided in practice. My own guess is that the pressure for recognising the economic underpinning of decisions will grow. If this is matched by increasing flexibility and openness in the professional economic advice going to the regulators, so much the better. We can also perhaps look forward to some vigorous public debate on the issues on occasions such as this conference provided.

---

[1] This division is explained more fully in a forthcoming book: M. E. Beesley, *Privatisation, Regulation and Deregulation*, London: Routledge & Kegan Paul, 1991.

155

PART THREE

ALTERNATIVES TO REGULATION

13

LAW AND ORDER
WITHOUT
STATE COERCION*

Bruce L. Benson
Professor of Economics,
Florida State University

IT IS NOT actually possible to describe what a system of privately produced law and order would be like in a modern society because one cannot describe what does not exist, and, more fundamentally, guesses based on historic privatised systems (and there have been many; some are referred to below) or current trends in privatisation may miss the mark substantially. The sophisticated crime protection and prevention equipment and the level of training and skill possessed by many crime prevention specialists today may be archaic compared to what would emerge as a result of the incentives created by full privatisation. For instance, at the turn of the century, who but the wildest, most fantastic science fiction writers could have predicted the revolution in communications and computer technology we are seeing today?

Some will no doubt consider the arguments that follow to fit in the category of science fiction too, but an attempt will nonetheless be made to describe how a modern society *might* function under a system of customarily produced and privately enforced and adjudicated laws. Some of the following predictions are made with considerable confidence after an extensive study of the scholarly literature on historical customary law systems, modern arbitration and mediation

*© 1990, Center for Libertarian Studies. Reprinted by permission. First published in the *Journal of Libertarian Studies*. This chapter draws from and consolidates material that appears in *The Enterprise of Law: Justice Without the State*, published and financed by the Pacific Research Institute.

processes, and other related issues, but others are no more than educated guesses. It should be added that mine is not the first effort to visualise such a system, so the following discussion draws heavily on work by people like Barnett, Friedman, Rothbard, Tucker, Smith, Sneed, Becker, and Stigler, among others.

Customary Law: The Unwritten Social Contract

James Buchanan has posed the following questions:

> '[If government is dismantled,] how do rights re-emerge and come to command respect? How do "laws" emerge that carry with them general respect for their legitimacy?'[1]

He contended that collective action would be necessary to devise a 'social contract' or 'constitution' designed to define the rights of the people in the first place and to establish a limited government to enforce them.[2] However, customary laws emerge spontaneously as a consequence of co-operation induced by reciprocities.[3] Reciprocity, in fact, provides the basis for recognition of duty or obligation under customary law.[4] Co-operation does not require collective (governmental) action. Furthermore, the rules of obligation recognised under all the customary law systems that have existed have always focussed on individual rights, including the right to private property. That has been the basis for customary laws from primitive societies[5] through the Middle Ages,[6] and for all the remnants of such law that exist today. As Tucker pointed out, in a free society without government imposition or enforcement of laws, 'man's only duty is to respect others' rights ... [and] man's only right over others is to enforce that duty'.[7] The many reasons to expect private property rights to be recognised as the dominant rules of obligation in a

---

[1] J. M. Buchanan, 'Before Public Choice', in Gordon Tullock (ed.), *Explorations in the Theory of Anarchy*, Blackburg, Va.: Center for the Study of Public Choice, 1972, p. 37.

[2] *Ibid.*, and see Buchanan, *Freedom in Constitutional Contract*, College Station, Tex.: Texas A&M University Press, 1972.

[3] See, for example, Bruce L. Benson, 'The Spontaneous Evolution of Commercial Law', *Southern Economic Journal*, Vol. 55, January 1989, pp. 644-61; Benson, 'Enforcement of Private Property Rights in Primitive Societies: Law Without Government', *Journal of Libertarian Studies*, Vol. 9, Winter 1989, pp. 1-26; Benson, *The Enterprise of Law: Justice Without the State*, San Francisco: Pacific Research Institute, 1990; or Lon L. Fuller, *The Morality of Law*, New Haven: Yale University Press, 1964.

[4] Fuller, *ibid.*, pp. 23-24.

[5] Benson, 'Enforcement of Private Property Rights in Primitive Societies', *op. cit.*; and Benson, 'Legal Evolution in Primitive Societies', *Journal of Institutional and Theoretical Economics*, 144, December 1988, pp. 772-88.

[6] David Friedman, 'Private Creation and Enforcement of Law: A Historical Case', *Journal of Legal Studies*, Vol. 8, March 1979, pp. 399-415; Joseph R. Peden, 'Property Rights in Celtic Irish Law', *Journal of Libertarian Studies*, Vol. 1, 1977, pp. 82-94.

[7] Benjamin R. Tucker, *Instead of a Book*, New York: Benj. R. Tucker, Publisher, 1893, p. 59.

customary law system will become apparent in the following discussion. Such law requires neither a written constitution nor legislative authority. Indeed, as Hayek suggested,

> 'Individual freedom, wherever it has existed, has been largely the product of a prevailing respect for such principles which, however, have never been fully articulated in constitutional documents. Freedom has been preserved for prolonged periods because such principles, vaguely and dimly perceived, have governed public opinion.'[8]

Lon Fuller maintained that customary law is appropriately viewed as

> 'a branch of constitutional law, largely and properly developed outside the framework of our written constitutions. It is constitutional law in that it involves the allocation among various institutions . . . of legal power, that is, the authority to enact rules and to reach decisions that will be regarded as properly binding on those affected by them'.[9]

Indeed, a privatised system of customary law based on reciprocity is not only possible, but has strong historical precedents.[10] The fact is that through much of history custom has been much more important in determining rules of conduct than written constitutions, legislation, or precedent.

Even members of primitive groups face strong incentives to develop a system of norms that, given enforcement, protects the rights and property of individual members of the group. Co-operative establishment of rules of conduct based on individual freedom and private property creates significant reciprocal benefits. The incentives for such development and the process itself are not much different from those of other institutions that promote effective and efficient co-operation within the system.[11] A spontaneous law-making process can be viewed as similar to the spontaneous development of language. Indeed, Fuller described customary law as a 'language of interaction'.[12] No government was ever instrumental in the development of a language. Languages in both spoken and written forms develop over time through the spontaneous interactions of many independent individuals – individuals with strong incentives to develop a common language that facilitates

---

[8] F. A. Hayek, *Law, Legislation and Liberty*, Vol. 1: *Rules and Order*, Chicago: University of Chicago Press, 1973, p. 55.

[9] Fuller, *op. cit.*, pp. 128-29.

[10] Benson, 'Enforcement of Private Property Rights in Primitive Societies', *op. cit.*; Benson, 'The Spontaneous Evolution of Commercial Law', *op. cit.*; and Leon E. Trakman, *The Law Merchant: The Evolution of Commercial Law*, Littleton, Col.: Fred B. Rothman & Co., 1983.

[11] See Hayek, *Law, Legislation and Liberty*, Vol. 1; Fuller, *The Morality of Law, op. cit.*; Fuller, *The Principles of Social Order*, Durham, N.C.: Duke University Press, 1981.

[12] Fuller, *ibid.*, p. 213.

interaction and co-operation. In fact, many other arrangements develop spontaneously for the same reasons – trading systems and markets, religious systems and congregations, extended family systems, clans, villages, cities, transport routes and customary law. Customary law based on widely held norms and equity emerges, as Berman wrote, 'on the ground' – it is 'less programmatic' than legislative law imposed from above.[13] Actually, many of the laws in modern societies that are widely respected and adhered to (that is, violated *relatively* infrequently) are laws that developed from the 'ground' because legislation is often the codification of customary law.

Characteristics of Customary Law

Offences in a stateless legal system would be treated as torts. Many 'crimes' would still be illegal, of course, particularly if they have victims. Nonetheless, certain types of activities that are currently defined as criminal would probably be permitted. Activities currently carried out in black markets (gambling, prostitution, the use and sale of marijuana and most other drugs) would probably be legal, for instance, since these actions generally do not have identifiable victims, and few people are likely to be willing to pay for their enforcement.

Of course, it is possible that a group may *voluntarily* co-operate (as opposed to being coerced into co-operating) to enforce a law where no identifiable victim exists if virtually everyone in the relevant group believes that the law should be enforced. But in a stateless system of law *and* enforcement, the allocation of enforcement resources would be determined by individual willingness to pay rather than by political strength or bureaucratic discretion over common pool resources.[14]

'People who want to control other people's lives are rarely eager to pay for the privilege. They usually expect to be paid for the service they provide for their victims.'[15]

A private system of law would clearly be strongly biased towards individual freedom when individual action does no harm to another's physical person or property.

---

[13] Harold J. Berman, *Law and Revolution: The Formation of the Western Legal Tradition*, Cambridge, Mass.: Harvard University Press, 1983, p. 274.

[14] For discussions of various aspects of government law enforcement as common pool resources, see Benson, 'Corruption in Law Enforcement: One Consequence of "The Tragedy of the Commons" Arising With Public Allocation Processes', *International Review of Law and Economics*, Vol. 8, June 1988, pp. 73-84; Benson and Laurin A. Wollan, Jr., 'Prison Crowding and Judicial Incentives', *Madison Paper Series*, No. 3, May 1989, pp. 1-21; and Richard Neely, *Why Courts Don't Work*, New York: McGraw-Hill, 1982.

[15] Friedman, *The Machinery of Freedom: Guide to a Radical Capitalism*, New York: Harper and Row, 1973, pp. 173-74.

The possibility of a community having its own law, differing substantially from other communities, does not mean that an irrational patchwork of entirely different law systems will exist. History demonstrates that standardisation of many aspects of customary law over very large geographic areas would arise. There certainly may be relatively minor differences, but perhaps even less differentiation would occur than exists from state to state and even city to city under the political system of law we currently have. Consider the privately developed English language, for example. The basic rules of English are such that people from Maine can communicate with people from Alabama, New York, Minnesota, Texas, Nebraska, and from the regions of Great Britain, Canada, Australia, New Zealand, and South Africa. Tremendous levels of standardisation dominate all the regional differences in language – and in customary law.

Punishment for Law Breakers

A significant advantage of a 'victim oriented' system of law is '... that specifying the victim has the practical function of giving someone an incentive to pursue the case'.[16] This incentive arises because of the nature of the 'punishment' that would exist. The goal of the private enforcement system, given a violation of the law, would be restitution for the victim, and thus punishment would typically take the form of a fine (payable to the victim) of at least sufficient magnitude to compensate the victim for all losses and cover the full cost of bringing the offender to justice. This prediction finds strong support in the historical evidence. All systems of privately enforced customary law have been restitution oriented in this fashion, with fines as the major form of punishment.

Advantages of Fines

Fines are very efficient compared with modern methods of punishment such as imprisonment, which use up resources like guards and other personnel, the capital and resources needed to build the prisons, and the prisoners' time.[17] Fines consume far fewer resources. Some offenders may require close supervision in prison-like workplaces to ensure payment, as noted below, but the prisoner's own time is not wasted in that he is working to produce goods and services that can be sold in order to pay off the debt.

[16] Friedman, 'Private Creation and Enforcement of Law: A Historical Case', *op. cit.*, p. 414; also see Randy E. Barnett, 'Restitution: A New Paradigm of Criminal Justice', *Ethics*, Vol. 87, July 1977, p. 293.

[17] See, for example, Friedman, 'Private Creation and Enforcement of Law: A Historical Case', *op. cit.*, p. 408; and Barnett, 'Restitution: A New Paradigm of Criminal Justice', *op. cit.*, p. 291.

Appropriately set fines can also provide a significant deterrent. Suppose fines are set equal to the full cost to the victim plus the full cost of bringing the offender to justice, all divided by the probability that the offender will be brought to justice, as suggested by Becker and Stigler.[18] Consider, for example, the fine for stealing a car. If half the car thefts are solved, costs borne by the victim and incurred in law enforcement would be divided by one-half or, in effect, multiplied by two. The fine would be double the damages. The benefit to the offender of stealing the car is the value of the car. Obviously, the expected cost of the crime is greater than the expected benefit if the courts set the same probabilities that the offenders perceive. Offenders, of course, may and probably do have a different perception of risk than victims, and perhaps judges, but the actual fine would still be quite large relative to the gain for the robber since the probability would clearly be less than one. Private courts may not determine fines in precisely the manner discussed here,[19] but private citizens who contract with courts and enforcers would be attracted to those firms that are effective at preventing (deterring) offences – that is, to enforcers who make significant efforts to recover for the victim and judges whose fines are clearly high enough to compensate the victim and the enforcer. (Naturally a judge will be concerned about recovering his own costs as well since the loser will pay the court costs under this sort of system.)

The fine and victim restitution emphasis of privately enforced law provides another reason to suspect that few laws against victimless crimes would arise, and even if they did, few resources would be devoted to their enforcement. It is certainly possible that fines could be dictated by some tightly knit community. Incentives could be created to enforce such laws as well, if, for instance, a right to the collected fine is given to a successful enforcer. Again, laws against drugs, prostitution, gambling, and so on, *could* arise under a system of customary law – they are simply not nearly as likely to arise as laws against the violation of another individual's rights.

Activities that clearly would be finable, and therefore deterred, are offences by private law enforcers against innocent citizens. Since falsifying violations, falsely charging innocent people of wrongdoing, and bullying citizens violate the rights of those who are innocent, a private, victim-oriented system of law would require full compensation from enforcers for anyone acquitted of a charge or mistreated. This

---

[18] See Gary Becker, 'Crime and Punishment: An Economic Approach', *Journal of Political Economy*, Vol. 76, March/April 1968, pp. 191-93; and George J. Stigler, 'The Optimum Enforcement of Laws', *Journal of Political Economy*, Vol. 78, May/June 1970, p. 531.

[19] For other possibilities see Barnett, 'Restitution: A New Paradigm of Criminal Justice', p. 288.

implies that the loser in a court case would pay the full cost of the court appearance.

Fines as Incentives

Fines as a primary form of punishment would also create incentives for those guilty of committing an offence to avoid unnecessary uses of court time, since fines levied by the courts would include court costs. Thus unsuccessful efforts by a guilty party to hide his guilt or drag out a trial would result in higher fines. This would encourage out-of-court settlements between offender and victim. Of course, this out-of-court settlement would not be like the plea bargaining of today's system. Victims would receive satisfactory restitution under private out-of-court settlements because the bargain would be between the victim and the offender, not between the offender and a *public* prosecutor. The offender would simply avoid the higher payment to cover court costs in this case, while modern plea bargaining typically 'forgives' a criminal for a certain portion of crimes committed in exchange for willingly admitting to and accepting punishment for the rest. Thus some victims do not even receive the satisfaction of knowing that the criminal has been punished, much less any restitution. Differential fines for those who admit guilt and those who try to hide it may even become a formal part of the customary law system. Such was the case in medieval Iceland's system of privately produced and enforced law, for instance, where

'... the difference between two sorts of offences provided a high "differential punishment" for the "offence" of concealing one's crime, an offence which imposed serious costs'.[20]

The preceding discussion suggests advantages to fines as the primary form of punishment for the offender as well. Imprisonment not only fails to compensate the victim, but typically requires the victim to bear more costs (for instance, the cost of co-operating in prosecution). Under these circumstances,

'it is not surprising . . . that the anger and fear felt toward ex-convicts who in fact have not paid their debt to society have resulted in additional punishments, including legal restrictions on their political and economic opportunities and informal restrictions on their social acceptance.'[21]

But because fines for restitution would 'restore' the victim, incentives for further revenge are significantly reduced.

Fines would be the primary type of punishment in a system of

---

[20] Friedman, 'Private Creation and Enforcement of Law: A Historical Case', *op. cit.*, p. 409.

[21] Becker, 'Crime and Punishment: An Economic Approach', *op. cit.*, p. 194.

privately enforced customary law, but they might not be the only type of punishment. Pre-13th century Icelandic[22] and primitive Kapauku[23] systems of law considered capital punishment appropriate for some crimes, for instance. Whether such punishment would arise in the customary law system of a modern society is difficult to predict. It is possible that the life of a perpetrator of a capital offence would be committed to working where the payments for such labour go to the victim or the victim's family, even though full restitution could never be achieved.

One individual property right that the law would recognise, as explained above, is the right to restitution when one's rights are violated. As with any private property right, the right to restitution would be transferable, which has been the case in virtually all the systems of privately produced law that have existed. A marketable claim by a victim implies that it can be sold to someone willing to pursue and prosecute the alleged offender.[24] This, in turn, could produce arrangements under which violators of the rights of the poor and the weak would be pursued and prosecuted. Private enforcement arrangements can be anticipated that would serve the poor, the wealthy, and those in between.

Private Law Enforcement Mechanisms

A wide variety of individual and co-operative arrangements can be anticipated that would emphasise the protection of persons and property (prevention) and the recovery of losses suffered by victims. Individuals may choose to protect themselves and their property by owning guns, installing burglar alarms, building fences, barring windows, and so on, much as they do today. The rights to do such things are private property rights that clearly would be supported by privately enforced customary law.

Co-operative arrangements by groups would also arise. The benefits to be shared by watching and patrolling geographic areas are considerable, and thus incentives are strong to support such efforts. In some communities or neighbourhoods where individuals' budget constraints are more binding than time constraints, residents would contribute their time to a voluntary patrol. In others, where budget constraints are less binding, people would contribute money to hire a private security firm or firms, which in turn would furnish patrols, watchmen, guards, electronic watching devices or whatever the community wished to pay for.

---

22 Friedman, 'Private Creation and Enforcement of Law: A Historical Case', *op. cit.*

23 Benson, 'Enforcement of Private Property Rights in Primitive Societies', *op. cit.*

24 Friedman, *op. cit.*, p. 414.

Although there may be free-rider incentives inherent in such localised watching, over time contractual arrangements would probably arise to internalise the deterrent benefits of patrol systems, thus eliminating the free-rider problem. This development might not actually take long in a highly mobile society like ours. Enterprising residential and business real estate developers would quickly see the benefit of establishing developments that offered, as part of the purchase price of a home or business location, a guarantee that everyone in the development has signed a legally binding contract to contribute to the community's security arrangements. Such communities already exist, of course. In some areas a person who buys property has to agree to pay a fee that covers the cost of the private guard and patrols (as well as street maintenance, street lighting, etc., if the entire community is privatised). As people move, for whatever reason, these sorts of contractual arrangements would attract increasing numbers, since such communities would be relatively safe from violations of individual property rights. This is particularly true since those least likely to free ride because of their strong concern for protection would find such contractual arrangements quite attractive, leaving relatively large numbers of free riders in other, non-contracting neighbourhoods.

Rising Cost of Free Riding

Voluntary arrangements without legally binding contracts (that is, those that allow free riding) would become relatively less effective, and neighbourhoods so characterised would face relatively greater threats to persons and property. As the threat increased more people would move out, or the cost of free riding would increase to a level such that more and more of those who remained would be willing to contract for joint purchase or production of protection. Free riders would face the increasing ire of their neighbours, ultimately backed by ostracism, and would be prevented from consuming any benefits of living in the area that they could be excluded from. Communities that failed to internalise the benefits of group protection because of free riders would find themselves at a competitive disadvantage with those that eliminated free riding. Property values would fall. The cost of free riding would rise tremendously under privatisation. Of course, none of this means that *all* free riding must be eliminated as *every* individual (or even every community) contracts to internalise the deterrent benefits of protection. Communities may conceivably exist and survive without developing such security systems, although their 'citizens' would probably have either very high levels of self-protection or have little they feel is worth protecting. (There clearly are people who have opted out of the current

167

legal and social system roaming the streets of most major cities and many of the nation's wildernesses.)

Individual security firms may simply offer protection services like patrols and guards, but they may also be vertically organised to offer recovery of losses (or restitution) as well. Some advocates of private law enforcement have hypothesised that the private security market would be organised much like a mutual insurance market. A firm or a co-operative surety (or pledge) group organisation would insure individuals and their property against violations.[25] This firm or organisation would therefore have strong incentives to prevent offences by supplying police services with an emphasis on patrolling, watching, and other deterrents. If an offence occurs against a subscriber to these services, the insurance would pay the subscriber's claim unless they recover all losses. In paying the subscriber, the firm or organisation, in effect, would purchase the right to collect at least some portion of the fine from the offender. Strong incentives would therefore exist to pursue the offender and to gather evidence for court prosecution.[26]

Of course, such insurance arrangements with vertically organised firms providing both protection and investigative services may not arise in every (or even any) case. Individuals may buy protection from one company and, in the event of an offence, contract with another to pursue the offender or offer a reward to attract the attention of a number of specialised thief-taking firms. Market forces of demand (reflecting the preferences of consumers) and supply (reflecting production technologies and costs) would dictate the actual industrial organisation that evolved.

Arbitration

Numerous other contractual arrangements can be anticipated under a system of private enforcement of law. For one thing, the contract with a particular protection firm may include an arbitration clause so that disputes between clients of that firm would be settled internally. The company may provide an arbitrator or arbitrators or contract with a particular dispute resolution firm. (The market for adjudication is examined in more detail below, following further consideration of enforcement.) An arbitration clause in a legal contract also would mean that refusal to submit to arbitration was unlikely since it would probably result in ostracism by the rest of the members of the community, loss of

---

[25] See, for instance, Friedman, *The Machinery of Freedom: Guide to a Radical Capitalism, op. cit.*; Murray Rothbard, *For a New Liberty*, New York: Macmillan, 1973, pp. 222-28; and Clarence L. Swartz, *What is Mutualism?*, New York: Vanguard Press, 1927, pp. 155-66.

[26] Rothbard, *ibid.*, p. 222.

protection services, and perhaps of ownership rights to property purchased under the contract (e.g., a residence or business location).

Similar contractual arrangements would probably arise between different communities and their (perhaps different) protection agencies. And even if a formal contract did not exist, the desire to avoid violence would lead to submission to arbitration in most instances. Such arrangements might be likened to formal or informal extradition treaties among political entities. Consider first an offence (or alleged offence) by a member of one group against a member of a different law enforcement organisation (firms, communities, etc.) where both law systems hold the act to be illegal. The organisation whose member is alleged to be the offender would have strong incentives to allow their member to be arrested and to apply considerable pressure on that individual to submit to arbitration. Sneed noted that a protection organisation (or firm) that refused to allow the arrest of a member (or client), given good cause, would suffer in several ways:

o   Other organisations would similarly resist attempts to arrest their clients, and thus the organisation's ability to protect its members would be reduced and the chances of violent confrontations would rise; either violent confrontations or reciprocal impotence would cause loss of membership (or clients);

o   Reciprocal working relationships for the pursuit and capture of geographically mobile offenders (co-operative information and apprehension networks, or an inter-group bounty system) would be very valuable and would undoubtedly develop, but refusal to co-operate in other areas would jeopardise the chance to participate in such arrangements; and

o   An organisation that refused to turn over members who committed offences would tend to attract members who intended to commit offences, thus placing the organisation in jeopardy because of ever-increasing confrontations.[27]

These incentives apply whether the member to be arrested is guilty or innocent. Thus every policing organisation would probably explicitly state that disputes between members of different organisations must be decided by impartial private courts or arbitrators.

That arrangements such as those envisioned by the Sneed argument, whether formal or informal, would arise is supported by historical evidence. For example, the extended families of the primitive Ifugao

27 J. Sneed, 'Order Without Law: Where Will the Anarchists Keep the Madmen?', *Journal of Libertarian Studies*, Vol. 1, 1977, p. 119.

applied pressure to their members to yield to mediation procedures when a dispute arose with a member of another family.[28] Formal procedures existed for resolution of disputes between members of different congregations in medieval Iceland and various *tuatha* in Ireland prior to subjugation by the British. Jurisdictional rules were well defined among the primitive Kapauku and the Anglo-Saxons before the Norman conquest. Medieval mercantile law was customary law enforced by the merchants themselves, and it was applied evenhandedly to foreign merchants and domestic merchants alike.

Bail Bonding

Sneed also suggested that bail bonds might be posted by an accused offender's protection company or organisation,[29] and this too has historical precedent. Under the surety system in medieval Ireland, a large fine levied against a member of a particular *tuath* might be paid by the group as a whole, and they in turn could collect from the offender. Similarly, Icelandic society prior to the 14th century 'provided their members with money to pay large fines'.[30] The Anglo-Saxon tithing system that existed before the Normans imposed their will on England also included effective credit and bonding.

Such bonding or credit arrangements have some very significant advantages. First, the victim's enforcement organisation would require a bail sufficient to compensate the victim or his heirs, and cover the organisation's costs associated with the case. Consequently, the victim and his organisation would be relatively unconcerned if the accused failed to appear. In fact, it would be the accused's own defence organisation which would be responsible for collecting from him if he were guilty. Ostracism must play a predominant rôle in inducing someone (particularly someone who is guilty) to submit to arbitration. This bail-bonding arrangement makes ostracism possible. If the members of an accused offender's own community or other mutual defence group have strong incentives to apply pressure on the accused to submit, then ostracism can be effective. Furthermore, in contracting with a particular organisation or firm for the option of bail, should it be required in the future, the individual may voluntarily agree to submit to confinement or yield a portion of his future income to repay the bond, should he be found guilty. At any rate, the onus would be on the

---

28 Benson, 'The Lost Victim and Other Failures of the Public Law Experiment', *Harvard Journal of Law and Public Policy*, Vol. 9, Spring 1986, pp. 399-427; and Benson, 'Enforcement of Private Property Rights in Primitive Societies', *op. cit.*

29 Sneed, 'Order Without Law: Where Will the Anarchists Keep the Madmen?', *op. cit.*, p. 119.

30 Friedman, 'Private Creation and Enforcement of Law: A Historical Case', *op. cit.*, p. 400.

members of the accused's organisation to collect if he were guilty, rather than on the victim.

A second desirable characteristic of the bail (or credit) arrangement as part of a contract with a particular protection firm or organisation is that organisations would have incentives to work on behalf of the accused in an effort to recover the bond. (Recall also that those who are acquitted of a violation would have the right to restitution of costs, including the cost of any investigation on his behalf.) Thus someone accused of an offence would

> 'regularly have investigative agencies working on his behalf which wield powers of the same order as those of the arresting company. Deliberate as well as accidental conviction of the innocent would be far less feasible. Falsification of evidence would be considerably more risky'.[31]

Problem of Law Violations in Distant Communities

The preceding discussion of reciprocal arrangements between different communities and different law enforcement organisations assumed that the violated law was common to both communities and their enforcement organisations, although, as observed earlier, some differences in law could arise across communities or groups. How might the private sector handle a member of one legal organisation who, while travelling in some distant community, violates a law unique to that legal organisation? Several possible arrangements can be conceived. For instance, a risk-averse individual who expects to be in situations where he may inadvertently violate an unknown law could insure himself against that possibility. Thus his protection company would pay his fine (or bail) and he would not suffer any exorbitant personal loss. Under this scenario, the relevant law is that of the group being violated rather than that of the violator.

A particular community's law could involve a fine that most people outside that group considered unreasonable, or the law itself may be commonly held to be unreasonable. However, if such a law is violated by someone from another community, both groups would still have strong incentives to avoid a violent confrontation. Imposition of laws on outsiders that are way out of line with those that exist in most communities clearly increases the chances of violence, and thus a negotiated or arbitrated settlement would, in most cases, lower the cost to the accused and his insurers below that which would induce violence. A community that insisted on strictly imposing its own morality and heavy penalties on outsiders would initially face continual clashes,

---

[31] Sneed, 'Order Without Law: Where Will the Anarchists Keep the Madmen?', *op. cit.*, p. 120.

followed by boycott sanctions as residents of other communities refused to travel to or trade with that community, or to enter into reciprocal arrangements to yield accused violators of their laws. A community that isolated itself would not survive in a competitive, free-market environment. Those who weakly adhered to the norms the community wished to impose would leave first, and as property values and trade-generated incomes declined, others would follow. In fact, then, if a community wished to impose laws differing substantially from the norm, it would have strong incentives to inform outsiders of the differences in order to avoid conflict and minimise the difficulty of maintaining non-standard laws. Part of the reciprocal agreements with other communities and enforcers for extradition, etc., might be explicit recognition of differences in laws and procedures for treating conflicts that arose under the different laws.

Undoubtedly some individuals would not join *any* co-operative law enforcement arrangement and would refuse to recognise *any* rules of law. After all, there are thousands of such people today. The incentives to co-operation and contract would be considerably stronger under a system of customary law and private enforcement than under public law and law enforcement (and, under a system dominated by private property, all those millions of acres of publicly owned land would not be available for such people to free ride on), but a relevant question remains: How would these people be treated under privatisation? First, they would be left alone unless they violated someone else's rights. Second, they would have to defend their person and property on their own, given their refusal to co-operate. But what would happen if they violated a law by infringing on someone else's rights? No form of ostracism or boycott sanction would be effective in inducing them to submit to arbitration or to pay whatever fine was levied, should they be found guilty. Actually, the same question applies to anyone who refuses to submit to the pressures of ostracism and pay a fine (or, perhaps, to go to arbitration).

The ultimate threat that underlies any system of property rights is that of violence. If someone refuses to yield to arbitration and/or accept the judgement of the courts, the system *(any system, including government)* moves to violence.[32] An individual who commits a major offence against someone else and then further refuses to yield to the legal justice system would be an outlaw. In primitive legal systems (as well as others that have not drawn their authority from a central state government), anyone

---

[32] Benson, 'Enforcement of Private Property Rights in Primitive Societies', *op. cit.*; Benson, *The Enterprise of Law, op. cit.*; and John Umbeck, *A Theory of Property Rights With Applications to the California Gold Rush*, Ames: Iowa State University Press, 1981.

was free to take an outlaw's life and property. Such a contingency would probably also arise in a modern system of privatised law and order.

Private Courts

It was suggested above that contractual arrangements for arbitration would probably arise within and between the groups and communities that organised for joint security. Furthermore, these various communities and agencies would have very strong incentives to seek out judges for both inter- and intra-community dispute resolutions who not only have reputations for impartiality, but for issuing clear, easily interpretable opinions available as a guide in settling future disputes – that is, precedents. Judges who provided such opinions would garner much more business (if not all the business) than judges who issued vague, uninterpretable, or secret opinions. Why? Simply because disputes are costly and always raise the spectre of potential violence. Both would be avoided if at all possible by private sector law enforcers. Note that the concern for a security agency or community representing some victim would be much stronger in this regard than the concern of *individual* disputants in our current system, since these firms or communities represent many potential victims and offenders, and therefore many possible future confrontations.

There is a second reason, beyond minimising the cost of future disputes, for demanding clear, well-founded decisions. Smith referred to it as the 'verification aspect'.[33] In order for a dispute to end satisfactorily, a decision has to be acceptable (verifiable) not just to the parties most directly affected, but to the groups or firms representing these parties and to groups who, although not directly involved, might be drawn into a confrontation with one of the groups in the dispute under consideration. The willingness of various other firms and organisations to enter into and honour reciprocal arrangements, such as extradition contracts, with those involved in the dispute would depend, in part, on the way this and other disputes were handled.

These contractual arrangements between dispersed organisations to encourage arbitration of disputes between their members also would increase the likelihood of standardisation of certain aspects of law. In effect, law would develop through dispute resolution to facilitate the interaction *between* groups – law based on common custom as reflected in previous judgements. Aspects of a particular group's law that proved

---

[33] George Smith, 'Justice Entrepreneurship in a Free Market', *Journal of Libertarian Studies*, Vol. 3, Winter 1979, pp. 422-24.

to be efficient would be revealed to another group in the process, and they could adopt it in turn, if they wished. Such a process characterised the standardisation of the Law Merchant throughout Western Europe during the 11th and 12th centuries, for example. Efficient rules adopted by one merchant community tended to spread to other communities quite rapidly.

Trial by Jury?

Critics of private adjudication systems are sometimes fearful that two desirable institutional arrangements of modern public courts might disappear in a private system. First, would there be trial by jury? If jury trials are demanded they would be supplied, assuming that the demand is sufficiently strong to pay the full cost of such a trial. Of course, our current system rarely comes close to reimbursing jury members for their time and effort. Jury trials would be relatively more expensive than judge-only trials, and consequently would be relatively less likely under privatisation. This is not necessarily a bad thing, however. As Person noted, jury trials '. . . are of great importance in the government courts as a means of protection from a hostile judge but of less importance when parties select their own judges'.[34] Indeed, juries were developed by Norman kings for inquisitional purposes and were ultimately accepted as a desirable institution because they served as a counter force to another royal institution – the judges of the king's courts. As a consequence, the demand for jury trials is likely to be considerably weaker in a privatised system, and when this is combined with their relatively high cost they become relatively unlikely.

Courts of Appeal?

The second institutional question that often arises is: Would there be courts of appeal? Again the answer is, if they are demanded. There would not be a single monopolised 'supreme court', of course, but there might be competitive appeals courts just as there would be competitive judges for the initial consideration of a dispute. Naturally, the next question is, given the existence of appeals courts but no supreme court of last resort, what will prevent a continuous, never-ending process of appeals so that an offender avoids submitting to a decision but is not declared an outlaw? The contractual arrangements for dispute settlement within a particular community or security organisation would, in all likelihood, specify an appeals procedure and put a limit on the number of appeals (the medieval Law Merchant allowed no appeals,

---

[34] Carl Person, 'Justice, Inc.', *Juris Doctor*, March 1978, p. 34.

for instance, because the costs in terms of delay and disruptions of commerce were considered to be too high). Since formal and informal contracts would arise between groups to establish procedures for intergroup dispute resolution, appeals procedures might be established for those disputes as well. Alternatively, as part of the agreement to submit to arbitration when prior arrangements did not exist, the parties might specify an appeals procedure and cut-off point.

Ostracism, Boycott Sanctions, Private Prisons, and the Collection of Fines

Why would someone pay a fine or pay off any debt if the coercive power of the state did not exist to force payment? The answer is basically the same as for the question of why someone, particularly someone guilty of an offence, would submit to arbitration in the first place – ostracism and boycott sanctions would convince many to pay their debts. The potential effectiveness of ostracism and boycott threats is enhanced under the contractual arrangements predicated above. If indeed part of the insurance arrangement is the provision of credit to pay bails or large fines, then the responsibility of collecting from the offender is shifted from the victim to the offender's own security organisation. Ostracism by one's own community can be an extremely effective method of inducing payment of debt. Outlawry would be the most severe form of ostracism, but less severe threats would often be sufficient to induce compliance.

The Effectiveness of Ostracism

Although ostracism has been effective through history as a means of inducing compliance with private court judgements, some might argue that it would not be effective in our modern mobile society. On the contrary, ostracism is likely to be even more effective today than it was in the historical situations alluded to here: 'Nowadays, modern technology, computers, and credit ratings would make such ... ostracism even more effective than it has ever been in the past.'[35] This does not mean that some guilty offenders would not flee and attempt to hide, just as many criminals do under our governmental system of justice. It simply means that, given the communications technology now available, the network of co-operative, reciprocal contracts between various communities and their justice agencies would probably prevent such an individual from obtaining the benefits of joining some other community, or at least severely limit the likelihood of such an

---

[35] Rothbard, *For a New Liberty, op. cit.*, p. 231.

occurrence. The Anglo-Saxon tithing arrangement excluded anyone from entering or dealing within a community who could not demonstrate that he was a member in good standing of some surety group. With modern communications technology, checking any stranger's claims of insurance would be much easier than it was then.

A more relevant concern is that offenders may be unable to meet their obligations. If an offender cannot be appropriately fined, would such a system break down? That was not the case historically. For example, Friedman, in his examination of medieval Icelandic justice, suggested that a variation on the Icelandic debt-thraldom would solve the problem of judgement-proof offenders. In particular, he proposed that

> 'an arrangement which protects the convicted criminal against the most obvious abuses would be for the . . . criminal . . . [to] have the choice of . . . accepting bids for his services. The employer making such a bid would offer the criminal some specified working conditions (possibly inside a private prison, possibly not) and a specified rate at which the employer would pay off the fine. In order to get custody of the criminal, the employer would have to obtain his consent and post bond with the court for the amount of the fine'.[36]

The offender would face a choice between ostracism or voluntarily working off the fine. Contracts between the debtor and the victim, or more likely the debtor's insurers, would specify the work conditions. If the insurers perceive little risk that a debtor will renege, they might simply allow him to continue in his trade and make periodic payments. If the risk of reneging is perceived to be large, varying degrees of security and supervision may be provided for in the contract. For example, the debtor may agree to report to a supervisor once a week or once a month (as parolees report to parole officers), or to return to and remain in a secure facility each evening (as in work-release programmes that are sometimes available today).

How to Cope with Renegers

If the risk of reneging is large enough, however, a 'penal specialist' would be employed. The protection agency-insurance company may have its own specialised penal subsidiary, of course, or separate firms may specialise in providing such services. Sneed predicted that a competitive penal system would arise wherein several firms would bid for employment of the convict under secure conditions.[37] Furthermore, the insurance company/convict would have the right to withdraw from

---

[36] Friedman, 'Private Creation and Enforcement of Law: A Historical Case', *op. cit.*, p. 415.

[37] Sneed, 'Order Without Law: Where Will the Anarchists Keep the Madmen?', *op. cit.*, pp. 122-23.

the resulting contract if the prison firm did not live up to its agreement, a right that would guarantee that the convict would make the highest possible wage (e.g., be paid the value of his marginal product) so he could earn his way out of prison as quickly as possible. Whether exactly these sorts of contractual arrangements would arise or not, it is clear that the private penal system would differ from current public prisons.

One important difference between prisons under a fully privatised system and current government prisons is that those who run private penal firms would have strong incentives to treat prisoners well. Such incentives are enhanced by an arrangement that ensures prisoner mobility, as Sneed emphasised, but they exist even without a high degree of mobility. After all, a person's productivity, and therefore the rate of debt repayment, under such a system is likely to be significantly influenced by his treatment. Since the penal firm would either contract with the debtor to assume the risk of debt payment or contract with insurers (or perhaps victims) who want the debt paid off as quickly as possible, a firm that has a reputation for mistreating prisoners in such a way as to reduce their productivity would clearly not receive much business. Along these same lines, increased effort by a prisoner would reduce the period of confinement, so the length of the term would be at least partly self-determined. Prisoner morale would improve, making eventual rehabilitation easier.

Effective Rehabilitation in Private Prison System

There actually are a number of reasons for expecting that rehabilitation would be far more effective under such a system than it is with current efforts, beyond the more humane treatment of prisoners and their relatively better morale.[38] Productive use of inmate time would provide them with incentives to develop new or strengthen existing marketable skills, and teach them the discipline needed to hold a job in the market-place after their release.[39]

Under the current system, prisoners are idle; they are bored. This

---

[38] See Barnett, 'Restitution: A New Paradigm of Criminal Justice', *op. cit.*, p. 293, for a discussion of physiological factors not discussed below.

[39] In fact, Sneed logically suggested that since the penal firms will be producing marketable products they will probably offer offenders continued employment after they have retired their debts ('Order Without Law: Where Will the Anarchists Keep the Madmen?', *op. cit.*, p. 123):

'It would be foolish to in effect fire a worker with experience simply because he has now regained his freedom. He will still remain employed by the penal agency but will become free of security restrictions and will be an ordinary worker. Indeed, an agency which does provide employment for "graduated" convicts would have a strong competitive edge in the recruitment process.'

This potential clearly reduces the likelihood of a return to illegal activities by a released prisoner and adds to the superior rehabilitation under privatisation, since many now return to crime out of virtual necessity – they have no marketable skills after release from prison and therefore they cannot support themselves in legal activities.

idleness and boredom reflects a lack of constructive outlets, and therefore encourages other outlets. In particular, violence and drug abuse are both significant problems in modern prisons. Neither are as likely in a privatised system. Drugs may reduce productivity and delay release, for example, and the risk of injury from a violent confrontation that significantly delays release would provide a substantial deterrent to violence.

In Sneed's words:

'[O]ur analogue to prison would not be, as today, a brutal institution primarily functioning to teach brutes how to be more brutish, but would become almost a treatment centre, a place to learn how to live peaceably in outside society. Our present system only teaches a person how to live in prison.'[40]

This is an important consideration for those who question the effectiveness of ostracism and boycott sanctions as sufficient inducements for offenders to submit to arbitration judgements, which may imply working under the supervision of a private penitentiary until the debt is paid off. The 'prison' experience under privatisation would not be at all comparable to the situation a convict faces in our 'modern', governmentally produced prisons. The incentives to avoid such 'punishment' would, therefore, be considerably weaker than under the current system.

Conclusions

The argument outlined above is that a system that emphasises individual responsibility and liberty can be established under customary law with private sector institutions for enforcement and adjudication. Such a system may not be perfect – for example, some free riding may occur. Thus some may suggest that limited government involvement, where government does those few things that it might do better than markets, would be superior to complete privatisation. Friedman answered this question in the following way:

'Perhaps it would be – if the government stayed that way ... One cannot simply build any imaginable characteristics into a government; governments have their own internal dynamic. And the internal dynamic of limited governments is something with which we, to our sorrow, have a good deal of practical experience ... the logic of limited government is to grow. There are obvious reasons for that in the nature of government, and plenty of evidence. Constitutions provide, at the most, a modest and temporary

---

[40] *Ibid.*, p. 123.

restraint. As Murray Rothbard is supposed to have said, the idea of a limited government that stays limited is truly Utopian.'[41]

Every aspect of government involvement in law and order started out to be very limited (or non-existent). Royal courts in England, for example, initially had very limited jurisdictions. Then they began competing with other courts in adjudicating increasingly more diverse laws. They had a 'competitive' advantage in that part of the cost of using them was not borne by litigants. Various interest groups were happy to shift their costs for protection services and the enforcement of their laws onto others by using government courts, and later government watchmen, police, prosecutors, and so on. Government entities were happy to oblige. The combination of power seeking and bureaucratic growth by government officials and transfer (or rent) seeking by interest groups inevitably turns limited government into big government.

---

[41] Friedman, *The Machinery of Freedom: Guide to a Radical Capitalism, op. cit.*, pp. 200-201.

14

THE MARKET REGULATION OF INDUSTRIAL SAFETY*

W. S. Siebert
University of Birmingham

1. Introduction

'The whole of the advantages and disadvantages of the different employments of labour and stock must, in the same neighbourhood, be either perfectly equal, or continually tending to equality ... Actual differences of pecuniary wages and profits are due partly to counter-balancing circumstances, and partly to want of perfect liberty.'

(ADAM SMITH, *The Wealth of Nations*, 1776)

IN COMPETITIVE MARKETS, workers whose jobs have undesirable characteristics – are dirty, dangerous, or tedious – demand and are paid wage premiums to compensate them for these undesirable aspects of the job. Workers must be paid more if firms are to attract labour to these jobs. This theory of wage determination is known as the theory of *compensating wage differentials*, and was first put forward by Adam Smith. The compensating wage differentials both reward workers for bearing risk, and penalise firms with poor accident records.

Industrial safety policy and regulation is based on a rejection of the theory of compensating wage differentials. It is claimed that dirty and hazardous jobs pay lower, not higher, wages, other things equal, and that the assumptions underlying the theory (good information, high

---

*I am grateful to Sir Henry Phelps Brown and Cento Veljanovski for comments, but retain responsibility for any remaining errors.

labour mobility and worker rationality) are unrealistic. Government must therefore intervene to protect vulnerable workers and improve workplace safety.

In this chapter I re-examine the theory and evidence to see whether market forces exist in modern labour markets, and the extent to which they can replace traditional forms of regulation. If we find workers in dangerous jobs are paid much more than in safe jobs, then the market itself penalises unsafe workplaces. In such a world the rationale for government industrial safety policy is different. It lies more in the provision of information (research into the labelling of dangerous chemicals, safety advice), than in direct monitoring of the workplace.

The issue of safety policy is particularly important today with the setting up of a supra-national European Community Safety, Hygiene and Health Agency (Social Charter Action Plan, 1989), and the proposed 'massive programme' of European Community health and safety Directives (Eberlie, 1990). National safety agencies have not interfered much on the shop-floor in the past, in part because they are closer to local industrial realities (Fenn and Veljanovski, 1988), and in part because the market is so effective (as will be seen). But a European-level agency would be further removed from local conditions, and would in any case be required to ignore costs of compliance so as to limit 'unfair' competition between countries (see Addison and Siebert (1991) for a general discussion of the EC Commission's aims to limit 'unfair' competition). Such an agency could make safety more expensive for firms. My survey of research results on the determinants of workplace safety will give a market context to these developments.

I first examine the logic of the market for industrial accidents. I then consider research findings, to see whether the market works. The final section summarises policy implications.

2. The Logic of the Market

A Simple Model

A simple model of compensating pay differentials can be constructed which shows what they are, and how they control accidents. Suppose we are analysing jobs in which there is a chance of dying in an accident at work. Then there should be some upward-sloping wage-risk-of-accident opportunity locus as in Figure 1. The opportunity locus starts at the risk-free wage, W_0, and increases as the chance of accident increases. For any particular accident risk, say R^*, the wage demanded by workers is higher than the risk-free wage and the compensating differential is $W^* - W_0$, as shown.

On the employer side there will be certain costs of accident

Figure 1: Determination of Accident Rate in Factory

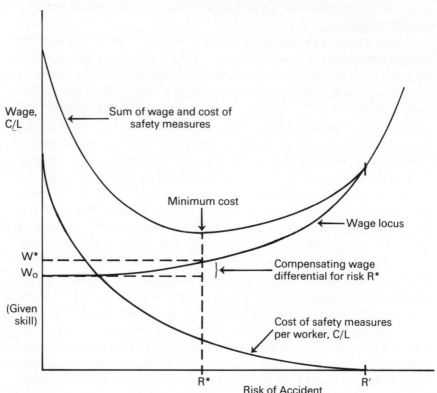

prevention. Costs of accident prevention per worker are shown as the C/L line in the diagram. (A per-worker formulation is used for comparability with the wage line, which is also per-worker – we assume the number of workers, L, is given.) The line is shown downward sloping because, as less is spent on prevention, accident risk rises. The C/L line will be determined by management skill – it shows the best that can be done for given safety expenditures. 'Slack' management would allow the C/L line to drift upwards. The C/L line is also technologically determined: a dangerous industry such as construction, for example, must have a C/L line displaced to the right of a 'safe' industry such as the selling of groceries.

The analysis can be applied to job risks other than physical injuries. For example, investment banking is physically safe, but it is risky in the sense of providing insecure jobs. Firms in the industry will need to compensate workers for the high risk of job loss. Measuring risk of job loss along the horizontal axis, the C/L curve of investment banking would be high relative to secure industries such as teaching. 'Safety expenditures' here would be contractual provisions to protect workers' jobs, rather than safety railings around machines. The C/L line would have the same downward-sloping shape because the more protected workers' jobs are, the more risky it will be for investors to invest in that firm, and the higher the cost of capital will be. While wages go down as risk of job loss falls, the cost of capital rises and the firm trades the two off.

We can picture the firm as wishing to minimise the sum of wages and safety equipment costs. The sum of the two costs are drawn in on Figure 1, with a minimum at R*. At the minimum, the slope of the wage locus equals the negative of the slope of the safety equipment costs line. At this point the employer is equating the marginal pound spent on safety equipment costs with the marginal pound saved on wage compensation for dangerous work.

The model demonstrates several points. *First*, it is the demand by workers for wage premia for danger which deters accidents. If the wage locus line were flat the incentive to buy safety equipment would decline to zero, and accidents would increase to R'. If workers under-estimated the chances of an accident, the wage locus line would be too flat, the compensating wage differential too low, and the accident rate would rise. The same would happen if, for some reason, workers were immobile, and could not move to the job which suited their preferences as between money and safety. Knowledge and mobility mean that the compensating wage differential $W^* - W_0$ exactly measures expected accident costs as evaluated by the marginal worker hired.

Secondly, at point R*, the amount spent on avoiding accidents approximately equals the expected accident costs as assessed by the workers involved (the compensating differential). This is prudent. It avoids the charge of 'negligence', which has been defined as taking precautions whose cost is less than the value of the injuries the precautions are designed to avoid (Veljanovski, 1990).[1] It is also not wasteful. At half R*, for example, much more would be spent on preventing accidents than was justified by the harm caused by accidents. Reducing accidents below R* would not be economic, in this sense.

A *third* point is that making firms strictly liable for damages resulting from accidents involving their workers could have the same effect as an upward-sloping wage locus line in preventing accidents. With employers strictly liable, the wage locus line becomes flatter since accidents are less damaging to workers. However, so long as firms' insurance premiums

---

[1] In other words, given C = cost of precautions, p = probability of injury, I = loss consequent upon injury, then $C < pI$ means negligence. In fact at R*, the cost of safety equipment per worker, C/L, need not be exactly the same as the compensating wage differential, but they will not diverge widely.

rise in accordance with their accident experience, that is, so long as there is 'experience rating', firms' (insurance) costs rise with their accident rates just as before. This prompts firms to take precautions against accidents. With fair insurance, there thus seems little to choose between the free market and Workers' Compensation.[2]

Experience Rating and Workers' Compensation

In practice, however, insurance is not experience rated. In the UK the Employers' Liability (Compulsory Insurance) Act of 1969 makes firms carry approved policies covering injury and disease of employees. But premiums are usually based on average experience in the particular line of business, and are not experience rated (Bartrip, 1987, p. 73). Moreover, the main industrial injury benefit is paid by the state and is not a cost to the employer at all (see below). In the USA there is more emphasis on experience rating, but even there it is mainly the large firms which are experience rated (Ruser, 1985, p. 488).

Workers' Compensation without experience rating breaks the link between a firm's accident experience and its costs. Making Workers' Compensation more generous should therefore cause not only (a) lower compensating wage differentials for industrial accidents, but also (b) higher accident rates since firms' costs are no longer so closely linked to accidents.

There are, admittedly, complicating aspects to the connection between Workers' Compensation and accident rates (Veljanovski, 1982). Imposing liability on employers via Workers' Compensation means that there will be 'adverse selection'. Workers will not be so careful about finding a job where they will face lowest injury losses, since all workers get compensated for injury losses. Similarly, workers will be less careful doing the job, once hired into it – the problem of 'moral hazard'. Both factors will increase costs and reduce employment. It is possible that reduced employment will drive injury rates down, since with fewer workers employed, only the least accident prone need be hired. A further point is that more generous Workers' Compensation will induce more reporting of accidents, even though the true frequency of accidents has not changed (Kniesner and Leeth, 1989).

---

[2] For example, suppose firms have to buy Workers' Compensation insurance costing £y a year per worker. The probability of a fatal accident is p each year, and the pay-out in the event of an accident is £I. Fair insurance requires approximately $y \cong p(1 + a)I$, where a, the insurance 'loading', is small. In other words, with $p \cong \cdot0001$, $I = £1$ million and $a \cong 0$, the premium would be about £100 a year. With rational workers knowing p and I, the compensating wage differential would also have been about £100 a year. Consequently, once there is a Workers' Compensation scheme, wages will fall by £100 (= pI). In terms of Figure 1, the wage locus line would become flatter if workers were reimbursed out of the insurance fund.

These points do not relate to the link between increased Workers' Compensation and lower compensating differentials for dangerous jobs. This link is strong, even though the link between Workers' Compensation and accident rates is not. However, if we see both links established in practice the logical point will receive corroboration: that Workers' Compensation (without experience rating) actually causes accidents.

A *fourth* point can be made in connection with the model in Figure 1. Injury rate R* minimises accident plus accident prevention costs. Therefore forcing a reduction in R by centrally imposing safety standards (noise standards, dust, toxic chemicals) raises costs. The higher-cost firms – for example, small firms – have to exit the industry, and the dangerous sectors, such as construction, contract relative to the safer sectors. The Chief Inspector of Factories has said that 'small companies are gaining an unfair advantage over their competitors' by failing to meet health and safety requirements (TUC, 1985, p. 132). Higher standards might thus have the effect of shutting down the small non-union firms. According to public choice analysis this could be why higher standards are proposed.

However, if the wage locus is 'wrong' because workers are poorly informed, or immobile, then the state might well wish to prevent accidents – though this is not easy, as will be seen. I now consider the wage locus in more detail.

The Wage-Job-Risk Locus

Much research effort has been expended on calculating the slope of the wage opportunity locus. The slope is essentially caused by the different attitudes to risk that people have – either due to their tastes or to their economic circumstances. It will be seen below that poor people can less afford to be choosy, and will ask for lower compensating wage differentials for given risk than richer people. Thus poorer people will tend to take the riskier jobs.

Because people are different, whilst we can compute an average compensating differential for some probability of injury, say R*, from the wage demands of individuals risking that level of injury, we cannot say that this compensating differential will be required by other workers. More risk-averse workers, for example, would require a bigger differential. Workers will 'self-select' into the jobs they prefer, and the wage the *incumbent* of a dangerous job will accept will generally be lower than the wage others not in the job can be prevailed upon to accept.

For example, we might find that a compensating wage differential

Figure 2: Density of Worker Tastes for Injury Risk

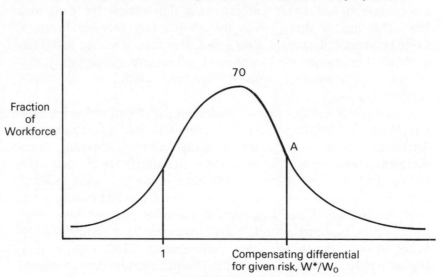

for a given dangerous job is low or even zero. This could mean market failure – lack of worker knowledge or mobility. But it could also mean that there are not many risky jobs relative to the size of the work-force. Figure 2 illustrates a distribution of worker tastes for a given risk of injury, as shown by the compensating differential (actual wage divided by risk-free wage) required. As drawn, some workers are risk lovers, and do not require any differential, but most are risk-averse. If there is a high demand by firms for workers in risky jobs, then a large fraction of the work-force will have to be induced to take up such jobs. The compensating differential would then be high – in a position such as *A*. If the demand for risky jobs fell, *A* would move leftwards, perhaps even to where no differential were offered. But this would not mean that the average person would not require a compensating differential. The important measurement point is that measured compensating wage differentials will provide only a *lower bound* to the true population-compensating wage differential.

Wealth and Risk

We noted above the rôle of poverty in driving people to take risks. On the basis of simple models of consumer behaviour, it seems that wealthier individuals will demand less risky jobs – or a higher premium for undertaking a job of given risk, which is the same thing. In other words, it appears that safety is a good that people demand more of as they grow richer. Thus in Jones-Lee's questionnaire study of the price

186

people would pay for safety improvements in transport, he found that a 10 per cent increase in the respondent's income went with a 3 per cent increase in the amount he would pay for a car safety feature that would reduce his chance of dying in a car accident from 1/10,000 to 1/20,000 (Jones-Lee, 1989, p. 84). Wealthier individuals can afford to forgo earnings in return for a safer job, but poor individuals cannot afford to do so.

There is likely to be a difference between wealth which accrues from non-labour sources and that accruing from labour sources. Non-labour sources are less likely to be affected by a work accident than are labour sources. It seems therefore that an individual with little human capital relative to his physical capital will be less risk-averse. In practice, individuals with high levels of non-labour income might tend to be more carefree since the job risks they take have less affect on their incomes.

Knowledge and Risk

The burning question is whether wages are based on informed worker choice. The answer given is often 'no'. It has even been said that 'people prefer to believe that their work is safe', even if it is not (Akerlof and Dickens, 1982, p. 308). However, it is hard to believe that such wishful thinking – called 'cognitive dissonance' – is widely prevalent.

Nevertheless, the informational task is certainly daunting: individuals must assess non-pecuniary aspects either through reports from fellow workers, or by directly experiencing the job. There is no recognised index for measuring non-pecuniary aspects such as dangers to health. Moreover, many accidents occur so infrequently that the small samples available to workers tell little. Steel erectors in Britain have a 1/2,000 annual chance of a fatal accident, as do shunters; for coal-miners the risk is 1/4,500, similarly for fishermen; fire brigade officers have a 1/7,000 chance. These are the biggest numbers – other occupations have much lower death probabilities, and the mean figure is 1/50,000 (Marin and Psacharopoulos, 1982). Then there are the occupational diseases which take many years to become manifest. There is thus ample room for mistakes in risk assessment.

However, we do not need to assert that workers know everything. They can have imperfect information, learn about job conditions while on the job, and quit if they do not like it. In fact, as Viscusi and O'Connor (1984) have argued, it is sensible in certain conditions for workers to enter jobs about which they have little information, because there is then a pay-off to learning. It is generally possible to leave, but if the experience is favourable one can stay and gain a higher wage. Workers'

187

choice among hazardous jobs is thus 'part of an on-going adaptive process' (1984, p. 948). In experiments with a sample of chemical workers, when they were told that the hazards of their job had gone up due to working with new substances (asbestos, TNT), they demanded higher wage premia, and were more likely to quit (1984, p. 955). People learn about jobs, and change when it suits them.

Viscusi has also used a learning framework to explain Lichtenstein's interesting 1978 study showing people's lack of knowledge about death risks. The study showed, for example, that the average person thinks tornadoes are bigger killers than asthma, even though the latter is 20 times more probable (though still very infrequent at 1/100,000) (Lichtenstein *et al.*, 1978, p. 555). More generally it was found that people systematically *over-estimated* small risks. Note how this finding contradicts the 'cognitive dissonance' view, and carries the implication that people demand *higher* risk premiums than are warranted. According to Viscusi, it is as though people assess infrequent events by starting with a prior assessment based on 'average' risk – which tends to be large. They average this with an assessment of the given event, coming up with a resultant which is above the true risk (Viscusi, 1985, p. 383).

Worker knowledge can be assessed in two ways. The first is direct: ask the people concerned. The problem with the direct approach lies in interpreting the answers – people might not interpret the questions in the same way, they might not try (questionnaire decision-making is costless), and they will not know much about injury risks. The last disadvantage can, however, be an advantage in that it enables statements about what the 'average' member of the public thinks. If a selected, knowledgeable sample were used there would always be the problem that this sample was unrepresentative – steel erectors, for example, are knowledgeable about the risks of their trade, but are presumably less risk-averse than average. Thus there is a place for carefully constructed questionnaire studies (for example, Jones-Lee, 1985). But given the difficulties, economists have traditionally preferred to look at what people do rather than what they say.

The alternative way in which knowledge can be assessed is by looking at what people do. It is termed the method of 'revealed preference', because the compensating wage differentials that people actually demand for different levels of risk reveal their valuations of risk in practice. The question is whether the pattern of compensating wage differentials squares with what is to be expected if workers are knowledgeable. Thus we assess whether there are 'reasonable' compensating differentials, whether these differentials shrink as predicted when

Workers' Compensation is increased, and whether the differentials are smaller for poor than for wealthy workers. Such an assessment is carried out below. To preview the findings, the evidence bears out the view that workers are knowledgeable. In particular, the implied values of a 'statistical life' are high – over £2 million in 1990 prices.

The Role of Trade Unions

We have been assuming that individuals are free to make individual bargains. However, large firms have internal labour markets so that employees can quit only at a cost: they are 'tied' to the firm. It is necessary to be careful here: both parties will foresee the tie, which will give rise to its own compensating differentials – so employees need not be disadvantaged (Siebert and Addison, 1991). Nevertheless, enterprise unions might be helpful in this context by revealing worker preferences to management (Duncan and Stafford, 1980, p. 357). In a large factory, safety is to some extent a public good: all are affected by a given safety policy, and unless there is a collective voice not enough will be done to represent workers' point of view since workers will free-ride on each other's efforts. In addition unions, because of their permanency, might know more about risks than workers.

No one knows how important the above considerations are in practice. One would expect a well-managed firm to be able to set up its own consultative safety committee without the help of a union if this lowered accidents and thus wages enough to make it cost effective.

It is true that unions are in the forefront of moves for legislation on workplace safety. But there could be several reasons for this apart from concern for worker safety *per se*. A safety programme for an industry could be supported because:

o   it would have the effect of driving out the smaller non-union firms (as already noted);

o   it could be a way of increasing full pay (the same pay packet, but less risk than when one first took the job is an increase in full pay);

o   it could be a way of gaining unions more power (as noted below, only a union representative can sit on a company safety committee set up in terms of the Health and Safety at Work Act of 1974).

Perhaps if compensating wage differentials are larger for union members than others, other things equal, it would indicate that unions are better informed about risks than individual workers (Marin and Psacharopoulos, 1982, p. 834). I shall look for this in the next, empirical section.

189

In sum, the problem is to assess whether accidents and other bad job characteristics have costs which are 'internalised' – which workers and employers foresee and for which they contract. The alternative is that bad job characteristics are like pollution – negative externalities imposed on non-consenting parties. Polluters do not have to pay. The question at bottom is whether firms using dangerous industrial processes have to pay.

3. Empirical Evidence on Compensating Differentials

In the previous discussion I showed that if workers were knowledgeable and mobile, the following predictions could be made:

o there should be compensating wage differentials for 'bad' job characteristics;

o compensating wage differentials for a given risk should be lower where Workers' Compensation is higher;

o accidents should increase as Workers' Compensation increases;

o poorer workers should be in the riskier jobs;

o young workers might demand smaller compensating differentials (evidence of misperception?) and unionised workers larger differentials (collective voice?).

Measurement Difficulties

Several measurement problems have to be confronted when testing the predictions. All lead to under-estimation of the compensating wage differential. So we must be wary of studies claiming to have found 'no differential'.

In the first place, *omitted variables*: other things must be held equal when fitting the wage locus. If there are omitted variables, such as ability, which are correlated with risk of death – as when more able individuals take safer jobs – then measurement of the effect of risk on wages will be biased downwards. This is because more able people achieve higher pay, and this pushes levels of pay up in the safer jobs (if richer people choose safer jobs), thus obscuring the effect of safety as such on pay levels. A way of overcoming omitted variables is to follow individuals over time. *Changes* in wages, for a given individual, consequent upon *changes* in accident risk cannot be due to omitted factors such as ability, so long as these themselves are not changing.

A second problem concerns *measurement error*: error in the measurement of accident risk (or other job characteristics) will also make the slope of the wage locus seem flatter than it is. Typically we do not know the actual risks people face, but have to assign them a risk based on their occupation or industry. However, the individuals concerned might not face the average risk in their industry – for example, surface workers in mining are safer than underground workers. If we lump together people who are doing safe work with those who are doing unsafe work, we will obscure the effects of danger on pay.

There are likely to be large errors in measurement of the dangers associated with particular jobs. If we are using accident or death rates by industry, one solution is to use only blue-collar workers, the assumption being that industry accident rates are more typical of manual worker experience. Another approach is to use workers' self-assessment of their working conditions. However, because there is no way of comparing such self-assessments with each other this technique also requires a longitudinal approach, following individuals over time and looking at changes in self-assessed working conditions and corresponding changes in wages.

A third problem is that of *selectivity bias*. As noted above, we can only measure a compensating wage differential based on the experience of people actually doing the job. But people doing the job will have selected themselves – they will be the ones who like doing it (or least dislike doing it). Measured compensating differentials will thus mark a lower bound to the premium that people in other jobs would require to induce them to move.

A way around the selectivity problem is to incorporate the selection process into the estimation of the wage locus. Statistical procedures have been developed (Rosen, 1986, p. 656) which basically revolve around the idea that the smaller the fraction of the population doing a job with particular characteristics, the less representative must be the current compensating differential for the characteristic. The measured differential is then adjusted upwards to show how much people in the population as a whole would need to do that job.

Examples of the above problems and the techniques used to overcome them are shown in the studies in Tables 1, 2 and 3 to which I now turn. Allowing for measurement and other error, do the results bear out the logic of the market outlined earlier?

The Evidence

Table 1 summarises the main findings of statistical studies of compensating wage differentials for risk of death and injury. The evidence bears out Adam Smith's view of the labour market.

Looking at the studies in turn, Olson (1981) finds the risk premium a

TABLE 1
FATAL ACCIDENTS: COMPENSATING DIFFERENTIALS
(Dependent Variable: Log Wage)

Study	Risk Data	Sample, Country Year	Co-efficient on deaths p.a. per 1,000†	Implicit Value of a Life*	Remarks
Olson, 1981	Deaths per 100,000 workers – matched by 3 digit industry	Full time workers, private sector US, 1973	·360	$3·2 to $3·4m ($8m for union, $1·5m for non-union)	Expected cost of workdays lost is $19 p.a.; risk premium is $850 p.a.
Veljanovski, 1981	Fatalities per 100,000 workers by industry	53 Manufacturing industries: UK, 1971		£0·8 to £1·1m (1971 prices) (£4·5m in 1990 prices)	Industry injury rate variable has perverse effect
Marin and Psacharopoulos, 1982	Fatal accident rate in respondent's industry (200 industries)	Male employees UK, 1975	·229	£0·6 to £0·7m (about £2·3m in 1990 prices)	Union premia lower
Dorsey and Walzer, 1983	Non-fatal accident rate in respondent's 3 digit industry	Blue collar employees US 1978	Positive for non-union workers, larger when firm liability controlled	n/a	Obtains insig. results for union workers
Duncan and Holmlund, 1983	Dangerous work self-assessed	Male employees, longitudinal, Sweden, 1968-74	Positive, signif. at 1% level	n/a	When data not entered in change form, result insignificant
Moore and Viscusi, 1983	Fatal accident rate in respondent's 2 digit industry	Non-farm employees, US, 1976	n/a	$6m (1986 prices)	Young workers demand higher premia
Garen, 1988	Deaths per 100,000 workers, matched to respondent's 3 digit industry	Blue collar males, US, 1981/2	·239 (OLS) ·547 (2 stage)	$4 million $9.2m	2 stage procedure makes choice of death depend on income
Brown, 1980	Fatal accident rate in respondent's occupation (zero assumed if occ. not hazardous)	Young males excluding college graduates, longitudinal, US	Insig.	Zero	No death risk premium

*Calculated as how much 1,000 people would pay, per year, for a 1/1,000 reduction in the probability of dying.

†Gives % increase in wage for increase in death risk from 0 to 1/1,000.

worker requires is ·36 of $9,200 (the annual wage) – that is, $3,300 for a 1/1,000 increase in death risk. The implication is that 1,000 people would pay $3·3 million to save one life a year. To look at it in another way, a firm employing 1,000 workers has to pay $3 million extra a year if it increases fatal risks in the factory from 0 to 1/1,000 and therefore kills one more worker a year. We can say that the 'implicit value of a life' – defined in this way – is over $3 million.

The study indicates a higher differential for unionised workers (the implied value of a life is $8 million for union members, $1·5 million for non-union), but this is not a universal finding (*cf.* the Marin and Psacharopoulos (1982) results, for example, which point to lower union differentials). This study also considers wage premia for days lost in non-fatal accidents. In the sample considered, about half a day is lost per person per year in such accidents, corresponding to a cash loss of about $19 (half a day's work at $37 a day). However, the premium actually demanded for this risk averages $850 a year, implying that earnings loss is only a small part of the cost to people of accidents, and that the 'pain and suffering' cost is much greater, as might be expected.

The next two lines give the only British results yet available. Veljanovski (1981) was the first study, using 53 industries as the unit of observation. Average male manual workers' wages were positively correlated with industry fatality rates, holding constant such factors as were measureable at the industry level, such as the average age of the industry's work-force. The implicit value of a life using 1971 data was found to be around £1 million, which is large (over £4 million in today's money). But the co-efficient on the industry injury rate was positive, which does not make sense. Interestingly, there were signs that industry wages were lower the higher were state Industrial Injury benefit pay-outs, which is as expected. However, correlations at the industry level have too many omitted variables to enable a fine test of our market hypotheses.

Marin and Psacharopoulos (1982) is more satisfactory in that they use data on individuals. A value of a life of £600,000 to £700,000 is found using 1974 data (£2 million in today's money). Note that the study finds that compensating wage differentials are apparently lower in unionised industries. However, the authors did not have individual level data on unionisation, and had to attribute to the individual the unionisation rate in his industry. Therefore, perhaps, the union result cannot be taken seriously – though it is repeated in the next study.

Dorsey and Walzer (1983) is significant because it shows how workers demand lower compensating wage differentials for jobs of given risk in States with more generous Workers' Compensation laws than in States with less generous laws. It will be recalled (above, p. 184, n.2) that a Workers' Compensation scheme promising £I will cost about £pI in liability insurance premiums where p is the annual chance of injury. It should also reduce the compensating wage differential by about £pI, if workers are knowledgeable and mobile. The authors find that workers in States with insurance premiums 1 per cent higher do indeed have compensating wage differentials for given injury risk about 1 per cent lower (1983, p. 648).[3]

Effect of Workers' Compensation on Compensating Differentials

The prediction that compensating wage differentials decline as Workers' Compensation increases is thus borne out. Viscusi and Moore (1987) obtain a similar result, using different data. In their sample the average injury risk was 3·8 cases per year per 100 workers – that is, approximately a ·04 annual risk. For every $1 increase in Workers' Compensation, wages should therefore decline by 4 cents (= ·04 x $1). The authors found in practice that increasing Workers' Compensation by $1 implied a wage decrease of between 9 and 18 cents for given injury risk (1987, p. 258). This is again the negative expected relation, but it is too sharp, given the risk rate of ·04. It seems as though employees want more Workers' Compensation – since they are prepared to give up more in wages than the expected benefits of the Compensation. Perhaps the reason more is not provided is the link noted above between Compensation and accidents. Higher insurance might mean more accidents, so insurance needs to be under-provided.

Notice how allowing for Workers' Compensation affects the value of a 'statistical life' as calculated by the revealed preference method. Where there is Workers' Compensation the compensating wage differential demanded by workers will be lower, as we have seen. One cannot therefore infer the value of a statistical life simply from the compensating wage differential in these circumstances. Arnould and Nichols (1983, p. 337) find that the value of a statistical life is 12 per cent higher once Workers' Compensation is properly accounted for.

Duncan and Holmlund (1983) use labour market data for Sweden. Their work is particularly interesting because the data are longitudinal, with individuals followed over time, so omitted variables such as ability do not matter. In addition, the accident risk measure is self-assessed, which gets around the risk measurement problem (i.e. assigning to

---

[3] The result only holds for non-union workers. However, the study has to attribute liability insurance premiums to each worker using the average for his occupation in the given State. In another study using data from 3,000 firms, where liability insurance premiums for each firm were known, the result also holds for union workers (Dorsey, 1983, p. 94).

people an accident risk solely based on their industry). A significant earnings premium in risky jobs is found. The premium disappears if longitudinal data are not used, which shows the importance of such data in minimising measurement and omitted variable errors.

Moore and Viscusi (1988) use detailed accident and Workers' Compensation variables. They not only find that wages respond positively to expected life years lost (probability of death multiplied by respondent's remaining work years), but also negatively to the capital value of the annuity the respondents' dependants would expect to receive in the event of death. Note also that the study gives a *higher* risk premium as being demanded by younger workers. This goes against the accepted wisdom that the young need to be 'protected from themselves'.

Garen (1988) is the only study which does not take death risk as exogenous, but takes into account the fact that poorer people – those with less schooling, and less non-labour income – will take the riskier jobs (see also Table 2 below). As can be seen, when allowance is made for the selectivity effect, the compensating differential is almost doubled to $9·2 million. Clearly, allowance for such selectivity effects is important and should really be included in all compensating differential studies. At any rate, if the imputed value of a life is of the order of $9 million, it can hardly be contended that the market does not generate pretty powerful incentives for work-places to be safe.

Finally, I turn to the study by Brown (1980), which is well known because it finds no premium for death risk. The result is worrying because the author has the advantage of special longitudinal data, enabling him to relate the change in wage of given individuals to the changes in occupation of those same individuals, so by-passing the omitted variables problem. A possible reason is the youth of the sample; wages of young workers are not representative of lifetime wages. The study also excludes college graduates, and is thus confined to poorer individuals. Such individuals can be expected to demand lower differentials, as noted above, so the sample is not representative. Finally, the author has to assume that individuals face accident risks based on the average risk in their industry, and so his accident measure is likely to have problems of mis-measurement.

Studies of Accident Rates

Table 2 summarises some results of studies of accident rates. The Garen study has already supported one aspect of market logic: that wealthier people are more likely to choose safer jobs. This is also borne out in the Viscusi study in the first row. The same effect is suggested using British

TABLE 2

DEPENDENCE OF ACCIDENT RATES ON
WORKERS' COMPENSATION
(Dependent Variable: Accident Rate)

Study	Sample	Remarks
1. Viscusi, 1978	Disabling injuries per million hours by respondents 3 digit industry, 1969	Significant negative relation with respondents' net assets, given education and colour
2. Chelius, 1982	Accident frequency rate, 2 digit industry, 36 states, 1972-5	Positive co-efficient on workers' compensation by state
" "	Days lost per accident, same sample	Negative co-efficient on workers' compensation by state
3. Veljanovski, 1981	Deaths per 100,000 workers per quarter, time series for manufacturing, quarterly, 1959-76	Industrial Injury payments positive, but not significant. Dummy for HSWA significantly negative. Fines increase accident rate
4. Ruser, 1985	Injuries per 100 workers per year, 41 states, 1972-79	Positive co-efficient on workers' compensation by state, co-efficient larger for small firms (whose insurance premiums are not experience rated)
5. Lyttkens, 1988	Accidents per hour, employees compared with self-employed, agriculture, Sweden	Employees have much higher accident rate than self-employed

data by Marin and Psacharopoulos, who find a negative correlation between earnings and accident risk (1982, p. 833).

Table 2 is also relevant to the question of whether better Workers' Compensation for accidents means more accidents. Are firms (and workers) more careless when their accidents are paid for? The famous study by Chelius has found that States with higher Workers' Compensation do indeed have higher injury rates, other things equal, as shown in the second row. There is also an indication that the same thing happens in Britain – see Veljanovski's results in the third row. Admittedly, reporting effects cast a cloud over these results. In other words, people must report more accidents when it pays them to. In a simulation exercise, Kneisner and Leeth (1989, p. 292) find that increasing Workers' Compensation benefit levels raises reported injuries – while actually *reducing* the true injury rate (which seems to prove too much).

Two research results question the importance of over-reporting. First, the study by Ruser (1985), reported on the fourth row, finds that generous Workers' Compensation raises small firms' accident rates more markedly than large. Both types of firm will be subject to reporting effects; the difference between the firms is that large firms are more likely to have insurance premiums that are experience rated. This suggests that it is the rise in Workers' Compensation unaccompanied by a rise in insurance premiums which matters, not reporting effects. Secondly, the Lyttkens study of Swedish farm workers, reported on the last line, is hard to explain in terms of over-reporting. In Sweden, employee farm workers are almost fully compensated for earnings losses due to injuries, but self-employed farm workers are not. Both face the same working conditions and occupational hazards. Yet employees suffer a much higher accident rate. It would be necessary for the self-employed to be reporting only about half their accidents to account for the difference in accident rates simply in terms of reporting (Lyttkens, 1988, p. 184).

Other Types of Compensating Wage Differential

Table 3 summarises the findings on further types of compensating wage differential. In the first row, King (1973/4) shows that wealthier people choose occupations with more variable incomes. This is a puzzle because it contradicts the findings in Table 2, showing that the better-off are attracted to safety. It could be that both the very rich and the poor act as risk lovers, and it is the people in the middle who are risk-averse (this is the Friedman-Savage (1948) utility function).

The Hamermesh (1977) study, in the second row, is interesting because it takes job satisfaction on the dependent variable. If we accept Adam Smith's theorem about the equalisation of the whole of the advantages and disadvantages of jobs, then there should be no systematic differences in job satisfaction. However, Hamermesh's analysis finds that older workers seem more satisfied. Essentially his explanation is that older workers know more about their jobs, while being paid at rates which have to be high to attract in the younger, uncertain workers. Adam Smith's proposition holds on entry into the workplace, but holds less exactly as individuals age.

Next consider the Duncan and Stafford (1980) study. The study is well known because it seems to suggest that part of the union pay differential is in fact a premium for the poor working conditions, in particular repetitive, machine-paced work, which union workers face. Not all the union pay differential is a rent, therefore, but part seems to be a compensating differential for 'alienating' work conditions.

Finally, consider McNabb (1989), the only modern British study of compensating wage differentials for poor working conditions. The study uses the 1975 General Household Survey, giving a large sample of 5,000

TABLE 3

STUDIES OF VARIOUS TYPES OF COMPENSATING DIFFERENTIAL

Study	Sample	Nature of Differential	Remarks
1. King, 1973/4	Professional Workers, 1960	Dispersion of income in respondent's occupation	Positive co-efficient on dispersion; wealthier family background associated with riskier occupation
2. Hamermesh, 1977	White collar employees, 1973	Job satisfaction	Satisfaction higher for older workers, *cet. par.*
3. Duncan & Stafford, 1980	Blue collar employees	Poor work conditions	Positive co-efficients on poor conditions; union wage advantage diminishes when work conditions included
4. Feinberg, 1981/2	Manufacturing employees, longitudinal 1971-76	Income variability	Positive differential for respondents with more variable incomes
5. McNabb, 1989	Manual workers, male UK, 1975	Poor work conditions	Positive co-efficients; no higher for workers in industries with high unionism

men. The important finding is that workers with self-assessed poor working conditions earn 3 to 4 per cent more per hour, holding constant education, experience, trade union coverage, race, marital status, and broad occupational category. The study thus indicates that the market compensates poor working conditions.

Summary

To summarise the empirical side:

o There do seem to be compensating differentials for bad job characteristics. When measured correctly the implicit value of a life could be as high as $9 million in 1986 prices (Jones-Lee gives a figure of £2·2 million in 1987 prices (1989, p. 96)). This means that a firm employing 1,000 workers would have to pay $9 million extra to increase the probability of a fatal accident by 1/1,000.

o Compensating wage differentials appear to decline as Workers' Compensation is increased. This is shown by the fact that compensating differentials for a given accident risk are lower in States with more generous Workers' Compensation. There are even signs that the compensating wage differential decreases by as much as the employer's liability insurance premium increases.

o Accidents do seem to increase as accident compensation increases. This could be merely a reporting effect, but the indications are that it is more than that.

o People with lower income are in the riskier jobs.

o The evidence on whether young workers, or unionised workers, obtain higher or lower compensating wage differentials is mixed.

4. Policy Issues

In all industrialised countries there is extensive state regulation of workplace safety. No country looks to market-established compensating differentials to deter accidents and compensate injured workers – the emphasis is rather upon regulation. In fact, however, we will see that the market is much more important than it seems. I will examine in turn the setting of safety standards, and Workers' Compensation laws.

Safety Standards

In England the first Factory Act, laying down safety standards, dates from 1838. This was also the time when prohibitions on child labour

Regulators and the Market

SAFETY REPRESENTATIVES BY WORKPLACE SIZE

Workplace Size	Private Sector Employment, full-times, 1983[a] %	% with Safety Representatives, 1987[b] %
1 – 10		1
11 – 25	60	6
26 – 50		20
50 – 100		37
101 – 250		69
251 – 500	29	88
501 – 1,000		94
1,000+	11	100
Total	100	9
		(4,715 plants)

Sources: [a] General Household Survey, 1983.   [b] Walters (1990, p. 11).

were introduced.[4] Since then the standards have become steadily more elaborate, with the setting up of the Health and Safety Executive (HSE) in 1974, and a stream of Directives on health and safety from the European Commission. The HSE administers an inspectorate to enforce standards with respect to clean air, noise, and poisons, and is assisted by company safety representatives appointed in terms of the Safety Representatives and Safety Committees Regulations of 1977 (regulations made as a result of the 1974 Health and Safety at Work Act). These latter regulations give trade unions exclusive rights to appoint safety representatives, with whom employers are obliged to consult, provide information, and co-operate in establishing joint safety committees. These safety representatives can be seen as an arm of the HSE, monitoring company compliance with regulations.

However, safety representatives are not much help for workers in small plants. Table 4 shows how safety representatives are much more likely to be found in large plants, even though 60 per cent of private sector workers are employed in small plants – that is, plants with fewer than 100 workers.[5]

---

[4] For a public choice analysis of this policy, see Marvell (1977). Child labour was banned, it seems, as a result of a successful campaign by steam mill-owners to advantage themselves against their competitors, the water mills, which were labour intensive. The prime aim was not the protection of children.

[5] Data on firms would be useful to supplement these data on plants, but are unfortunately not available. In fact, about 40 per cent of the private sector work-force is estimated to work in firms employing fewer than 100 (Siebert and Addison, 1991, Table 1).

It is true that this might change, since in 1989 the EC issued a Directive designed to extend the powers of safety representatives. The Directive requires that countries change their laws so as to require employers to designate a safety representative (not necessarily a trade unionist) who would have to be trained and be immune from victimisation (see Walters, 1990, Appendix 1, for a summary). In practice, however, the safety representative has until now had little impact on the working conditions of most workers.

The uneven distribution of safety representatives, and the paucity of factory inspectors, underline a major difficulty with the setting of standards: they are difficult to enforce – and penalties actually levied are small. A fine of only £1,000 is used by Fenn and Veljanovski in their study, and the expected fine (= actual fine x probability of conviction) is much smaller (1988, p. 1,061).[6] Only so many firms can be visited per year by the inspectors who in any case do not know of the new dangers (standards tend to be out of date – and we have already seen that safety representatives can be of help only in large firms). In addition, inspectors might well be 'captured' by the firms they police.

Fenn and Veljanovski (1988) have put forward a model which disputes the 'capture' view. They note that fines could be low because negotiation rather than prosecution is a cheaper way of bringing about compliance. A fine requires prosecution which takes up more days of an inspector's time than does negotiation. Also costs of compliance with an 'over-inclusive' law might be thought to be too high by inspectors, who will want to use their discretion. The authors show that disciplinary action is indeed less likely in high unemployment areas, where the employment consequences of strictly enforcing the law would be high (1988, p. 1,068). Inspectors are not 'captured'; rather, they are behaving in a way akin to the market, recognising that poor areas, like poor people, can less afford to be choosy. Inspectors are on a knife-edge, it seems, fearing to be too easy on firms, while at the same time mindful of bankrupting them.

Contrast the necessarily crude regulatory effects with the precisely targeted incentives generated by the market's compensating differentials. If market incentives are working well, every dangerous workplace has to pay more, whether or not an inspector knows of the workplace and the danger. Olson (1983, p. 180) calculates that blue-

---

6 Recently ICI was fined £250,000 and ordered to pay £92,000 costs for admitting to contravening safety regulations and causing an accident in which a fireman died, and 93 people were injured. Tate and Lyle has also been fined £250,000 for the death of an employee in a sugar silo (*Financial Times*, 12 April 1990). These figures may seem large, but one accident injured nearly 100 people, and actual fines are much larger than expected fines.

collar workers are paid 14 per cent more per week as a result of the average chances of death and of losing days in an injury. The average expected penalty for violating a safety standard is by comparison small.

Whether it be because inspectors are tentative, or fines small, or – most likely – market forces are overwhelmingly strong, American results indicate that inspections make little difference to safety (see McCaffrey, 1983, p. 137). We can compare the annualised injury rate of firms which were inspected a certain time ago (say, six months) with that of firms currently being inspected. (It is not correct simply to compare inspected with non-inspected firms because the latter will be less hazardous – inspections are triggered by complaints.) If inspections make an impact, those which were inspected six months ago should have lower injury rates. But they do not. The implication is that inspections have little effect.

There are further difficulties associated with the setting of standards. *First*, standards concentrate on inputs (asbestos, noise) to the accident process, rather than outputs – the number of accidents. If accidents themselves can be discovered, and a fine or tax (or compensating wage differential) imposed, accidents are deterred, and at the same time firms have an incentive to find the cheapest way of avoiding them. For example, if the emphasis were on asbestos-related deaths, rather than on asbestos in the air, firms might be able to protect employees just as well with gas masks rather than expensive air-conditioning systems. There could still be a place for standards, but it would rather be in the area of occupational health where it is often difficult to know on whom to place a tax or fine.

Secondly, standards can be expensive to comply with, and disproportionate to the quantity of the danger. For example, the British blue asbestos standard is so rigid that the use of such asbestos is effectively ruled out. Safety measures following the 1988 Piper Alpha oil-rig disaster, in which 167 people were killed, might add 10 to 15 per cent to the cost of oil-rig operations (*Financial Times*, 28 April 1989). The OSHA arsenic standard costs perhaps $70 million a life saved (Viscusi, 1986, p. 129). This is far higher than the values calculated in Table 1.

Thirdly, standards are the outcome of a political lobbying process. Industries often themselves initiate requests for regulation.

'One might suggest that wherever a standard is written by an industry committee, watch out. The examples I think of concern fire water pumps and flammable gas detectors, where altruistic gentlemen framed standards which trampled competitor firms or sectors' (Ashmore, 1990).[7]

---

[7] Dr F. S. Ashmore, Safety and Fire Consultants Ltd., personal communication, 5 March 1990.

US standards for bottles, lawn mowers, fire extinguishers, are also examples (Cornell *et al.*, 1976, p. 493). Safety standards could thus be a way of restricting entry. We have already seen how British trade unions see the small firm as the safety 'culprit' – but it is the small firm which provides non-union competition. Safety might be a 'cover story' for limiting competition.

Workers' Compensation

The movement towards Workers' Compensation began around the turn of the century. Britain led the way in 1897 with the first Workmen's Compensation Act which provided 'no fault' compensation for employees, at the same time as limiting employer liability. The Act was to become a model for US practice (Bartrip, 1987, p. xi). In both countries the common law doctrines of contributory negligence and voluntary assumption of risk made it difficult for workers successfully to sue firms in the courts. It might be noted as well that the causes of occupational diseases are more difficult to pin down than those of industrial accidents, due to the long latency period of disease. Thus the drawing up of a tariff of recognised industrial diseases such as lead poisoning – but excluding lung cancer or heart disease which are not clearly industry related – simplifies proof.

The question arises as to whether compulsory Workers' Compensation should replace market-generated compensating differentials as a means of compensating for (and reducing) accidents. In a way, as we have seen, they come to the same thing. If there were zero transaction costs, the parties would decide whether employees should 'buy their own insurance' (premium = compensating wage differential), or whether employers should provide workers' compensation. The outcome would be that the party which could most cheaply insure would do so – whether or not the courts placed legal liability for accidents on one side or the other. This is the Coase theorem (see Veljanovski, 1982). In practice, as we have seen, there really is replacement: the workers' compensation is not added on to the higher wage in the riskier jobs, but that wage itself declines. The wage decline is pretty much equal to the increase in employers' liability insurance premiums, at least in the USA.

So why have Workers' Compensation laws been such a popular policy? The answer could be the greater apparent certainty of Workers' Compensation. Public opinion does not seem to believe in the practical existence of compensating wage differentials, and can see only the very real difficulty that workers face in proving injury in the courts – 'if no fault could be proved, if the injury appeared to be the result of a pure accident or of some action taken by the worker himself, then the victim had to bear his own losses' (Brown, 1982, p. 1). Public opinion emphasises explicit contracts.

However, the British scheme of compensation for industrial accidents is not simple Workers' Compensation as we have analysed it to this point. The British system, as it has evolved, breaks the link between compensation for an accident, and the workplace in which that accident occurs, and actually *encourages* accidents.

The coming of the welfare state in Britain after the Second World War called into question the philosophy of paying injured workers on a different basis from other people on low incomes. Why specially compensate those who had been injured more than those who are unemployed, or those who are sick? A specific 'injury benefit' was initially retained at a higher level than state grants for unemployment or sickness, but in 1967 this difference was frozen in monetary terms, and consequently has now faded away. Accompanying the change in philosophy, a worker's injury compensation has come to be paid out of taxes, like any other state benefit. It is no longer related to the firm's accident experience. The fact that accidents, unlike sickness, are a consequence of *choice* is ignored.

State Subsidised Injury

At the moment, if a worker suffers an industrial injury, he or she is entitled to Statutory Sick Pay (SSP), paid by the state (currently £53 a week for those earning more than £125, £40 otherwise). Absence due to injury is treated exactly like absence due to any illness. Thus the financial penalty for the firm when it has an accident is reduced. Admittedly, many firms have sick pay schemes which top up the SSP amounts to normal basic rates (56 per cent of private sector employers offer such schemes, and all public sector employers do (Incomes Data Services (IDS), 1989, p. 5). But SSP still acts as a type of subsidy for injuries.

In America, on the other hand, the various state systems function more like proper insurance schemes, with firms paying insurance premiums averaging about 3 per cent of payroll (Dorsey and Walzer, 1983, Table 1), according to their risk rating. These risk ratings are imperfect, but it can be seen that the American system should act as more of a deterrent to accidents than the British. British firms do in fact buy a little insurance against being sued by their workers. But workers do not sue much because of the difficulty of proving fault. British firms' insurance against court claims only comes to about 0·3 to 0·4 per cent of their total labour costs (Department of Employment, 1990, p. 432). The low level of British premiums indicates that firms do not in practice face much chance of being successfully sued by accident victims.

In sum, the British system of compensation for industrial injury does not harmlessly replace *ex ante* compensating wage differentials with *ex post* state compensation. The firm does not pay more if it has more accidents, so more accidents will occur – particularly since workers are compensated (to some extent) for accidents. The system ignores the essential framework of choice within which accident rates are determined, as shown in Figure 1. It is necessary to return to a proper insurance-based scheme, imposing costs on workplaces with accidents, if we wish to harness market incentives to reduce accidents instead of to increase them.

5. Conclusions

In this chapter it has been argued that labour markets are self-regulating. The evidence from a number of statistical studies using official data indicates that wages reflect risk.

If one examines Tables 1, 2 and 3 one cannot help being impressed by the weight of the evidence. It is not so much the mere fact that compensating differentials exist, as that they change in the expected direction when Workers' Compensation laws become more generous. Moreover, once we make more careful measurements – controlling for an individual's ability, allowing for sample selectivity bias – the compensating wage differential becomes substantial. A sum of several millions is hardly insignificant.

Compensating wage differentials are important because they are the way in which the market itself deters accidents and rewards risk-bearing. Such differentials are precisely targeted. They are policed by the worker concerned, and by the firm (and the firm's insurance company). This form of deterrence does not depend upon an outside agency which might not know of the risk. It applies in small firms without union safety representatives as well as large firms. Moreover, the deterrent effect is considerable – hundreds of times greater than the expected penalty for violating a safety standard.

What the research therefore suggests is that market incentives to safety are so strong that we do not depend much upon government regulation for deterring accidents. This is why regulations – for example, the new Regulations on Noise at Work, and the Control of Substances Hazardous to Health – cause little difficulty in industry. But it need not be like this, and overly expensive safety regulations are always possible – beware of the Action Programme on workplace safety put forward by the European Commission. Instead of more regulations, a definite safety improvement would be achieved by linking industrial injury pay-outs to firms' accident experience via an insurance scheme, so harnessing market incentives.

REFERENCES

Addison, J. T., and W. S. Siebert (1991): 'The European Community Charter of the Fundamental Social Rights of Workers: Evolution and Controversy', *Industrial and Labor Relations Review*, pp. 597-625.

Akerlof, G., and W. Dickens (1982): 'The economic consequences of cognitive dissonance', *American Economic Review*, pp. 307-19.

Arnould, R., and L. Nichols (1983): 'Wage-risk premiums and Workers' Compensation', *Journal of Political Economy*, pp. 332-40.

Bartrip, P. (1987): *Workmen's Compensation in the Twentieth Century*, Aldershot: Avebury.

Brown, C. (1980): 'Equalizing differences in the labor market', *Quarterly Journal of Economics*, pp. 11-34.

Brown, J. (1982): *Industrial Injuries*, London: Policy Studies Institute.

Chelius, J. (1982): 'The influence of workers' compensation on safety incentives', *Industrial and Labour Relations Review*, pp. 235-42.

Commission of the European Communities (1989): *Action Programme Relating to the Implementation of the Community Social Charter of Basic Social Rights of Workers*, Brussels, COM (89)569 final.

Cornell, J., R. Noll, and B. Weingast (1976): 'Safety regulations', in H. Owen and C. Schultze, *Setting National Priorities*, Washington: Brookings Institution, pp. 457-504.

Department of Employment (1990): 'Survey of Labour Costs, 1988', *Employment Gazette*, September.

Dorsey, S. (1983): 'Employment hazards and fringe benefits: further tests of compensating differentials', in J. Worral (ed.), *Safety and the Workforce*, Cornell: ILR Press.

Dorsey, S., and N. Walzer (1983): 'Workers' compensation, job hazards and wages', *Industrial and Labour Relations Review*, pp. 642-54.

Duncan, G., and B. Holmlund (1983): 'Was Adam Smith right after all?:

Another test of the theory of compensating wage differentials', *Journal of Labour Economics*, pp. 366-77.

Duncan, G., and F. Stafford (1980): 'Do union members receive compensating differentials?', *American Economic Review*, pp. 355-71.

Eberlie, R. F. (1990): 'The New Health and Safety Legislation of the European Community', *Industrial Law Journal*, Vol. 19 (2), June, pp. 81-97.

Fenn, P., and C. Veljanovski (1988): 'A positive theory of regulatory enforcement', *Economic Journal*, pp. 1,055-70.

Friedman, M., and L. J. Savage (1948): 'The Utility Analysis of Choices Involving Risk', *Journal of Political Economy*, Vol. 56, August.

Garen, J. (1988): 'Compensating wage differentials and the endogeneity of job riskiness', *Review of Economics and Statistics*, pp. 9-16.

Hamermesh, D. (1977): 'Economic aspects of job satisfaction', in O. Ashenfeller and W. Oates (eds.), *Essays in Labor Market Analysis*, New York: John Wiley.

Hicks, J. (1932): *Theory of Wages*, London: Macmillan, 2nd edn. 1963.

Incomes Data Services (1989): *Sick Pay Schemes*, London: Incomes Data Services.

Jones-Lee, M. (1989): *The Economics of Safety and Physical Risk*, Oxford: Basil Blackwell.

Jones-Lee, M., M. Hammerton and P. Philips (1985): 'The value of safety: results of a national sample survey', *Economic Journal*, pp. 49-72.

King, A. (1973/4): 'Occupational choice, risk aversion, and wealth', *Industrial and Labour Relations Review*, pp. 586-96.

Kniesner, T., and J. Leeth (1989): 'Separating the reporting effects from the injury rate effects of Workers' Compensation insurance: a hedonic simulation', *Industrial and Labour Relations Review*, pp. 280-89.

Lichtenstein, S., P. Slovic, B. Fischoff, M. Layman and B. Combs (1978): 'Judged frequency of lethal events', *Journal of Experimental Psychology*, pp. 551-78.

Lyttkens, C. (1988): 'Workers' compensation and employees' safety incentives', *International Review of Law and Economics*, pp. 181-85.

Marin, A., and G. Psacharopoulos (1982): 'The reward for risk in the

207

labor market: evidence from the United Kingdom and a reconciliation with other studies', *Journal of Political Economy*, pp. 827-53.

Marvell, H. (1977): 'Factory regulation: a reinterpretation of early English experience', *Journal of Law and Economics*, pp. 379-402.

McCaffrey, D. (1983): 'An assessment of OSHA's recent effects on injury rates', *Journal of Human Resources*, pp. 131-46.

McNabb, R. (1989): 'Compensating wage differentials: some evidence for Britain', *Oxford Economic Papers*, pp. 327-38.

Moore, M., and W. Viscusi (1988): 'The quantity adjusted value of life', *Economic Inquiry*, pp. 369-88.

Olson, C. (1981): 'An analysis of wage differentials received by workers on dangerous jobs', *Journal of Human Resources*, pp. 165-85.

Rosen, S. (1986): 'The theory of equalising differences', in O. Ashenfeller and R. Layard (eds.), *Handbook of Labor Economics*, Amsterdam: North Holland.

Ruser, J. (1985): 'Workers' compensation insurance, experience rating and occupational injuries', *Rand Journal of Economics*, pp. 487-96.

Siebert, W. S., and J. T. Addison (1991): 'Internal Labour Markets: Causes and Consequences', *Oxford Review of Economic Policy*, Spring, pp. 16-72.

Smith, A. (1776): *Wealth of Nations*, Chicago: University of Chicago Press (Cannan Edition, 1976).

Trades Union Congress (1985): *Report of the Annual Conference*, London: TUC.

Veljanovski, C. (1981): 'Regulating Industrial Accidents: An Economic Analysis of Market and Legal Responses', D. Phil, Oxford.

Veljanovski, C. (1982): 'Employment and safety effects of employers' liability', *Scottish Journal of Political Economy*, pp. 256-71.

Veljanovski, C. (1990): *The Economics of Law: An Introductory Text*, Hobart Paper No. 114, London: Institute of Economic Affairs.

Viscusi, W. (1985): 'Are individuals Bayesian decision-makers?', *American Economic Review*, Papers and Proceedings, pp. 381-85.

Viscusi, W., and C. O'Connor (1984): 'Responses to chemical labelling: are workers Bayesian decision-makers?', *American Economic Review*, pp. 942-56.

Viscusi, W., and M. Moore (1987): 'Workers' compensation: wage effects, benefit inadequacies, and the value of health losses', *Review of Economics and Statistics*, pp. 249-61.

Walters, D. R. (1990): *Worker Participation in Health and Safety*, London: Institute of Employment Rights.

15

FRANCHISING, NATURAL MONOPOLY, AND PRIVATISATION

Antony W. Dnes

*Virginia Polytechnic Institute and
State University, Blacksburg, Virginia*

1. Introduction

NATURAL MONOPOLY arises where a product or group of products can be produced most cheaply by one large firm. The industries believed to be affected by such cost conditions are mainly utilities like telecommunications, electricity and water, and transport industries like railways. Usually, the cost of duplicating some facilities is avoided if there is just one firm. Natural monopoly raises the issue of organising an industry so as to gain the potential efficiency advantage of production by a single firm without creating the conditions for monopolistic conduct or losing incentives for management control of costs.

The franchise solution to problems of natural monopoly, first suggested by Chadwick and promoted by Demsetz, avoids certain pitfalls connected either with traditional regulation of such industries or with their nationalisation. A Chadwick-Demsetz auction requires producers to bid for the right to offer the service in terms of the price they will charge customers for a particular quantity and quality of products. Competition for the field then ensures that these prices to customers are minimised subject to the franchisee covering his costs. In this paper I assess whether franchising can be an alternative to regulating or nationalising natural monopolies.

To help us analyse the franchising of natural monopoly, we must briefly consider some problems associated with more traditional methods of its organisation. One traditional solution is for the state to nationalise the natural monopoly. This is how telecommunications, gas, electricity and water were supplied in the UK before the 1980s. In principle, the nationalised industry can be ordered to refrain from monopolistic conduct. Disenchantment with nationalisation is now widespread in the UK, where such industries developed a reputation for inefficiency and problems of control.[1] This inefficiency more than offsets any allocative advantage which might be claimed in the case of a natural monopoly for a public enterprise operating under conditions of decreasing cost (here the advantage claimed is that marginal-cost pricing leads to efficient allocation even though it causes the enterprise to make a loss which no private firm could bear). Among the utilities, the Government has privatised telecommunications, gas, water, and electricity. It is doubtful whether natural monopolies like railway travel will remain nationalised.

US Solution to Natural Monopoly

Another traditional solution to natural monopoly leaves such industries in private hands with the state regulating against monopoly abuses. This model has been followed in the USA, where rate-of-return regulation has been applied to utilities in the hope of encouraging monopolists not to increase profits by reducing output. In the USA, there is little nationalised industry, the best-known example being the Post Office; although some regulated industries have a mixed ownership form as in electricity supply.

In the UK, the Government has subjected newly privatised companies to regulation. It would be unfair to describe this as moving in the direction of US methods as the system differs in attempting to avoid some of the pitfalls of rate-of-return regulation. In the USA, regulation is thought to have distorted incentives for cost efficiency as firms may try to increase the capital base upon which a rate of return is calculated so as to increase absolute profits (the Averch-Johnson effect).[2] British regulation places limits on prices that may be charged (price capping); the principle was first suggested for telecommunications, was subsequently extended to gas and water, and is also being used for

---

[1] *Cf.* Richard Pryke, 'The Comparative Performance of Public and Private Enterprise', *Fiscal Studies*, Vol. 3, 1982, pp. 68-81, and Stephen Littlechild, 'Problems of Controlling State Enterprise', in *State Enterprise and Deregulation*, Special Study No. 5, Centre of Policy Studies, Monash University, Melbourne, 1983.

[2] Harvey Averch and Leland L. Johnson, 'Behavior of the Firm under Regulatory Constraint', *American Economic Review*, Vol. 52, 1962, pp. 1,052-69.

electricity. The idea is that cost savings may still work to the benefit of the regulated firm and will be encouraged. Price capping is based on the RPI minus X system in the UK. As applied to British Telecom, an index of prices for trunk calls, local calls, business equipment, line rental, domestic rentals and connections must remain 4·5 per cent below the annual change in the Retail Prices Index.

Vulnerability of the Regulator to 'Capture'

However, all regulatory régimes may be vulnerable to capture by organised interest groups, particularly by those whom the regulation seeks to control.[3] The British régimes for telecommunications and gas were set up in consultation with the managements of the previously existing nationalised industries and with an eye on the proceeds from the sale of shares to the public. It is intended that consultation will continue over future regulation of prices. This will encourage the companies to devote resources to influencing the regulatory outcome. There is a very serious problem if regulators start to choose X in the RPI-X formula with a rate of return in mind; for then price capping converges on rate-of-return regulation.[4]

We show that a franchising scheme has real advantages compared with nationalisation and traditional regulation. We also consider below whether natural monopolies could be simply privatised with no use of franchising, but conclude against this solution. However, no analysis of franchising could fail to notice certain problems with the method. Authors have expressed concern over the likely complexity of contracts designed for dealings between the winner of a Chadwick-Demsetz auction and the auctioning body, over the need to establish parity between competing firms, and over the repercussions of long-lived investments when franchise contracts may be shorter lived. We argue that such pessimism is not justified. However, it is vital to design franchise contracts in relation to these problems.

2. Some Principles

The Demsetz/Chadwick Analysis

Basing his analysis on the much earlier work of Chadwick, Demsetz questions the necessity for regulation (or nationalisation) of natural

---

[3] G. Stigler, 'The Theory of Economic Regulation', *Bell Journal of Economics*, Vol. 2, 1971, pp. 3-21.

[4] See Michael E. Beesley and Bruce Laidlaw, *The Future of Telecommunications*, Research Monograph 42, London: IEA, 1989, and John Burton, 'Privatisation: the Thatcher Case', *Managerial and Decision Economics*, Vol. 8, 1987, pp. 21-29, for analyses of capture. Stephen Littlechild recognises the convergence problem in 'Economic Regulation of Privatised Water Authorities and Some Further Reflections', *Oxford Review of Economic Policy*, Vol. 4, No. 2, pp. 40-60, but does not believe this has happened.

monopolies.[5] Demsetz quotes the following textbook account of natural monopoly before showing that it is based on poor logic:

> 'If a product is produced under [decreasing] cost conditions such that larger rates ... mean lower average costs per unit ... only one firm could survive; if there were two ... one could expand to reduce costs and ... thereby eliminate the other. ... But if there is only one, that incumbent ... may be able to set prices above free entry costs for a long time.'[6]

This line of reasoning traditionally led to the conclusion that regulation or nationalisation of the industry would be required to control such monopoly abuse. Demsetz regards the traditional view as a special case of the argument that there is a connection between the number of firms in an industry and their conduct. In fact, there is no necessary connection of this sort as the threat of entry and potential competition will ensure that a firm does not adopt monopoly pricing. According to Demsetz:

> 'The theory of natural monopoly is deficient for it fails to reveal the logical steps that carry it from scale economies in production to monopoly price in the market-place.'[7]

Attempting to provide these steps by no means supports traditional conclusions.

Under the assumptions that inputs may be bought in competitive markets and that the costs of firms colluding are prohibitively high, Demsetz shows that potential competition leads a firm to price output well below the monopoly price (these assumptions are required for most economic theory). There would be many rivals ready to enter into sales contracts with buyers, with the firm offering the best terms obtaining patronage. In a natural monopoly this will lead to production by a single firm: but the natural monopolist finds his pricing constrained by the availability of other would-be suppliers. To beat off his rivals the natural monopolist is driven to price at average cost, which is the policy just enabling him to cover costs. Marginal-cost pricing would lead to losses as decreasing average cost means that marginal cost is below average cost. Nevertheless, average-cost prices are a much better result than the much higher monopoly prices that traditional theory predicts.

Demsetz's analysis is based upon Chadwick's distinction between competition 'within the field' and 'competition for the field'. Where

---

5 Harold Demsetz, 'Why Regulate Utilities?', *Journal of Law and Economics*, Vol. 11, 1968, pp. 55-65. The earlier work is Edwin Chadwick, 'Results of Different Principles of Legislation in Europe: of Competition for the Field as Compared with Competition within the Field of Service', *Journal of the Royal Statistical Society*, Series A22, 1859, pp. 381-420.

6 Armen Alchian and William R. Allen, *University Economics*, Belmont, Ca.: Wadsworth, 1964, p. 412.

7 Demsetz, *op. cit.*, p. 56.

competition is not possible within an industry, competition for the right to be the natural monopolist may be an adequate substitute. Demsetz gives some illustration of his principle of rivalry in which the authorities award a franchise to a producer offering the lowest price for a given quality and quantity of product. More generally, he argues that much natural monopoly would arrive at the same result if simply left alone by government. In this last respect, Demsetz is a forerunner of later contestability analysis.

Contestable Natural Monopoly

A market is said to be contestable if it is vulnerable to hit-and-run entry by firms seeking profits.[8] The principal requirement for this is that entry into and exit from the industry should be free. In particular, there should be no sunk costs attached to operation in the industry. Sunk costs are outlays that could never be recouped if a firm left an industry, such as expenditure on industry-specific training for a workforce. Sunk costs must be distinguished from fixed costs, which simply do not vary with output. Thus, an aeroplane operating a route has a fixed cost of purchase that does not vary with the number of passengers carried; but it is not a sunk investment as it could be moved to another route at near-zero cost. Sunk costs impose a penalty on a firm if it leaves an industry. Clearly, other devices such as entry restrictions imposed by governments in industries like telecommunications also cause problems. However, contestability analysis emphasises sunk costs as the major deterrent to entry. Perfect competition, as expounded in elementary economics textbooks, is a special case of perfect contestability. But, the classic results of perfect competition, which give marginal-cost pricing, zero pure profits, and allocative efficiency, may be extended to industry structures with fewer firms. Given the threat of free entry, any profits above a normal return on investment will attract entrants causing adjustments among profit-maximising firms that lead to the competitive result.

Monopoly is 'sustainable' in contestability analysis only if it is natural. However, natural monopoly must be carefully defined. A single-product industry may be a natural monopoly as a result of decreasing cost, as it is normally treated in elementary textbooks. It may also be one where costs are not decreasing but where a one-firm industry has absolute cost advantages over two or more firms: utility companies faced with the full costs of establishing a distribution network would yield a lower industry

---

[8] Contestability is comprehensively explained in William J. Baumol, John Panzer and Robert D. Willig, *Contestable Markets and the Theory of Industrial Structure*, New York: Harcourt Brace Jovanovich, 1982.

cost function if they were to merge, even though average operating costs might be constant as output varies. When a multi-product industry is considered, a firm may enjoy economies of scope as well as economies of scale or absolute cost advantages. Economies of scope arise when it is cheaper to produce products together than separately. Natural monopoly may then derive from any of these three sources.[9]

If a contestable market is characterised by natural monopoly, then production by a single firm can be sustained due to inherent cost advantages, notwithstanding freedom of entry. However, the natural monopolist must charge no more than the lowest prices that allow him to cover costs or he may lose sales to an entrant. These 'Ramsey prices' maximise consumer welfare subject to the firm making a normal return on investment; in the case of a single-product, decreasing-cost industry, average-cost pricing is Ramsey optimal. There is no rôle for active public policy towards contestable natural monopolies. In considering the legal monopoly usually conferred on nationalised industries, Baumol comments:

> 'If the state enterprise is operated efficiently and the monopoly is indeed natural, then such prohibitions are redundant . . . The entrants will not long survive.'[10]

Baumol goes on to speculate that the legal monopoly will in fact cause problems with the efficiency of the operation by removing the threat of competition for the field.

Is Franchising Required?

Is there a case for active policy towards natural monopoly? If industries like telecommunications could be shown to be reasonably contestable, then they might simply be privatised with no regulatory framework and without any special franchising scheme. I shall argue that ideas of contestability analysis are of limited value in dealing with natural monopoly.

Demsetz's argument that rivalry prevents monopolistic behaviour depends upon the absence of incentives for collusion among firms. In general, one could not exclude the possibility of collusion. Demsetz is of course correct to answer that all textbook theories of competition assume no collusion. However, such an assumption may not take us far in considering public policy towards industry. A deliberate system of

---

[9] The interested reader is referred to Gavin C. Reid, *Theories of Industrial Organization*, Oxford: Blackwell, 1987.

[10] William J. Baumol, 'Natural Monopoly and Contestable Market Analysis', in *State Enterprise and Deregulation, op. cit.*, p. 16.

franchising a natural monopoly may be able to devise means to hinder collusion. Demsetz's analysis of natural monopoly is in any case compatible with deliberate franchising; indeed, it has often been interpreted in that way.

Baumol has written that he does not believe any industries are characterised by perfect contestability.

'No one who has written on the subject believes it to be an all-pervasive attribute of industries in reality. On the contrary, . . . no industry is perfectly contestable.'[11]

As a consequence, perfect contestability becomes something of an ideal standard rather than a piece of predictive economics. It then becomes relevant to consider means for improving the contestability of industries. The analysis serves as a guide to what might be achieved with careful design of economic institutions, and rules out such things as legislated monopoly. Natural monopolies are often seen as having large sunk investments attached to them, which immediately violates the requirements for contestability. An advantage of franchising is that it enables competition for the field to occur before sunk investments have to be made.

Problems of Contract Specification

If a franchise system for natural monopoly is to be successful, much depends upon contract design. This point cannot be over-emphasised. Posner has argued that the major problems of contract design concern adaptation to changing circumstances and the transfer of long-lived assets between different franchisees.[12] He suggests that long-term contracts are unlikely to cope adequately with uncertainty and that the use of recurrent short-term contracts is better. If there are errors in specifying contracts, the franchising agency can simply correct matters at the next franchising round. However, short contracts give rise to a problem: many assets are likely to be longer lived than the franchise contract. The incumbent franchisee may be able to outbid any rival who would have to build a plant from scratch. How do we then ensure parity among bidders at the renewal stage for the contract?[13] This may be important to gain the continuing benefit of competition for the field. Posner believes that the problem can be overcome by stipulating in the contract the terms under which assets must be

---

11 Baumol, *ibid.*, p. 5.

12 Richard A. Posner, 'The Appropriate Scope of Regulation in the Cable Television Industry', *Bell Journal of Economics and Management Science*, Vol. 3, 1972, pp. 98-129.

13 This matter is also raised by Alan T. Peacock and Charles K. Rowley, 'Welfare Economics and the Public Regulation of Natural Monopoly', *Journal of Public Economics*, Vol. 1, 1972, pp. 227-44.

transferred to a successor company, although it should be borne in mind that investment may be deterred if the contract creates uncertainty.

Williamson argues that Posner takes 'too sanguine' a view of problems of asset transfer.[14] Williamson believes that the original cost of assets can be manipulated to a would-be entrant's disadvantage (if an incumbent were corruptly to arrange false costs with suppliers, for example). In addition, human capital is very difficult to transfer. If it is costly to replace experienced managers or workers, then the incumbent franchisee may be able to block a franchise re-assignment. An entrant may know that it is disadvantaged but may lack precise data on which it could try to attract the right workers. In contrast, the incumbent may have all sorts of informal understandings that assist in this endeavour.

A further problem with asset transfer is the possibility that a successor franchisee might try to purchase assets at their value in the next-best non-franchised use. Assets will often reflect sunk investment, in that a part of any outstanding value is specific to the franchised use. Thus a franchisee losing his franchise may be vulnerable to attempts to purchase his assets at knock-down prices. We might add that an unscrupulous franchising authority might also use asset specificity as a lever to force down returns to the franchisee once a contract had been agreed: for example, the authority could claim that costs had changed and that failure to revise prices downwards broke some part of the contract giving grounds for termination. These hold-up possibilities reflect opportunism and may make franchisees reluctant to invest in franchise-specific assets, when these in fact offer cost advantages. Opportunism refers to the human tendency to exercise guile and to be self-seeking.[15]

Williamson also considers the use of long-term contracts, which might avoid some of the problems caused by contracting periods that are shorter than the life of most franchise-specific assets. However, these also face execution problems. Litigation costs and the probable reluctance of franchising authorities to admit errors may discourage efforts to displace an unsatisfactory franchisee. Latitude over contract performance is certain to be granted to franchisees because of the infeasibility of contracting for every eventuality. Franchisees will be expected to adhere to the spirit of any agreement. This implies a need for a monitoring apparatus.

With longer-term contracts, there may be greater incentive for

---

[14] Oliver E. Williamson, 'Franchise Bidding for Natural Monopolies: in General and with Respect to CATV', *Bell Journal of Economics and Management Science*, Vol. 7, 1976, pp. 73-104.

[15] Oliver E. Williamson, *The Economic Institutions of Capitalism*, New York: Academic Free Press, 1985, p. 64.

adventurous bids by would-be franchisees. The temptation is to bid a high service quality at a low price and then, once a contract is written, to try and renegotiate. Such post-contract opportunism would rely on the disruption costs faced by the franchise agency: to avoid these the agency might renegotiate to improve the returns to the franchisee. It is not enough to argue that the contract is enforceable in the courts. The commercial world is full of cases in which claims that costs have changed are used as the basis of price renegotiation subject to an implied threat that otherwise the supplier will fail.

Williamson concludes pessimistically that the problems of Chadwick-Demsetz franchising are severe, and concern details of the contracts. A 'fundamental transformation' applies in which a highly competitive pre-contract situation is turned into one of limited competition thereafter; the threat of franchise loss may not be as great a discipline on incumbent franchisees as Demsetz and Chadwick argued. Williamson also notes that efforts to strengthen continuing potential competition may cause franchising to converge on regulation solutions to natural-monopoly problems.[16] I argue below that Williamson is too pessimistic.

The Costs and Benefits of Franchising Natural Monopoly

Compared with regulation, franchising of natural monopoly should avoid problems of regulatory capture. Franchise contracts would be awarded for a period of time during which there would be no scope for altering their general terms. At renewal times, competing companies would have every incentive to advertise their suitability to become the franchisee. This should not be misinterpreted, however, as the provision of information is a valuable activity. As long as the terms of the franchise award are clearly specified to avoid excessive discretion on the part of the franchise-awarding body, there should be no incentive for would-be franchisees to go beyond informative advertising in their efforts to secure a franchise.

Compared with nationalisation, franchising reduces the scope for political interference in the management of the natural monopoly. There would be no scope for *ad hoc* intervention of the kind practised by UK governments in, for instance, requiring the CEGB to buy British coal regardless of its competitiveness. To be fair, it would be possible for franchise contracts to contain details protecting some cherished aspiration: for example, requirements for nuclear generation could be written into power franchises. Also, some regulatory interference could

---

16 See also Victor P.Goldberg, 'Regulation and Administered Contracts', *Bell Journal of Economics*, Vol. 7, 1976, pp. 426-48.

occur as issues arise that are not covered in the contract. However, any dilution of economic efficiency is placed clearly into the open. Such policies may then be more easily resisted by the consumers whose interests are harmed.

Assuming franchise contracts that specify maximum prices for set qualities of goods or services, the cost efficiency of the natural monopoly is encouraged compared with nationalisation or rate-of-return regulation. We should remember that price capping, as in the RPI-X system, may be reduced down to rate-of-return regulation when X is renegotiable. A franchise contract will encourage cost efficiency as all cost savings accrue to the franchisee during the life of the contract. Similarly, all gains from developing new business opportunities accrue to the franchisee. Adaptation to a changing environment is therefore also encouraged. Competition for the field ensures prices are as low as possible whilst allowing the franchisee to cover his costs (including a normal return on investment). Such prices have already been described as Ramsey optimal. Franchising can achieve optimal pricing even when sunk costs rule out contestability, as competition for the field occurs before firms commit themselves to investment programmes.

3. Some Experience

In this section, we consider some areas of practical experience with franchising. Unfortunately, there is only limited experience with franchising natural monopoly and this is restricted mainly to historical attempts at municipal franchising. However, there is well-documented experience of franchising local cable-television networks in the USA. This is worth analysing as issues of contract design are similar even though cable may lack natural-monopoly characteristics: falling costs of cable provision and the growth of competing transmission media like direct-satellite broadcasting would produce competition over the provision of entertainment in an unregulated environment. Local authorities in the USA have created artificial cable monopolies for control and revenue-raising reasons. Nevertheless, this experience is interesting because of the contractual issues it has raised.

I also examine some examples of municipal franchising.[17]

---

[17] It would be possible to consider further areas of experience with franchising. Companies like Cable and Wireless are subject to franchise contracts on their overseas operations. Commercial franchising yields some transferable lessons. Defence contractors enter into near-franchise arrangements with governments. However, our examples are sufficient to draw out the main issues.

Cable Television

Williamson analyses the experience of the City of Oakland in franchising community antenna television (CATV) services, otherwise known as cable television, beginning in 1969.[18] Interestingly, the franchise was non-exclusive. A franchise fee of 8 per cent of annual turnover was to be paid to the City, subject to a minimum payment of $125,000. An automatic fine of $750 per day would be incurred by a franchisee whose promised establishment of programmes was delayed. The City could terminate a franchise contract for good cause with 30-days notice and a public hearing. In disputes between the City and a franchisee, the City Manager was authorised to act as adjudicator. The City could acquire the CATV system at its renewal cost in the event of a termination (or voluntary exit) during the 15-year franchise term.

By 1970, bids had been made for the provision of CATV services. The lowest bid came from Focus Cable Inc., which was duly appointed as franchisee. Construction of the system was due to be completed by the end of 1973. However, this did not go as well as planned and, furthermore, subscriptions to Focus were fewer whilst construction costs appeared higher than anticipated. Focus pressed for a revision of terms. It is possible that Focus had put in an adventurous bid, as its bid had been around one-half of that of its nearest rival.

The City had the problem of whether to quote the original contract or to revise its terms. Revision was chosen, even though the City disputed many of Focus's claims over escalated costs and attributed problems to poor management. The City was against public ownership of the system, for 'philosophical and financial reasons'.[19] It believed that a replacement franchisee would be unlikely to offer more than a minimal CATV system. Legal action against Focus was considered too costly. Eventually, the City agreed to Focus reducing its scale of operations, lowered the penalty rate from $750 to $250 for delays up until mid-1974, approved a lengthened construction schedule, but increased the minimum franchise fee by $25,000. Williamson regards the renegotiation practised by Focus as a case of post-contract opportunism, as do some other commentators on the case.[20] However, the facts are also consistent with ignorant bidding, where Focus may have genuinely

---

[18] Oliver E. Williamson, 'Franchise Bidding for Natural Monopolies', *op. cit.* Detailed material on the cable-television industry both in the USA and UK is contained in Cento G. Veljanovski and William D. Bishop, *Choice by Cable – the Economics of a New Era in Television*, Hobart Paper 96, London: IEA, 1983.

[19] Williamson, 'Franchise Bidding for Natural Monopolies', *op. cit.*, p. 96.

[20] Williamson, *ibid.*, pp. 92-103. See also Veljanovski and Bishop, *op. cit.*, p. 88, and Richard Schmalensee, *The Control of Natural Monopoly*, Lexington, Ill.: D.C. Heath and Co., 1979, p. 73.

misjudged costs. In the latter case, the subsequent moves would reflect efficient adjustment of the contract to new information as it became available.

Efficiency of Franchise Bidding in Cable TV

In a recent systematic study of cable television, Mark Zupan uses survey results and statistical methods to show that early pessimism over franchising is not justified.[21] The study reports the results of a survey of 66 cable systems and draws on other work using samples of up to 216 systems, all in the USA. This moves us away from observations based solely on an individual case study. An initial observation is that most franchising exercises generate a sufficient number of bidders to sustain competition. In one study upon which Zupan draws, the average number of applicants was found to be 5·2.[22] Zupan's statistical results then show that the number of bidders significantly reduces cable prices, supporting the claim that organised potential competition constrains monopoly practices.[23] Zupan also analyses the question of whether opportunism undermines cable franchising, noting as we have that Williamson's example of renegotiation is consistent with honest mistakes. By careful examination of the trade press, he could find fewer than 60 cases of operator reneging relative to over 3,000 systems franchised between 1980 and 1986. Using further statistical analysis, Zupan shows that opportunism is controlled by the operator's wish to maintain a good reputation in future dealings or in other contractual relations.[24]

In the UK, government policy is to franchise cable television stations.[25] However, Chadwick-Demsetz methods are not adopted. Instead, the Cable Authority (CA) has awarded 134 franchises on the basis of factors like the perceived ability of a company to offer a set programme schedule. The authorities have exercised much discretion and have not sought the lowest-cost supplier of a set output mix. The Government intends to auction cable franchises to the highest bidder after 1992.[26] This

---

[21] Mark Zupan, 'The Efficiency of Franchise Bidding Schemes in the Case of Cable Television: Some Systematic Evidence', *Journal of Law and Economics*, Vol. 32, 1989, pp. 401-56.

[22] Robin Prager, *Firm Behavior in Franchise Monopoly Markets*, Ph.D Dissertation, Massachusetts Institute of Technology, 1986.

[23] Zupan, *op. cit.*, p. 416.   [24] Zupan, *ibid.*, p. 435.

[25] *Cf.* Cento Veljanovski, 'Cable Television: Agency Franchising and Economics', in R. Baldwin and C. McCruddin (eds.), *Regulation and Public Law*, London: Weidenfeld and Nicolson, 1987, and Michael Waterson, 'Issues in the Regulation of Cable TV', *International Journal of Law and Economics*, Vol. 4, 1984, pp. 67-82.

[26] Home Office, *Broadcasting in the 90s: Competition, Choice and Quality – the Government's Plans for Broadcasting Legislation*, Cm. 517, London: HMSO, 1988. A similar auction system is proposed for all commercial TV, whether based on cable, microwave, direct satellite, or terrestrial (UHF) broadcasting methods.

proposal should select the most cost-efficient firm prepared to apply monopolistic pricing (where marginal cost equals marginal revenue rather than price). There appears to be no justification for this other than the desire to extract monopoly profits for the Exchequer.

In contrast, a Chadwick-Demsetz auction would select the lowest price to viewers or advertisers and would be associated with a higher level of provision of the service. There can be no justification for restriction based on the need to conserve a scarce resource since cable channels and competing means of delivering entertainment services are potentially unlimited in availability. In fact, in the case of cable, it may be difficult to sustain arguments for either regulation or any kind of franchising providing we look at the provision of entertainment services as a whole. Then, given the availability of competing media for transmitting programmes, unregulated competition is indicated. However, the US franchising experience gives useful lessons for contract design in other industries.

Municipal Franchises

Municipal authorities in a number of countries often conferred franchises on private firms in the 19th and early 20th centuries. These were clustered in gas supply, railway and tram operations, water provision, and electricity distribution. The contracts sometimes loosely obeyed Chadwick-Demsetz principles, although there were also instances of selling monopoly privileges.[27]

In 1907, the city of Paris franchised its gas industry. Bids were received from 13 companies wishing to operate municipally owned plant. This is an example of an operating franchise, where the franchisee does not own the assets, and avoids asset-transfer problems as the municipal authority could simply transfer its plant to a replacement franchisee. The operating franchisee simply supplies day-to-day management skills in such a case. Paris gas illustrates the problem of designing a franchise contract to encourage efficient operation over a lengthy period when costs may change. The Paris contract fixed a maximum price for gas and guaranteed a minimum profit for the operator. Changes in the cost of coal then led to gas costs rising above the maximum price. The municipal authority subsidised gas production until 1918, when it became possible to revise the contractual details.[28] This contract really required some formula to permit price to change with cost conditions.

---

27 The interested reader is referred to Schmalensee, *op. cit.*, upon which I have drawn, for further history.

28 Schmalensee, *ibid.*, p. 51.

The inflation of World War I caught out a number of franchise contracts. In the USA, many utilities were franchised on fixed-price terms but without profit guarantees. Franchisees renegotiated terms. In some instances, this led to franchising being abandoned in favour of regulation. In general, the experience of those years suggested the use of contracts with price-change formulae. However, excessive attention to guaranteeing the income of franchisees can lead to their inefficient operation. This is a problem of 'moral hazard': the franchisee may fail to achieve the lowest possible operating costs, knowing that the authority will vary the permitted prices.

Further examples of operating franchises can be found: the New York, Boston and Paris underground railway systems were originally leased in this way. Schmalensee notes that, apart from the need for price-revision formulae, there were two common problems. First, misleading investment incentives could be created by the fixed-term nature of contracts. Also, it could be difficult to enforce contracts. Operating franchises solve asset-transfer problems including the removal of any bidding advantage for incumbents. However, the franchisee has little incentive to maintain equipment towards the end of a franchise contract as this may revert to the authority. Common observations were that maintenance slackened off in this way and, also, that franchisees could not find long-term financing for their ventures.[29]

Finally, historical experience points to the need for enforcement of the franchise contract. Schmalensee notes that 'Under any workable scheme for the control of a natural monopoly, some entity . . . must act as buyers' agent.'[30] The franchisee may try to reduce the quality of his service once prices have been fixed in a contract and the franchisor may not wish to rely on regard for reputation to control this tendency. However, it is important that the buyers' agent is not able to force just any terms upon franchisees.

The world has largely moved over to the nationalisation or regulation of natural monopoly. This is for many reasons and is not necessarily a response to contractual difficulties with early franchise schemes: for example, the post-war Labour government in the UK sought *political* control of key industries. Given the modern experience of problems with nationalisation and regulation, the question is whether contracts can be designed that overcome historical difficulties with franchising. Our understanding of contractual relationships has improved since the early experiments.

---

[29] Schmalensee, *ibid.*, p. 53.

[30] Schmalensee, *ibid.*, p. 54.

Experience of Competitive Tendering for Local Authority Services

Since 1980, local authorities in the UK have been required to purchase services like catering, maintenance and refuse collection through competitive tender, rather than automatically using directly employed labour. The tendering operates along Chadwick-Demsetz lines with bidding in terms of the lowest price at which a service will be offered; and, although natural monopoly is not involved, useful lessons can be drawn from this experience.[31] Local authorities can refuse to accept the lowest bid only on specific grounds such as the likely financial failure of the bidder. Contracts usually set service levels, sometimes contain provision for cost-related price changes, and have often been enforced using financial penalties. Current recommendations from professional bodies like the Chartered Institute of Public Finance & Accountancy urge movement away from 'bonding' practices, with the substitution of financial vetting for penalty clauses. I shall concentrate on the experience with privatising refuse collection.

A government study in 1984 found that refuse collection became approximately 20 per cent cheaper when contracted out.[32] Tendering appears to have weeded out some very inefficient local authority direct-labour departments. Curiously, the study concluded that contracting out was not necessary to ensure efficiency as many direct-labour departments were as efficient as average outside contractors. However, this conclusion overlooks the competitive discipline exercised by the procedure. A more sophisticated academic study carried out in 1986 by Domberger, Meadowcroft and Thompson also suggested savings of around 20 per cent.[33] This study analysed the experiences of 305 local authorities, controlling for contractual details that could also affect costs (such as whether or not refuse bags were used). Generally, by the late 1980s, a picture of consumer savings was arising from experience with contracting out refuse collection. However, my main interest is in contract enforcement.

A potentially valid general criticism of tendering, raised by Ganley and Grahl, is that contractors may attempt to revise prices once they have been hired.[34] We dealt with this issue in depth in discussing cable TV. In the local-authority case, we note that Ganley and Grahl point to

---

31 See Ken Cheong and Robin Foster, 'Auctioning the ITV Franchises', in Gordon Hughes and David Vines (eds.), *Deregulation and the Future of Commercial Television*, Aberdeen University Press for the David Hume Institute, 1989, pp. 91-125, for a review of this experience.

32 Audit Commission, *Further Improvements in Refuse Collection: a Review by the Audit Commission*, London: HMSO, 1984.

33 Simon Domberger, Shirley Meadowcroft and David Thompson, 'Competitive Tendering and Efficiency: the Case of Refuse Collection', *Fiscal Studies*, Vol. 7, 1986, pp. 69-87.

34 J. Ganley and J. Grahl, 'Competition and Efficiency in Refuse Collection: a Critical Comment', *Fiscal Studies*, Vol. 9, 1988, pp. 80-85.

just two examples of this type of behaviour: in South Kesteven, Exclusive Cleaning sought a 2·5 per cent revenue increase almost as soon as the contract was awarded and the Waste Management Company applied for a 13·2 per cent revision within its first year of operation in Taunton. These are isolated cases in the context of the many hundreds of contracts that exist, which is a similar observation to one made for cable franchising.[35] Contract revision may occur because of genuine mistakes in predicting costs.

4. The Design of Contracts

We now turn to the design of a practical scheme for franchising a natural monopoly, assuming that this applies to an industry like telecommunications or electricity supply in which there is a mixture of natural-monopoly and other elements. In telecommunications, local networks are likely to be subject to natural monopoly. However, natural monopoly is under erosion in other areas of the business such as long-distance calling. In electricity supply, the national grid appears to have natural-monopoly characteristics but generation and local distribution do not.[36] The general idea I put forward is to 'ring fence' natural-monopoly elements and franchise them whilst allowing unrestricted competition everywhere else in an industry.

All manner of separate and competing firms may be expected to generate power. Mostly, these will wish to plug into a national grid, although sometimes direct sales to final consumers may be possible where an electricity generator is located close to an end-user and it is economic to run special lines. A diverse set of distribution companies could exist, purchasing power and selling to final customers. In addition, the grid or network may wish to deal directly with final customers. Distribution and generating companies could be jointly owned if merger saves costs: this possibility was not considered in the UK White Paper on electricity privatisation.[37] Although the power grid has natural-monopoly aspects and can be franchised, the option of bypassing the grid should not be removed. As a result of the structure, consumers

---

[35] See also Trades Union Congress, *Contractors' Failures*, London: TUC Publications, 1984, for further isolated cases.

[36] For further consideration of the extent of natural monopoly in these industries, see John Vickers and George Yarrow, *Privatization: An Economic Analysis*, Cambridge, Mass.: MIT Press, 1988, p. 187 and pp. 290-312, and Veljanovski and Bishop, *op. cit.*, pp. 73 and 74. However, Walter Primeaux disputes the existence of natural monopoly in electricity in the USA on the grounds that the protection of natural monopoly leads to poor cost control by management: see 'An End to Natural Monopoly', in Cento Veljanovski (ed.), *Privatisation and Competition*, Hobart Paperback 28, London: IEA, 1989.

[37] Department of Energy, *Privatising Electricity*, Cm. 322, London: HMSO, 1988.

would shop around for services and use the grid where it has definite advantages. We require a Chadwick-Demsetz auction of the right to be the common carrier of the system and to offer non-discriminatory access to the grid for producers, distributors and consumers. Since alternatives to using the grid are not closed off there is no enforced separation of production and distribution.[38]

Franchising the Telecoms National Network?

In the case of telecommunications, there are no direct equivalents to the generation companies in electricity. However, technical change has eroded natural monopoly and makes it possible to have competitive suppliers of some circuits. At present, Mercury supplies mainly long-distance services in competition with British Telecom. The application of a franchise scheme would require an end to the current duopoly policy in telecommunications. The 'grid' for telecommunications is a national network containing local exchanges; this is where we find natural monopoly at present and this is the part to be franchised. Companies specialising in value-added network services (VANS), such as the transmission of electronic mail, are best seen as being located at the retail end of the business. Further 'distribution' companies could be expected to emerge by permitting resale of leased telephone capacity, which is currently illegal. Nothing in the scheme would prevent mergers between firms located at different levels in the industry and bypassing the 'grid' would be possible.

It is worth dealing with a possible objection to the basic scheme before moving on to consider details of an outline franchise contract. It might be argued that the proposed structure enables competition to erode some of the benefits from one-firm operation in a natural monopoly. Natural monopoly could arise in an industry because it is cheapest to produce a bundle of goods or services together. However, it may be profitable for a firm to market some of these in competition with the natural monopoly, practising 'cream skimming'. It is often claimed that a natural monopoly must be protected from all competition or else its joint production at overall least cost would be disrupted. The argument implicitly assumes that sunk costs are less than expected profits for the entrant. There are a number of reasons why the cream-skimming argument does not convince.

In particular, we need to examine a link like the one from electricity generation to final distribution. If a generating company could separate some services and profitably bypass the grid, it suggests that there is no

---

38 Proposals for enforced separation are rightly criticised by Veljanovski and Bishop, *op. cit.*, p. 84.

natural monopoly. Otherwise, the grid operator should be able to ensure that the generator continues to use the grid. Suppose bypassing were to occur. The grid operator can respond by mirroring the generator's strategy, lowering the price of supplying the distributor, and closing off the opportunity. The grid operator may need temporarily to alter his pattern of production away from the optimal one in order to do this. It should be borne in mind that the grid has large sunk costs attached to it; the operator faces great losses if his business is undermined. The bypassing generator knows all of this, 'entry' would not occur, and no actual adjustments would be needed in the industry.[39] The case is different when the generator has a genuine advantage that lowers industry costs: then natural monopoly has been eroded and the grid operator will not be able to resist bypassing. Without legislated monopoly, there is a continuing market test of the existence of natural monopoly in some part of an industry.

Suggestions for a Practical Scheme

In assessing bids for the right to be the common carrier, the franchising authority would need to construct a price index along the lines of current RPI-X regulation. Firms could then bid in terms of X. Initial weights and prices for the index could be taken from the sales figures achieved in the year prior to franchising (with additional estimates for any newly proposed activities). Thereafter weights and prices would be self-generating. The figure for X should be binding for the life of the agreement as a minimum amount once it is accepted by the authority. This prevents adventurous bids from being beneficial to a would-be franchisee. In the unlikely event of a tie between bidders, a lottery could be used rather as in recent US processing of cellular telephone applications.[40] Bidders would have full details of any non-price terms of the franchise contract available to them prior to bidding. The successful franchisee would also be required to purchase the assets of the previously nationalised industry with the proceeds going to government funds.

Indexing prices according to RPI-X protects franchisees from cost increases outside their control. The bidding method generates a price-adjustment formula of the kind required in historical examples of municipal franchising. There is no need to incorporate special cost protection of the kind used in the regulated gas industry in the UK. Gas is protected from increases in fuel inputs, although such costs do not

---

[39] See Schmalansee, *op. cit.*, p. 36, for further consideration of this type of argument.

[40] *Federal Register*, Washington, Vol. 54, 1989, p. 50,699.

affect the natural-monopoly parts of the industry. The use of a general price index is appropriate.

The franchise term would be for a period of approximately five years, which is a figure suggested by conversations with individuals experienced in setting up telephone networks. The fixed term allows details to be revised later if they are misjudged initially. At each renewal point, the authority would receive bids including one from the incumbent. As long as a franchisee believes himself capable of sustaining his tenure of the franchise, sunk investment should not be discouraged. If the franchise were lost to another bidder, sunk investment would be lost. However, I propose conditions below whereby the authority would take over the assets if it refused to renew an agreement, and this should maintain correct investment incentives.

Automatic renewal rights for an efficient incumbent would lead to the problem of deciding when an auction was not required. This exercise of judgement would give the franchise authority too much discretion, which risks encouraging efforts for its capture. Any re-assurance to the franchisee is as easily given by the asset-transfer and valuation conditions specified below. Service quality need not be specified in the written contract. Indeed, it may be foolish to be too specific here given that technology can be very fast changing. Rather, the agreement would be incomplete and require the franchisee to achieve reasonable service standards set by the franchising authority. 'Reasonableness' could be disputed in the law courts or through arbitration facilities that I discuss below so as to prevent the franchising authority from contriving faults to pressurise the franchisee into accepting a less favourable revision of the contract.

The non-franchised aspects of an industry, such as electricity generation and local distribution, would simply be privatised. Liberalisation of the industry, allowing entry into areas lacking natural monopoly, would be required before the Chadwick-Demsetz auction of the natural monopoly. Finally in this area, companies operating at the production and/or local distribution level would not be prevented from bidding for the natural monopoly. However, their connection and continuing charges would be required to be identical for all firms.

Discouraging Discrimination – Liability for Damages

Discrimination against certain users was a concern of the UK White Paper on electricity privatisation, where it was first proposed to make the national grid the joint property of local distribution companies.[41] This

---

[41] *Privatising Electricity*, Cm. 322, *op. cit.*

may be a basis for collusion among distributors. In contrast, given the manner in which the franchise bid is made, such difficulties are much less likely. However, to be sure of discouraging discrimination, with firms perhaps claiming that the services being sold differ slightly from those detailed in the bid or by their delaying connection to the system, they could be made liable for a multiple of the damages imposed on a customer. Such cases could be dealt with in the normal law courts. Liability for damages would have prevented the delays suffered by Mercury over inter-connection with British Telecom.[42]

There are costs of finding and establishing a suitable franchisee. Once an agreement has been reached it is vulnerable to disruption, as the costs are faced again if a new franchisee has to be found. This makes it possible for the franchisee to behave opportunistically and attempt to revise prices upwards under the threat of leaving the business. As long as each franchisee is charged a lump-sum fee covering the costs of establishing the franchise, such opportunism will be checked. It is then the case that the franchisor does not face uncompensated disruption costs. The costs of establishment are properly part of the cost of operating the natural monopoly anyway and should not be paid through taxation. There is no need for a franchise renewal fee.

The necessity to minimise disruption costs suggests that the franchise agreement should contain provision for repurchase of the grid or network by the franchise authority. If the franchisee leaves the business or proves unsatisfactory so that the agreement is terminated or not renewed, the authority would have the right to buy assets at prices that are set independently. There is then effectively no cost for re-establishing the network. The alternative is to confer a user franchise, with the state retaining ownership of the capital assets of the natural monopoly. However, a user franchise creates incentive problems because the franchisee may have an incentive to run down his rented assets without proper maintenance.[43] This implies additional problems of monitoring and control. If the franchisee owns the assets then he has an incentive to look after them. If the authority did take over a network because of problems with the franchisee, this would be a temporary step whilst a new operator was sought: there must be no permanent re-nationalisation.

Protecting Franchisees' Assets and Franchisors' Rights

These considerations suggest some rules governing the franchisor's right to purchase assets. First, whenever they are purchased, assets should be

---

[42] As detailed by Michael E. Beesley and Bruce Laidlaw, *op. cit.*, p. 27.

[43] Schmalensee, *op. cit.*, p. 69.

subject to independent valuation, using the services of individuals like chartered surveyors to assess their current value in the franchised business. A contractual clause of this kind prevents opportunism on the part of the franchise authority, since no purchase of assets at knock-down prices would be possible, and prevents creative accounting by the franchisee. However, if the authority wishes to terminate an agreement for good cause or wishes not to renew, then it should be obliged to purchase the sunk assets. Otherwise, it may attempt to renegotiate terms on the basis that the franchisee incurs a sunk-cost penalty if assets are not bought.

If the franchisee should fail (or wishes to leave) during an agreement, then the authority should be free to choose whether or not to take the assets. The sunk assets then become a 'hostage' in Williamson's terms and act as a screening device.[44] It may also be important to prevent the franchisee from being active in any aspect of the industry for a period of around two years, should he fail during the term of an agreement. Any human or brand-name capital that the franchisee has attached to the natural monopoly is then rendered worthless to him. Penalties for failure that bite hard during the term of the agreement encourage the franchisee carefully to assess his bid and capabilities, reducing honest mistakes: this is what is meant by screening. However, if the franchisee decides not to renew his agreement, then the franchise authority must be obliged to buy the sunk assets. Otherwise, refusal to purchase could be used to negotiate for very low renewal prices relative to the rates available from competitive Chadwick-Demsetz bids. Without this condition, sunk investment would be discouraged.

Human capital is difficult but not impossible to include in this valuation process. The majority of a firm's expenditures on human capital consists of investment in training. The value in the current use of the investment may be estimated by calculating the expenditure necessary to produce the same effect. The position is similar with brand-name capital. If a firm builds up a valuable brand image that is specific to operation of the natural monopoly, this would have to be transferred to a replacement franchisee. The value of the brand name can be estimated, as is frequently done in the commercial world when companies are valued on the stock exchange or prior to their sale. Brand-name capital that is specific to the operator could not be transferred; but nor is there any requirement that it should be. This is the kind of unique advantage that would lead us correctly to select one franchisee rather than another.

---

44 Williamson, *The Economic Institutions of Capitalism, op. cit.*, p. 169.

Finally in this section, we should act on Demsetz's suggestion that there be access charges for digging up streets to lay cables and pipes.[45] The franchise authority could usefully perform the function of exacting these charges based on estimates of the value of time delays caused to travellers and the environmental nuisance to residents in urban areas.

Enforcement Issues

Contracts depend for their effectiveness upon an appropriate set of institutions. The best plan would be for one franchise authority to be established for all natural monopolies in a country. In the first instance, one industry could be organised in this way as an experiment; obvious candidates in the UK would be electricity or rail travel. The franchising authority should be established as an independent body subject to an annual audit to ensure its cost efficiency. The authority would operate auctions and monitor franchisee performance during the life of contracts. It would be subject to the law and would be ultimately governed by the statutes that established it. Having one authority rather than copying the UK practice of establishing a monitoring body for each industry (e.g. OFTEL), should lead to cost savings.

An independent arbitration body would be needed. Disputes over asset valuation and compliance with franchise terms could be referred to this body, which would be composed of both legal and technical personnel. Arbitration should be compulsory but not necessarily binding. Parties may be left free to appeal against decisions in the normal law courts. It is not likely that cases would go beyond arbitration, which usually saves costs for the parties. However, claims for penal damages for failure to supply would be best dealt with in the normal courts. The normal application of competition law would continue and would be additional to the contractual governance proposed here.

Possible Objections to the Scheme

It might be objected that the franchise scheme outlined above is so complex and detailed that it has converged on regulation. This is a point made by Williamson and also by Goldberg in considering details of such schemes.[46] However, we may note a significant difference between the franchising scheme and regulation. There is substantial external governance of the franchising scheme, which is controlled by normal legal process. There is no question of regulators being left with considerable discretion.

---

[45] Demsetz, *op. cit.*, p. 62.

[46] Williamson, 'Franchise Bidding . . .', *op. cit.*, p. 92, and Victor P.Goldberg, *op. cit.*, p. 441.

A further objection is that would-be franchisees could collude to obtain monopoly profits for the successful franchisee. The franchising system does not remove a need for the vigilant application of a country's competition law. However, practical difficulties would arise for a successful franchisee which wished to reward an unsuccessful one that colluded. Furthermore, there is an ever-present temptation for a firm to break ranks once it has colluded in order to obtain the contract at slightly lower prices than it had agreed to support. This tendency reinforces the desired level of competition.

It could be argued that the costs of preparing a franchise submission are relatively high for an inexperienced franchisee and may limit competition. This argument may be valid but requires careful interpretation. It may be that competition is limited relative to some completely unattainable, hypothetical norm. In the spirit of Demsetz's analysis of barriers to entry, we may argue that if incumbents can put proposals together most cheaply, this reflects an efficiency advantage that they possess. It is then appropriate that the high-cost entrant be excluded.[47] This is rather like the exclusion of any inefficient firm from a perfectly competitive industry, and is desirable.

Yet another objection to franchising is that it may be afflicted by the 'winner's curse'. This notion refers to an alleged tendency that auctions have to select the least-informed bidder.[48] Where information is imperfectly distributed across individuals, the danger is that the well-informed will drop out from an auction process knowing that cost and demand conditions cannot support the terms that are emerging. In a Chadwick-Demsetz auction, the authorities are then lumbered with a franchisee who will fail. The winner's curse refers to 'common-value auctions', where the value of the auctioned thing is the same for all bidders, but where some over-estimate this value. In fact, the Chadwick-Demsetz auction of a natural monopoly is an example of a private-value auction, where different would-be franchisees have unique advantages and, therefore, the franchise really has a different value to each one. In general, there would anyway be no means of distinguishing a cursed winner from a well-informed one with cost advantages who then fell victim to changed circumstances.

5. Conclusions

Given that natural monopolies are characterised by high sunk costs, potential competition is unlikely by itself to discipline an incumbent

---

[47] Harold Demsetz, 'Barriers to Entry', *American Economic Review*, Vol. 72, No. 1, 1989, pp. 47-58.

[48] *Cf.* Vickers and Yarrow, *op. cit.*, p. 111, and Martin Cave, 'The Conduct of Auctions for Broadcast Franchises', *Fiscal Studies*, Vol. 10, No. 1, 1989, pp. 17-31.

natural monopolist. To avoid monopolistic conduct, potential competition 'for the field' must be organised along Chadwick-Demsetz lines. This requires the establishment of a franchise authority and the franchising of the natural monopoly. The rôle of the state here is best seen as setting the rules for an appropriate form of competition. The problems of devising a practical franchising scheme revolve around the need to protect the franchisee's sunk investment from opportunism by the authorities. In addition, the disruption which could be caused by a franchisee threatening to close down must not be allowed to become a bargaining lever for him. The guidelines I have just given address these problems and the history of related schemes gives grounds for cautious optimism.

Finally, much public discussion of the merits of franchising compared with regulation or nationalisation is necessarily speculative. Little is known of the costs of regulation or of administering the relationship between a government and a nationalised industry. This information is required so that the costs and benefits of schemes could be more carefully assessed, which is a plea for more open government in this respect. For franchising, contemporary costs and benefits could be precisely known by experimenting with a Chadwick-Demsetz scheme in an area like electricity supply, telecommunications, water provision, or the railways. Such experiments are urgently required.

THE AUTHORS

THE AUTHORS

THE AUTHORS

Michael Beesley is a founding Professor of Economics at the London Business School. He was Lecturer in Commerce at Birmingham University, then Reader in Economics at the LSE; he later became the Department of Transport's Chief Economist for a spell in the 1960s. He started the Small Business Unit at the LBS. At the other end of the scale, he has advised on company problems of monopoly and restrictive trade practices and on the relationships between nationalised industries and their Ministries.

His widely known work in transport economics and telecoms policy has taken him to such countries as Australia, USA, India, Pakistan, Hong Kong, South Korea, Cyprus and many in Europe. His independent economic study of *Liberalisation of the Use of British Telecommunications' Network* was published in April 1981 by HMSO and he has since been very active as an advisor to the Government in telecoms, the deregulation of buses and the privatisation of the water industry.

He has been a Visiting Professor at the Universities of Pennsylvania (1959-60), British Columbia (1968), Harvard Business School and Economics Department (1974), McQuarie, Sydney (1979-80). He was appointed CBE in the Birthday Honours List, 1985; and he became Director of the PhD programme in the same year. In 1988 he became a member of the Monopolies and Mergers Commission.

Bruce L. Benson received his PhD from Texas A&M University in 1978. He is a Professor of Economics at Florida State University, as well as a Research Fellow at the Pacific Research Institute, an Associate of the Political Economy Research Center, an Advisory Board Member for the James Madison Institute, and an Associate Editor of the *Journal of Regional Science*.

Professor Benson was awarded an F. Leroy Hill Fellowship from the

Institute for Humane Studies in 1985, a 1991 Earhart Fellowship and the 1989 Georgescu-Roegen Prize for the best *Southern Economic Journal* article. He has contributed many articles to learned journals, including the *American Economic Review*, the *Economic Journal*, *Economic Inquiry*, the *Journal of Legal Studies*, and *Public Choice*; he is also the author of *The Enterprise of Law: Justice Without the State* (1990); co-author of *American Antitrust Law in Theory and Practice*; and has contributed chapters to several other books.

Sir Gordon Borrie, QC, took up his first five-year appointment as Director General of Fair Trading in June 1976. He was re-appointed for further five-year terms in 1981 and 1986, and in 1991 was re-appointed for one year. He was knighted in the 1982 Queen's Birthday Honours List and was appointed a Queen's Counsel in March 1986.

Now aged 60, Sir Gordon was born in Croydon and was educated first at the John Bright Grammar School, Llandudno, and then at the University of Manchester where he graduated LLB (Hons.) in 1950 and LLM in 1952. The University awarded him an honorary LLD in 1990. After further studies in the Middle Temple, where he was Harmsworth Law Scholar, Sir Gordon was called to the Bar in 1952. (He was elected a Master of the Bench of the Middle Temple in 1980.) After practising as a barrister in London until 1957, Sir Gordon became a Lecturer at the College of Law in London; in 1964 he moved to the University of Birmingham, where he became Professor of English Law in 1969 and was Dean of the Faculty of Law 1974-76. (He was given the honorary title of Special Professor in 1989.)

He was a member of the Council of the Consumers' Association from 1972-75, and also served on a number of government bodies including the Parole Board for England and Wales and the Consumer Protection Advisory Committee.

He is the author or part-author of a number of publications dealing with legal and consumer matters, including *Commercial Law* (6th edition, 1988), *The Consumer, Society and the Law* (with Professor A. L. Diamond, 4th edition, 1981), and *Law of Contempt* (with N. V. Lowe, 2nd edition, 1983).

Ian Charles Rayner Byatt was appointed as the first Director General of Water Services on 1 August 1989. He is an economist and an expert on the regulation of public utilities. His previous post was a Deputy Chief Economic Adviser to the Treasury (1978-89). He was born in 1932 and educated at Kirkham Grammar School and at St Edmund Hall and Nuffield College, Oxford. He also studied at Harvard University as a

Commonwealth Fund Fellow. He has lectured in economics at both Durham University (1958-62) and the London School of Economics (1964-67).

He joined the Civil Service in 1967 as Senior Economic Adviser to the Department of Education and Science. His career in the Civil Service also included spells at the Ministry of Housing and Local Government and the Department of Environment, before joining the Treasury in 1972. In 1986 he chaired the Advisory Committee on Accounting for Economic Costs and Changing Prices.

His publications include *The British Electrical Industry 1875-1914* (1979).

Sir Bryan Carsberg has been Director General of the Office of Tele-communications (OFTEL) since 1984, and was re-appointed for a further five years from 1 July 1987. He was knighted in 1989.

He qualified as a Chartered Accountant in 1960. After four years in private practice, he became a Lecturer in Accounting at the London School of Economics and Political Science (LSE) and a visiting lecturer at the University of Chicago. He gained an M.Sc. (Econ.) at the LSE in 1967. In 1969 he was appointed Professor of Accounting and Head of the Department of Accounting and Business Finance, University of Manchester, and later Dean of its Faculty of Economic and Social Studies. From 1978 to 1981 he was Assistant Director of Research and Technical Activities and Academic Fellow with the Financial Accounting Standards Boards, USA. In 1981 he became Arthur Andersen Professor of Accounting at the LSE and part-time Director of Research for the Institute of Chartered Accountants. He is the author of numerous accountancy publications and has also undertaken various consultancy assignments in accounting and financial economics.

Antony W. Dnes was educated at the Universities of Leicester (BA, 1976), Aberdeen (M. Litt., 1978), and Edinburgh (PhD, 1988). He was formerly a Lecturer in Economics at the University of Buckingham. He is presently Assistant Professor of Economics at Virginia Polytechnic Institute and State University in the USA. Dr Dnes's research interests are in the economics of organisation. He has published a number of journal articles.

David Glencross became Chief Executive of the Independent Television Commission when it was established on a statutory basis on 1 December 1990. He joined the Independent Broadcasting Authority (IBA) as Senior Television Programme Officer in 1970; he was appointed Head of Programme Services in 1976, Deputy Director of Television in 1977, and Director of Television in 1983.

He was born in 1936 and educated at Salford Grammar School and Trinity College, Cambridge. He joined the BBC in 1958 as a general trainee, and worked in both radio and television in London, Birmingham, and Manchester, and in the External Services at Bush House, specialising in current affairs and documentary production.

Mr Glencross is a Fellow of the Royal Television Society and a Fellow of the Royal Society of Arts.

Stephen Littlechild was appointed the first Director General of Electricity Supply on 1 September 1989. He has been Professor of Commerce, University of Birmingham, since 1975. He was formerly Professor of Applied Economics, University of Aston, 1973-75, and sometime Consultant to the Ministry of Transport, the Treasury, World Bank, Electricity Council, American Telephone & Telegraph Co., and Department of Energy.

He is author or co-author of *Operational Research for Managers* (1977), *Elements of Telecommunication Economics* (1979), and *Energy Strategies for the UK* (1982). For the IEA he wrote *The Fallacy of the Mixed Economy* (Hobart Paper 80, 1978, Second edn. 1986), and contributed to *The Taming of Government* (IEA Readings 21, 1979) and *Agenda for Social Democracy* (Hobart Paperback 15, 1983). He has been a Member of the IEA Advisory Council since 1982. He was commissioned by the Department of Industry to consider proposals to regulate the profitability of British Telecom. His Reports, *Regulation of British Telecommunications' Profitability*, and *Economic Regulation of Privatised Water Authorities*, were published in 1983 and 1986.

James McKinnon was appointed as the first Director General of Gas Supply on 24 June 1986. The term of appointment has been extended to 1994. He has over 30 years' experience of international business in general and financial management. Recently he has been consulted on the development of the gas supply business in Eastern Europe. The unique developments in the UK gas market have created a high level of interest in various parts of the world.

Mr McKinnon is a member of the Institute of Chartered Accountants of Scotland and was its President in 1985-86. He is also a member of the Institute of Cost and Management Accountants. He has written several publications, including a series of books on Management Accounting for the Institute of Cost and Management Accountants' examination students.

Sir Alan Peacock is Executive Director of the David Hume Institute, Edinburgh, and Research Professor of Public Finance at the Esmee Fairbairn Research Centre, Heriot-Watt University, Edinburgh. He was the Chairman of the Committee on the Financing of the BBC (which produced the 'Peacock Report', 1986), and formerly Principal and Professor of Economics, and later the first Vice-Chancellor, University College at Buckingham, 1978-84; Professor of Economics and Head of Department of Economics, University of York, 1962-77; Chief Economic Adviser, Departments of Industry, Trade and Prices and Consumer Protection, 1973-76. Formerly a member of the IEA Advisory Council, now a Trustee of the IEA. He was knighted in 1987.

He is the author of numerous books, including *Economic Analysis of Government* (1979); *Economy of Taxation* (1981); *The Regulation Game* (1984); *Public Expenditure and Government Growth* (1985); (with Jack Wiseman) *The Growth of Public Expenditure in the UK* (1961); *Income Redistribution and Social Policy* (1954); (with G. K. Shaw) *Fiscal Policy and the Employment Problem* (1971); co-author (with C. K. Rowley) of *Welfare Economics: A Liberal Restatement* (1975). For the IEA he has written: (with Jack Wiseman) *Education for Democrats* (Hobart Paper 25, 1964); (with A. J. Culyer) *Economic Aspects of Student Unrest* (Occasional Paper 26, 1969); *The Credibility of Liberal Economics* (Seventh Wincott Memorial Lecture, Occasional Paper 50, 1977); 'Trade Unions and Economic Policy', in *Trade Unions: Public Goods or Public 'Bads'?* (Readings 17, 1978).

Dr Stanley Siebert was born in Central Africa, graduated with first-class honours in economics from the University of Cape Town, and then gained his PhD from the London School of Economics in 1975. He is a Senior Lecturer in Economics in the Department of Commerce at the University of Birmingham and Visiting Professor at the University of Wisconsin-Milwaukee.

Dr Siebert was co-author of *The Market for Labor* (1979); *Labour Economics* (1985); and of *The Economics of Earnings* (forthcoming). His writings on labour economics and industrial relations have also been published in the *British Journal of Industrial Relations, Economica*, the *Economic Journal*, the *Industrial and Labor Relations Review*, the *Oxford Review of Economic Policy*, the *Scottish Journal of Political Economy*, and the *Southern Economic Journal*. For the IEA he has contributed articles to *Economic Affairs* on minimum wages (April/June 1985), discrimination in South Africa (October/November 1986), and comparable worth (October/November 1989). He is currently investigating the labour market implications of the restrictions on freedom of contract proposed in the European Community's new Social Charter of Fundamental Workers' Rights.

Dr Irwin M. Stelzer is Director of Harvard University's Energy and Environmental Policy Center; US economic correspondent for the *Sunday Times*; and Associate Member of Nuffield College, Oxford. He founded National Economic Research Associates, Inc. (NERA) in 1961 and served as its President until a few years after its sale in 1983 to Marsh & McLennan. He was a Managing Director of Rothschild Inc., investment bankers, and is now a Director of Putnam, Hayes & Bartlett, Inc. Dr Stelzer has served on numerous government committees investigating the regulated industries and competition policy and as a consultant to most of America's regulated companies. He has been named to the Advisory Panel of the President's National Commission for the Review of Antitrust Laws and Procedures.

He has published work on competition in regulated industries, the organisation of cable broadcasting, and anti-trust economics. He has served as Economic Editor of the *Antitrust Bulletin*, is a member of the Editorial Board of Telematics, and is the author of *Selected Antitrust Cases: Landmark Decisions* (7th edition, 1986).

Sir Christopher Tugendhat is Chairman of Abbey National Plc, a non-executive Director of The BOC Group Plc, of LWT (Holdings) Plc, and Eurotunnel Plc. He is also Chairman of the Royal Institute of International Affairs (Chatham House). He was knighted in 1990.

From 1986 until May 1991 he was Chairman of the Civil Aviation Authority. From 1981 until 1985 he was a Vice-President of the Commission of the European Communities and from 1977 until 1981 a Member of the Commission. His responsibilities included the Budget; Financial Institutions and Taxation; and Financial Control. From 1970 until 1976 he was Conservative Member of Parliament for the City of London and Westminster South, and from 1960 until 1970 a Feature and Leader writer on the *Financial Times*.

Sir Christopher is the author of *Oil: The Biggest Business* (1968); *The Multinationals* (1971), which won the McKinsey Foundation Book Award in the United States; *Making Sense of Europe* (1986); and (with William Wallace) *Options for British Foreign Policy in the 1990s* (1988).

Dr Cento Veljanovski was Research & Editorial Director of the IEA from 1988-91; he is now a Director of Lexecon Ltd. and Senior Research Fellow in Law and Economics at the IEA. He has previously been in private practice; Lecturer in Law & Economics, University College,

London (1984-87); and Junior Research Fellow, Centre for Socio-Legal Studies, Oxford (1978-84). He has held visiting posts at a number of North American universities and worked for a short period after graduation with the Australian Treasury. He was educated in Australia and the UK, holding several degrees in law and economics (B.Ec., M.Ec., D.Phil.). He has advised government and industry on privatisation, regulation and the media. He is a founder member of the European Association of Law and Economics.

Dr Veljanovski is one of the few exponents of the economics of law and was the first economist appointed to a law lectureship in the UK at the University of London. He has written widely on the subject, including several books: *The New Law and Economics* (1983); (with A. S. Ogus) *Readings in the Economics of Law and Regulation* (1984); and more than a dozen articles in scholarly journals, including the *Modern Law Review* and the *Economic Journal*. He is the author of *Selling the State – Privatisation in Britain* (1987), (with W. Bishop) *Choice by Cable* (Hobart Paper 96, 1983), and edited and contributed to *Privatisation and Competition: A Market Prospectus* (Hobart Paperback 28, 1989), and *Freedom in Broadcasting* (Hobart Paperback 29, 1989). His most recent publication for the IEA is *The Economics of Law* (Hobart Paper No. 114, 1990).